# The Yankee West

# Susan E. Gray

The University of North Carolina Press

Chapel Hill and London

# The Yankee West

COMMUNITY LIFE ON THE MICHIGAN FRONTIER

Library of Congress Cataloging-in-Publication Data

Gray, Susan E., 1952–

The Yankee West: community life on the Michigan

frontier / by Susan E. Gray.

p. cm. Includes bibliographical references and index.

ISBN 0-8078-2301-5 (cloth: alk. paper).

ISBN 0-8078-4610-4 (pbk.: alk. paper)

1. New Englanders—Michigan—History—19th

century. 2. Community life—Michigan—History—

19th century. 3. Frontier and pioneer life—Michigan.

4. Michigan—History, Local. I. Title.

F566.G788    1996                              96-7269

977.4'04—dc20                              CIP

The paper in this book meets the guidelines for
permanence and durability of the Committee on
Production Guidelines for Book Longevity of the
Council on Library Resources.

00 99 98 97 96   5 4 3 2 1

To my parents,
Jack and Caroline Gray

# Contents

# Preface

This book began more years ago than I care to remember as a paper for a University of Chicago graduate seminar on the social history of the nineteenth-century Midwest, directed by Kathleen Conzen. The year before, I had watched in envy and dismay as fellow students in a seminar on colonial American history dug up fascinating records from their various hometowns on the east coast with an eye to contributing to the colonial community studies then in vogue. They spoke of local historical societies and gravestone rubbings with an easy intimacy that I, confined by family and finances to the Midwest, could not hope to emulate. "Very well," I thought, "I'll find my own community in the Midwest." The pioneering aspect of this decision was particularly appealing: unlike the East, and especially New England, the Midwest was hardly overrun by ambitious graduate students. And as a suitable place to study, where better to look than in my own backyard?

This spurt of filiopietism was aided and abetted by my parents, Jack and Caroline Gray, who pointed me toward the Regional Historical Archives of the state of Michigan at Western Michigan University in Kalamazoo. They also remembered Roy Nichols. He was probably in his late eighties at the time, as was his wife, Joyce, but my memory of him is fixed in my childhood: pats on the head and nickels occasionally pressed into my hand after Sunday morning services at the Richland Presbyterian Church. Once the local banker, he was known to be extremely tight with larger sums. Roy Nichols's nickels, however, were not what gave my parents pause. They remembered that while serving as supervisor of Richland in the 1950s he had saved the earliest township records from destruction when the board burned its nineteenth-century proceedings in the interests of tidying up. The historical vision illuminated by his rescue was probably genealogical. Roy Nichols was proud of his family's role in the settlement of Richland; the first township record book contains his ballpoint pen annotations, including an asterisk after the name William J. Humphrey and the notation at the bottom of the page, "Roy Nichols's grandfather."

What Roy Nichols saved from the bonfire, particularly the township record book and justice of the peace court dockets, was the making of my seminar paper, subsequent dissertation, and now this book. How he came to agree to lend the records to me for as long as I liked and then to turn them over to the Regional Historical Archives has become part of local folklore, and it was the beginning, long before I read Clifford Geertz, of my understanding of why local knowledge matters. Local knowledge, I came to realize, meant more than my graduate student's desire to achieve scholarly authority; more than my need to tell stories, even while, as a tyro social historian, I built my data base; and even more than my midwestern chauvinism. For however many times we move in our lives, we remain rooted in place, a fact that is no less true in the late twentieth century than it was for Yankee settlers like William J. Humphrey, who descended on Kalamazoo County some 150 years ago. What we know is how we live where we live, and to study people in past times and places is to confront our local knowledge with theirs.

Roy and Joyce Nichols lived on the old Humphrey homestead in a Greek Revival house high on a hill overlooking Gull Lake. My dad offered to take me out to visit them. "You'll never get the records unless I go with you," he said, and feeling about eight years old again, I agreed. We had to wait to gain admission to the house until Roy had disarmed his burglar alarm system—a baseball bat, a hammer, and a broom stacked against the door. Once inside, we pushed aside several of the piles of clothing heaped on every available surface and sat down. Joyce served stale coconut cream candies with pastel icing. My father explained the purpose of our visit. First Roy said he didn't have the records (not likely). Then he said he wouldn't be able to find them (all too likely). Finally, he said he guessed he could look; he'd call my dad. We left, and nobody, including Roy, knew what would happen next. But he did find the records and call my dad, and I wrote my paper and kept on writing.

I could tell many more stories about writing this book. Like the time I was trapped with the Christmas decorations in the cavernous and windowless basement of the Kalamazoo County courthouse, where I had gone to sample deeds, when someone shut off the lights and closed the door. But the interest that accrued on my memory of nickels from a Nichols makes the point. This is a book about people who tried to replicate their old experience of community in a new place. It is about the power of communal and kinship ties in the creation of personal, ethnic, and ultimately regional identities. Writing this book meant coming to terms with my own sense of place.

During the writing of this book, I made many friends and racked up many debts that, although I can never repay, I want at least to acknowledge. Robert Ferguson, while exhorting me to tend to the literary qualities of my dissertation, complained about its awkward title and in a flash of inspiration suggested "The Yankee West." I am grateful for his advice, and not only about the title. My dissertation advisers, Kathleen Conzen and Ted Cook, and my editor at the University of North Carolina Press, Lewis Bateman, maintained their faith in me and the project. Middlebury College provided funds for summer research and subsidized a leave of absence. The Charles Warren Center at Harvard University made it possible for me to spend a year thinking, doing still more research, and writing. At the Warren Center, I had the good fortune to find in Jim Sellman an exceptionally able research assistant and an invaluable friend.

Research for this book was conducted at the Regional Historical Archives at Western Michigan University, the State of Michigan Archives in Lansing, the Regenstein and Newberry Libraries in Chicago, and the Title Bond & Mortgage Company in Kalamazoo. I gratefully acknowledge permission to cite from the collections of the Bentley and William L. Clements Libraries in Ann Arbor, the Baker Library at Harvard University, and the Amistad Research Center at Tulane University. I thank the staff at all of these institutions for their assistance. An earlier version of a portion of Chapter 3 was published as "Limits and Possibilities: Indian-White Relations in Western Michigan in the Era of Removal," *Michigan Historical Review* 20, no. 2 (Fall 1994): 71–92.

I also thank my colleagues in the History Department at Arizona State University for their friendship and support, especially Peter Iverson, whose office is across the hall from mine and who therefore spends much time dispensing advice; Al Hurtado, whose interest in another historiographic patriarch, Herbert Bolton, matches my own in Frederick Jackson Turner; Rachel Fuchs, *femme formidable*; and Brian Gratton, who gave several chapters tough, incisive readings. Trace Baker, Timothy Braatz, Marianne Hess, Lonette Janes, Jennipher Rosecrans, and Colleen Stitt provided excellent research assistance. Andrew R. L. Cayton has long been a friendly critic and a critical friend. And, finally, I extend my deepest gratitude to my boon companions Shank Gilkeson and Teddy.

The Yankee West

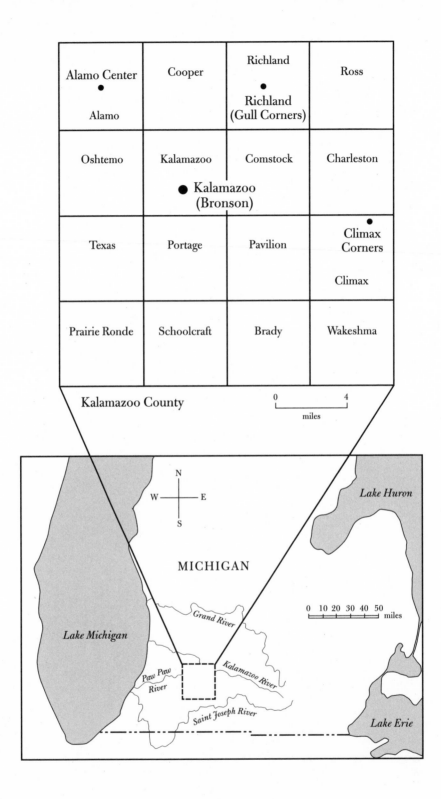

| Alamo Center<br>●<br>Alamo | Cooper | Richland<br>●<br>Richland<br>(Gull Corners) | Ross |
| Oshtemo | Kalamazoo<br>●Kalamazoo<br>(Bronson) | Comstock | Charleston |
| Texas | Portage | Pavilion | ●<br>Climax<br>Corners<br>Climax |
| Prairie Ronde | Schoolcraft | Brady | Wakeshma |

Kalamazoo County

0        4
miles

N
W —— E
S

MICHIGAN

Lake Huron

Grand River

Lake Michigan

Kalamazoo River

Paw Paw River

0 10 20 30 40 50 miles

Saint Joseph River

Lake Erie

# Introduction. The Yankee West and the "Universal Yankee Nation"

This is the story of three townships on the antebellum southwestern Michigan frontier. Richland, Climax, and Alamo are located in Kalamazoo County and are roughly equidistant from Kalamazoo, formerly Bronson, the county seat. Throughout the nineteenth century and well into the twentieth, the economy of the townships was agricultural. None of the villages established in the townships—Gull Corners (later Richland), Climax Corners, and Alamo Center—ever became more than low-level centers for the exchange of goods and services. The townships acquired inhabitants in a manner consistent with their development as farming communities; the population of each grew from a few hundred souls in the 1830s, the first decade of settlement, to roughly 2,000 individuals by 1880, then stabilized. One could write the early history of Richland, Climax, and Alamo as the mundane march of the farm boy who collects the herd in the back forty and drives it resolutely toward the barn and not be far from the mark, except for two considerations: the circumstances under which the townships were settled were by no means mundane, and the settlers saw themselves as anything but plodders.

Richland, Climax, and Alamo are located near the heart of a culture region known in the late nineteenth century as "Greater New England," more recently as "Yankeeland," and in this work as the "Yankee West." In the nineteenth century, this region extended west from New England along roughly longitudinal lines through upstate New York, Ohio's Western Reserve, the southern half of Michigan's lower peninsula, northern Indiana and Illinois, and southern Wisconsin to southeastern Minnesota. It was settled in stages between the American Revolution and the Civil War by New Englanders and their ever westward-moving descendants. The Yankee West received its first scholarly attention in 1909 in Lois K. Mathews's still invaluable *Expansion of New England*, and it has been mapped with increasing sophistication for several decades now by geographers, linguists, and students of material culture interested in both the actual migration streams and the diffusion of folkways.[1]

As the Yankee West took shape in the antebellum period, Yankees and non-Yankees alike referred to migrants from New England as the "universal Yankee nation," and they saw them, for good or ill, as cultural imperialists. Through their migration, Yankees were imposing New England values and institutions as the template of all American culture. Whereas non-Yankees heaped opprobrium on the "universal Yankee nation," New Englanders saw it as cultural compensation for their region's loss of preeminence in national politics.[2] Whether a term of praise or abuse, the "universal Yankee nation" connected geographical mobility to the heart of a culture perceived as distinctive: where there were Yankees, there would be New England. The cultural persistence of Yankees depended upon self-replication over time and through space. Yankee culture was at base a culture of hegemonic aspirations.

The significance of the Yankee West and the "universal Yankee nation" is obviously tied to the history of two regions, the Old Northwest and the Midwest, but in not so obvious ways. The confusion arises over the extent to which the Old Northwest and the Midwest can be considered as one. The assumption is intuitively irresistible, but the facts of the matter indicate otherwise. The Old Northwest—the states of Ohio, Indiana, Illinois, Michigan, and Wisconsin carved from the federal domain north of the Ohio River between 1803 and 1850—is a discrete entity in time and space. The Midwest, by contrast, is a timeless place bounded by where and what it is not— the East, the South, the West, and Canada.

In his 1989 study of the popular connotations of "Midwest," or "Middle West," from its coinage in the antebellum period to the present, the geographer James R. Shortridge demonstrates how a simple, geographical referent acquired persistent ideological freightage that enabled it eventually to encompass a vast section of the interior of the United States. The term was first applied in the early nineteenth century by the travel writer Timothy

Flint to Kentucky and Tennessee and literally meant the middle of the trans-Appalachian West. It reappeared in newspaper editorials in Kansas and Nebraska in the 1880s, once again denoting the middle of the West or the high plains then being settled. In the 1890s, however, in the midst of a severe economic depression, the Middle West received its now long-standing moral charge: it became associated with pastoralism—a youthful, virtuous, agrarian world of small producers, the true America that the aged, corrupt, industrial East had ceased to be. Endowed with these attributes, the Midwest again moved, so that by World War I, it and the Old Northwest, the West of Frederick Jackson Turner, were one and indivisible. Then, at the moment of its greatest triumph, the Midwest became, in Frederick J. Hoffman's phrase, a "metaphor for abuse," a dull land of middle-class Babbitts. Since the 1920s, Shortridge shows, these Janus-images of the Midwest have been locked in competition, and to the extent that the pastoral characterization has prevailed, it is because the region itself has moved back to where it came from—away from the rust belt to Minnesota, Iowa, Nebraska, and Kansas.[3]

How does this ideological equation of region with nation, so powerful as to move the region, relate to the Yankee West and the "universal Yankee nation"? The answer turns on the relationship between the peculiar identity of the Midwest and the equally peculiar historiography of migrating Yankees. This historiography has two overlapping parts: a mid-nineteenth-century view coeval with the creation of the Yankee West and an interpretation that reigned from the 1890s to about 1950, to which the works of Frederick Jackson Turner are central. The historiography can be deconstructed to recapture the cultural reality of Yankees in the time and space of their West. Yankees are treated here as an ethnic group, which means, following Frederik Barth and Werner Sollors, that they defined themselves, and others defined them, oppositionally by singling out cultural markers as emblematic of their distinctiveness.[4] There was widespread agreement on these markers; what differed was the moral meaning ascribed to them. For Yankees and their detractors, the positive and negative connotations of the cultural markers were flip sides of the same coin. The cultural markers of Yankeeness can be divided into two principal categories: market involvement and communal institutions. The connotations of the first can be roughly described as greed versus "go-ahead"; the connotations of the second pitted the sanctimony and hypocrisy of Yankee morality expressed through insistence upon key communal institutions—church, school, and local government—against a view of the same institutions as the bulwark of communal order, without which barbarism—irreligion, ignorance, and anarchy—would reign on the frontier.

In this examination of the transplantation of a regional culture, the location of Richland, Climax, and Alamo in the heart of the Yankee West is of no small moment. The southern half of Michigan's lower peninsula has played a prominent role in earlier interpretations of the Yankee West and the "universal Yankee nation." Yankeeness was long considered the area's defining characteristic. Thanks largely to the opening of the Erie Canal in 1825 and the appearance of steam-powered traffic on the Great Lakes, Michigan was overwhelmingly and rapidly settled by New Englanders and to an even greater extent by the children of New Englanders from upstate New York. Moreover, the state did not acquire a substantial foreign-born population until after the Civil War, a fact much applauded by antiquarians and historians alike until well into the twentieth century.[5] In Michigan, Yankees had their way, and a good thing it was, too. Although, ironically, today the state is one of the most ethnically diverse in the union, it was long known as the "third New England"—the second being New York. Michigan very early was recognized, moreover, as the first Yankee-dominated area outside New England in which the New England–born constituted a minority of the population, thus directly posing the question of what constitutes Yankeeness.

Regional stereotypes were pervasive in the antebellum period. The classic work on the Old Northwest is Richard Lyle Power's *Planting Corn Belt Culture* (1953), which examines how upland southerners and Yankees perceived the differences between them in such aspects of material culture as techniques of cultivation, house design, and housekeeping. These morally freighted perceptions reinforced the more general regional stereotypes analyzed by such scholars as Constance Rourke and William R. Taylor. As a concrete example, consider the editorials of the *Kalamazoo Gazette* in the twenty-five years before the Civil War that praised Yankees for their steadiness and moral probity but condemned them for their penny-pinching and mean-spiritedness, the effects of unrelenting toil on worn-out, rocky farms, and that lauded southerners for their easy manners and generosity but lambasted them for their indolence and profligacy, the effects of plantation slavery. Westerners—virtuous, frugal, go-ahead, and independent—had the best, but none of the worst, features of the inhabitants of older regions.[6]

Since the southern population in Michigan was negligible whereas a good many of the *Gazette*'s readers were New Englanders, one wonders about the audience for this bombast. A work that specifically addresses the composition of the settlement population and Michigan's future offers a clue. Here is James Lanman in his 1839 *History of Michigan*:

The mass of the population of Michigan is comprised of emigrants from New England and New York. . . . The sober, careful, and straightforward perseverance of the New England states is so mixed with the more daring enterprise of New-York, as to give vast impulse to the character of the people, and momentum to the projects which necessarily belong to the rapid progress of a new country. The character of Michigan is . . . generous and republican. . . . In New England . . . society is divided . . . into clearly defined castes. Prescribed forms of opinion, strengthened by age and influence, are marked out; and the youth are confined to the shadows of the cloisters; large masses of wealth are accumulated and hoarded up. Here it is far otherwise.

Warming to his oratory, Lanman explained the reasons for this difference: the land was "bounteous" and wealth could easily be acquired, so no one need fear social hierarchy; therefore, men were truly independent in mind and means. Thus, enterprising spirits were released to drive the engine of material progress.[7] Thanks to the work of scholars too numerous to name, but in Lanman's case particularly Henry Nash Smith, this rhetoric is easily recognizable as an expression of an ideology variously known as republicanism, Jeffersonian agrarianism, and pastoralism. It underpins not only popular conceptions of the Midwest but also, as Andrew R. L. Cayton and Peter Onuf have recently demonstrated, nineteenth-century views of the Old Northwest and, as Robert Berkhofer showed nearly thirty years ago, the Turner thesis.[8] Of interest here is the role that the characterological attributes of the settlers were supposed to have played in the creation of an ideological Eden. Lanman's notion, crudely put, is that New Englanders contributed "values" and New Yorkers—here a breed apart—"drive."[9] This constitutes an early formulation of the dialectic between the two congeries of Yankee cultural markers: the market and morality.

Later versions of the Yankee impress were more elaborate but in some ways not that different from Lanman's. Paradoxically, if not coincidentally, the first attempt to define more precisely the Yankee impress occurred in the two decades before World War I, the period in which the drums beat loudest for the equation of the Midwest with the Old Northwest and of the region with true America. Two examples link this effort to xenophobia aroused by large-scale foreign immigration. "Michigan," wrote E. P. Powell in *New England Magazine* in 1895, "is peculiarly interesting as being the furthermost western point where New England reappears distinctively. Beyond that state, the foreign element begins to make itself a preponderant factor in society." He then applauded Michigan's abundance of Calvinist institutions, educational system ("the common school as developed in New England at the bottom; the Jeffersonian university at the top"), and township system of local government. Michigan, he trumpeted, "is New England amended and perfected." Powell concluded his essay by sighing that although soon New England itself would have none of the "original blood" left, its institutions and "Puritan conscience" would live on in the West.[10]

Twenty years later, George N. Fuller of the University of Michigan stated flatly at the conclusion of his massive *Economic and Social Beginnings of Michigan*: "Owing to the great foreign immigrations to New England in later times, Michigan represents today more truly the blood and ideals of the Puritans than does any one of the New England states. The foreign immigrants who came after 1848, finding Michigan already largely occupied, moved further west to Wisconsin, Minnesota and Iowa. As a result of the early immigration from New York and New England, Michigan probably has a larger percent of original New England stock than has any other state in the Union."[11] Like Powell, Fuller emphasized the triumph of Yankee institutions in Michigan—church, school, and local government—but his appraisal of the character of these institutions and of the "stock" that established them was distinctly Turnerian. Indeed, he acknowledged his debt to Turner. It is therefore appropriate to consider Turner's interpretation of the Yankee West not only for its own sake but because it pervades the three classic studies of Yankee migration—Mathews's *Expansion of New England*, Lewis Stilwell's 1937 *Migration from Vermont*, and Stewart Holbrook's 1950 *Yankee Exodus*—as well as shorter works in state historical journals.[12]

Turner's writings about Yankees tell a consistent story with an inconsistent logic. Despite his environmental determinism, he never got rid of germ theory, an argument for the ancient European origins of American institutions and ideals. In fact, he needed this theory because his vision of the Midwest as true America in part depended upon the fact that the region was peopled by "Yankee stock," of which he himself was a proud offspring. Turner saw the eastern seaboard as having been divided in the seventeenth century by "physiography and the different colonizing peoples" into three sections: "New England, the Middle Region, and the South." Despite his phrase, often quoted as proof of his environmental determinism, about settlers "pouring their plastic life into geographic moulds," he argued later in the same 1925 essay for a "geography of culture": "As a rule there has been . . . a connection of the stock, the geographic conditions, the economic interests, and the conception of right and wrong that all have played upon each other to the same end." The mechanism of this interaction Turner never elaborated because his conception of its constituents was so shallow.

By geographical conditions, Turner mostly meant primeval forest, as Robert Berkhofer has shown. By stock, economic interests, and conception of right and wrong, Turner meant irreducible American values exemplified by institutions.[13]

"New England," Turner declared in "The Significance of the Frontier in American History," "stood for a special English movement—Puritanism." Four years later in "Dominant Forces in Western Life," he came as close as he ever would to defining Puritanism when he linked westward-moving Yankees to populism: "The center of discontent seems to have been men of the New England and New York current." "If New England looks with care at these men," he continued, "she may recognize in them the familiar linea-ments of the embattled farmers who fired the shot heard round the world." "Spiritual kinship" tied the populists not only to the "frontier farmers of the Revolution" but also to the "levelers and sectaries of Cromwell's Army." The lineage was derived from the "ideals of individual opportunity and democracy" that in turn had their roots, Turner wrote in 1914, in "the Calvinistic conception of the importance of the individual, bound by free covenant to his fellow man and his God."[14]

In four essays written between 1896 and 1914, Turner elaborated a genea-logical geography of Puritanism in America.[15] The general process that he described was one of declension as liberation, of New Englanders loosening their collars and rolling up their sleeves but somehow keeping on their Puritan shirts as they moved west. First in western and northern New England, then in central and western New York, and finally in the Old Northwest, Yankees "spread their ideals of education and character and political institutions," which in the last region meant for Turner a notion of education as a public trust, moral probity, and local self-government. Be-cause the pioneers were not of "the class that conserved the type of New England civilization pure and undefiled," they carried with them not spe-cific institutions but ideals that animated institutions created anew in the West.[16] The New Englanders who peopled the Old Northwest and formed the "dominant element in Michigan and Wisconsin" were "a distinctly modified stock."[17]

The modification of Yankee stock occurred in New England before the Revolution. Turner spelled out the transformation in his 1908 essay, "The Old West," with an interpretation of the history of colonial New England that received its fullest elaboration in Roy H. Akagi's *Town Proprietors of the New England Colonies* (1924). The Congregational establishment and the corporate, proprietary system of land distribution created on the New En-gland frontier of the seventeenth century a distinctive "community type of settlement"—the town. When land became scarce in the eighteenth century, the proprietors refused to share their property with other town inhabitants, giving rise to class conflicts that found some release in the creation of new settlements with a "Western flavor." With the advent of the auction system, the religious and social ideals embedded in the means of land distribution were replaced by political and economic ideals. The new land policy spurred migration, provoked "individualistic speculation," and, by the late colonial period, engendered new values of "individualism" and "the self made man."

At the time of the Revolution, there were two New Englands—one coastal, commercial, and Congregational; the other, agrarian, democratic, and pluralistic in religion. Vermonters had shown that New Englanders could become "democratic pioneers"—individualists who retained a sense of community through group settlement. Vermont, and Vermont through New York, peopled the Old Northwest, and the modified Yankee stock made their values stick in the region. "Native stock and foreigners in the Midwest," Turner wrote in his 1914 essay, "The West and American Ideals," became an "assimilated commonwealth." In the Northeast, by contrast, foreigners were now taking over from the "descendants of the Puritans."[18]

Fourteen years later, Turner seemed not so sure that the values had stuck and therefore less certain about the meaning of the Midwest as true America. His 1926 essay, "The Children of the Pioneers," is a painfully defensive example of history as autobiography. "The Children of the Pioneers" is a significantly belated rejoinder to the late Senator Henry Cabot Lodge's 1891 compilation by regional origin of over 14,000 individuals listed in Appleton's *Cyclopedia of American Biography*. Naturally, New England had produced the greatest number of men of high achievement, with 5,486; followed by the Middle States, with 5,021; then the South, with 3,125. The West—or the rest of the United States—was responsible for a mere 641. The figures outraged Turner's patriotic pride in his origins: "As a descendant of the New England stock, I regret to say that there were certain flies in this statistical ointment." He then produced his own count, drawn primarily from the states in the Old Northwest, to demonstrate the intellectual as well as material achievements of what he called the "children of the pioneers," or the "children . . . of the New York–New England stock," or the "Middle Western Yankee and his neighbors." By these last, Turner meant the children of foreign-born settlers in the Midwest who had become part of the "assimilated commonwealth," founded in part upon the ideals carried to the region by the New York–New England stock.[19]

The bulk of Turner's essay—some twenty pages—is a list of names, including Turner's, of midwestern men and a few women from every walk of professional life. "The Children of the Pioneers" ends abruptly with a brief, worried assessment of the parade of achievement: "the children of the Middle Western pioneers" show in "their work the Lincolnian quality—the interest in the common man." They are involved in mass production and cheap communication and write realistic fiction and social and economic history. They are reformers, "constructive" capitalists, and "socialist labor leaders." But, Turner concluded, in all this achievement lurks "a danger of the loss of individuality, originality." If the next generation continues their parents' trend toward standardization, "they will be false to the radical spirit of the pioneers."[20] In the 1920s, of course, such fears about the stifling effects of standardized society were hardly unique to Turner. What is interesting here is how well Turner's anxiety fits the negative popular image that had emerged in that decade of the Midwest as a dull land of middle-class Babbitts. The "assimilated commonwealth" was losing touch with the very ideals that had brought it into being.

Since Frederick Jackson Turner, few scholars have taken Yankees in their West very seriously, except as a reference point. And, of course, the Midwest itself is perhaps the most understudied portion of the United States. Thus, as Brian Q. Cannon and Kathleen Conzen demonstrate in two recent examinations of studies of rural immigrants to the Midwest, Yankees are routinely conflated with native-born Americans, and their presumed individualistic behavior—rapid adoption of commercial farming techniques, high rates of population turnover, and general lack of commitment to perpetuating family farms—is held out as a standard for measuring immigrant assimilation.[21] At the other extreme, evidence of highly communal behavior on the part of Yankees in the Midwest has been portrayed as a Puritan relic, a vestige of the seventeenth century in an entrepreneurial, pluralistic world. A 1961 essay by Morris C. Taber, "New England Influence in South Central Michigan," is a typical effort. Taber holds out as essentially Yankee a seventeenth-century standard of a town, communally founded and comprehending three fundamental institutions—Congregational church, town meeting, and common school—against which he judges several actual settlements. Those most closely approximating the ideal failed economically; the economic successes failed the communal test of Yankeeness.[22] In either case, whether Yankees are held as the standard of judgment for the experience of rural immigrants or themselves judged by a reified Puritan past, the dialectic between market and morality remains firmly in place.

Stereotypes are powerful and long-lived because, however much they distort, they contain a piece of the truth. Why these images should have come to be so closely associated with Yankees becomes apparent if we locate Yankees, as earlier commentators did not do, in the time and space of their West. Consider, first, the formation of a Yankee landscape in the Midwest.[23] Long before Yankees arrived in southwestern Michigan, for example, what James E. Vance has called a potomac system of settlement was already in place in the form of fur-trading posts at the principal fords and at the mouths of three more or less parallel, navigable rivers that debouch into Lake Michigan. The settlers quickly adopted these entrepôts as the first elements in their location geography. They were also interested in finding prime land— in this case, small prairies—and water power for local milling and in determining transportation routes among all of these "natural" sites of settlement. Imposed over the entire area, moreover, was the township grid system that dictated how land would be bought and that ensured, at least for political purposes, that each thirty-six-square-mile plot would contain a town.

Finally, the landscape with which the settlers were familiar was itself dynamic. New England towns that in the colonial period had been relatively uniform in spatial distribution and in the limited goods and services they offered were, under the impact of regional market integration, nucleating into commercial villages, arranged throughout the countryside in an emerging system of central places. What we think of as Yankee settlements in the Midwest—towns platted around greens lined with churches and shops—are the New England commercial villages of the early nineteenth century. Most townships in the Midwest, however, never acquired commercial villages. Yet these townships, with their dispersed settlement, containing little more "center" than a crossroads or "corners" with a church and a shop, show no less the effects of the simultaneous imposition, within a grid, of both potomac and central-place systems of settlement, geared to both translocal and local trade. It is not necessary—indeed, it would be wrong—to claim the landscape produced by these settlement systems as distinctively Yankee. More to the point is the fact that this landscape betokens the settlers' unwillingness to rest content with subsistence-plus agriculture. It shows the settlers' sensitivity to market connections, which in this pre–Civil War era meant a water route to the East.[24]

Such market sensitivity in turn suggests the relationship between the state of transportation and communications technology and the nature of Yankee migration itself. The point of departure is the much vaunted geographical mobility of Yankees that has been considered somehow emblematic of their moral character. That these people were movers and had been so for generations is not in dispute. That this migration was family based often gets lost in discussions of Yankees outside New England. Scholars like to focus in the

Midwest on the Puritan relic of the colony bound by compact and led by its minister. No fewer than three articles, for example, two published since 1960, examine the colony that founded Vermontville, near Lansing, Michigan.[25] The normative Yankee migration, however, was chain migration, usually, but not always, in family groups.

In and of itself, of course, chain migration is a poor determinant of group distinctiveness because it has characterized both foreign- and native-born migration generally in the United States. As Kathleen Conzen has written, "Not chain migration alone, but also migration systems, migrant selectivity, and place characteristics—to be understood particularly in comparison with other places to which immigrants might have gone—are important in the creation of ethnic cultures."[26] At this level of specificity, the distinctiveness of Yankee migration begins to emerge. In the first place, unlike the contemporaneous clan-based migration of upland southerners and the highly atomistic movement of planters to the cotton South, the Yankee migration system was extremely flexible.[27] Yankee migration took a variety of forms ranging from highly organized colonization companies, operating under written charters, that made group purchases of land, to more voluntaristic emigration societies, to assorted family groups. The actual kinship relations within these groupings varied tremendously.

The flexibility of the Yankee migration system was in part a function of the existence of a water route west via the Erie Canal and the Great Lakes. Because of this route, Yankee migration was far more rapid—only a few weeks—and far less arduous than for either southern migrants or European immigrants. The water route also helps to explain why Yankee settlement was so consistently "prospected." Yankees moved not just to a particular area, county, or township but often to an exact tract of land already staked out by an advance party.

Second, with regard to migrant selectivity, movement along lines of longitude both focused where Yankees settled in the West and delineated the source region for the migration from the East, as it did for all native-born, white Americans before the Civil War. Yankee migrants were drawn from Vermont, western Connecticut, and Massachusetts and from the Yankee population continuum along the Erie Canal. Theirs was a rural-rural migration. They left communities in the throes of market integration that had brought heightened prosperity yet restricted opportunities for landownership. In the West, Yankees sought the benefits of a market connection in conjunction with the renewed availability of land. Economically, they were a middling sort. If farm-making costs estimated at between $500 and $1,000 discouraged the very poor, the Yankee West also did not attract many gentlemen farmers.[28] Finally, the Yankee migrants tended to be evangelical Protestants, especially Presbyterians, Congregationalists, and Baptists.

This religious orientation points to the peculiar reliance of Yankees on local institutions in the creation of new settlements. As we have seen, moreover, institution building has long been considered a defining characteristic of Yankeeness. The concern of Yankees with the triumvirate of church, school, and township government distinguishes them from migrants from the upland South who were slow to develop local institutions, except for churches.[29] What is significant about Yankee institutions, first, is that they were ways of drawing the like-minded, even those without kinship ties, into the orbit of community life. Institutions, rather than clans or autonomous planter households, were at the foundation of Yankee settlements. And this, in turn, helps to explain the relative flexibility of the Yankee migration system. Community for Yankees was far more than the sum of family ties. Institutions did not grow out of the web of kinship but were as portable as the family ties themselves.

Second, the comprehensiveness of Yankee institutions distinguished Yankee settlements from European communities organized around a parish church. In some European settlements, churches did over time take on educational and governmental functions. Other European settlements that managed to remain homogeneous and cohesive while gaining population were able to take control of schools and governments from the native-born.[30] In Yankee settlements, such comprehensive control of local institutions was present from the beginning.

Finally, the Yankee migration system and migrant selectivity help to explain the peculiar balance that Yankees struck between the market and familial and communal relations. Yankees were prepared to embrace the market and not to see it as a threat. They viewed farming both as a business and as a way of life, and they saw land both as a commodity and as an earmark of local status. For them, the world had always been composed of similar small places that by the antebellum period could be more easily replicated than ever before. There was no need for rootedness in a particular community because communal life could be easily reestablished elsewhere.

In other words, capitalism for Yankees seemed to promise not the destruction but the intensification of familial and communal ties. The commodification of land did not challenge but eased the portability of status. Concerned primarily with the accumulation of capital and only secondarily with the creation of permanent farmsteads, Yankees, unlike immigrant settlers, made little attempt to perpetuate their families in their communities from one generation to the next. Unlike planter families, movement to the frontier does not seem to have caused Yankees a great rupture of kinship ties. And Yankees, unlike upland southerners located some distance from markets, did not build capital simply by clearing more land each year.[31] Yankees' interest in commercial farming is clear, signaled by their early specialization in wheat production and rapid adoption of new farming technology.

Like the migration system, Yankee inheritance practices were predicated upon very close yet extremely flexible family ties. As fathers and sons and as brothers, Yankees worked their farms cooperatively, sharing land, livestock, and equipment. The persistence of individuals in a community was highly correlated with their involvement in family farming. The object of these ventures was the accumulation of capital to provide retirement portions for parents and stakes for sons and brothers that would in turn finance new family farms elsewhere in the community or further west. Thus, although the object of family farming was not the perpetuation of the family in its community, such was often the result for some of its members.

All of which is to say that Yankee culture, as a culture of self-replication, was peculiarly suited to the adoption of values and behaviors associated with the market. There was, of course, a catch to this adaptability. For Yankee culture to be predicated on the conceit that capitalism intensifies community, the dialectic between market and morality had to be an encounter between equals. Communal institutions had to restrain rampant economic individualism, but they did not always do so. Some family members took their capital and left their communities and farming altogether.

These men are the source of the stereotype of the Yankee as deracinated entrepreneur—the anonymous confidence man, as I have elsewhere argued. By the 1830s, large numbers of young men were moving west alongside actual family groups. Many of them, the county histories attest, had achieved early independence by "buying their labor from their fathers" so that they could leave home before they were of legal age. My evidence shows clearly that they were considerably more mobile than the family migrants. In some cases, they were mobile because they were so poorly capitalized that they found it difficult to support themselves anywhere for very long. But in other cases, their mobility was a function of their constantly changing investments in nonfarming enterprises on the underdeveloped frontier—land speculation, milling, merchandising, hotel keeping, and banking. The pursuit of capital for its own sake required a continuous search for investment opportunities.[32]

It is wrong to see these men as a breed apart from the communities in which they found their opportunities, though they certainly were agents of capitalism in the countryside. In the first place, some were also engaged in farming. Second, they were builders of local infrastructure that the settlers badly wanted; they were the middlemen who forged the links between the central-place and potomac systems of settlement. Finally, they were also bound by family ties that facilitated both their migration and their entrepreneurial schemes.

From the perspective of these ties, no sharp line existed between the world of the farm and the world of the entrepreneur. Nevertheless, the pursuit of capital for its own sake was economically and culturally volatile. Unlike farming, it rooted no one in the community for very long. Here, perhaps, is the source of the agitated New England polemic, analyzed by William R. Taylor, that Yankees could (and should) leave their New England farms to pursue capital yet remain uncorrupted by the wealth they attained if they were sufficiently inoculated with agrarian values. Here, perhaps, is also the explanation for Lanman's distinction between New England values and New York drive. It is, moreover, as Cayton and Onuf and others have shown, part of the link between small and large "r" republicanism in the Old Northwest. And, finally, it helps to explain why Frederick Jackson Turner could uphold a fundamentally pastoral vision of his West while saluting the "captains of industry."

What, then, was so Yankee about Yankeeness? This work argues that the answer turns on locating Yankees in the space and time of their West. Only through a case study does the experience of migrating Yankees acquire the historical and cultural specificity that a century and a half of celebrating or decrying their "contributions" has erased. What is distinctive about Yankees in their West is their peculiar role in its capitalist transformation. The most striking characteristic of the settlers of Richland, Climax, and Alamo Townships was their ambivalence toward social and economic change. Participants in a brave new economic world, they were not, in a social sense, pioneers.

From the moment of their arrival, Richland, Climax, and Alamo settlers attempted to unite a collective social tradition of frontiering with a program for the rapid economic development of their townships. In this merger, tradition often emerged as the poor partner, but the settlers' apparent willingness to compromise community in the pursuit of self-interest did not signal the failure of tradition to sustain itself against the rush of economic modernity. The settlers equally embraced new economic ends and old social means without ever seeing the contradiction between the two. They did not, moreover, represent a lesson in the hard death of old habits, what one historian has called the persistence of "micro-units" despite "alterations in the macro-structure of a society."[33] Richland, Climax, and Alamo settlers were clear about what they were doing. They were not confused, but their objective was fundamentally ambivalent: to create traditional rural communities of unlimited potential for economic growth. They wanted more of the same, only better. In realizing their goal, however, they altered forever the dialectic between market and morality. Those who were more materially successful contributed to the creation of a rural bourgeoisie. Others found their particular vision of how to usher in the future challenged and ultimately defeated.

By way of a conclusion, a few words about the architecture of this work are appropriate. Relatively few literary records survive for the townships, and they are not evenly distributed. Therefore, the narrative does not discuss each township in a series by topic. Instead, it either treats all three townships simultaneously or shifts among them. These shifts, moreover, reflect more than the potluck that all historians take in seeking records; they are indications of the social and economic characters of the townships. Only Richland, for example, had an organized church before the end of the period of initial occupancy, and church records from the generation of settlement exist only for Richland. Enough is known about religious life in the other two townships to explain why churches were for so long unorganized and, hence, why records are so scarce.

The most important records for this work, however, are fully comparable for all three townships. This work rests on extensive nominal record linkage among the population and agricultural censuses, annual township tax rolls, and abstracts of all land transactions from federal alienation through the early 1860s. Such linkages underpin both my reconstruction of the biographies of individuals and families and my construction of social and economic profiles of the townships' settlement populations. Short of citing every instance in which I have used a particular source of this type, I have indicated in either the text or a note the records from which I combined data.

Finally, because the chapters are organized topically, the narrative moves back and forth from the beginning to the end of the generation of settlement. Chapter 1 establishes the settlers in the townships by examining the complex interaction among Yankee traditions of frontiering, the settlers' perceptions of the geography of settlement, and the federal land system. Chapter 2 locates the frontier economy of the townships within a regional context and describes the settlers' adjustment of their expectations of commercial farming in the aftermath of the panic of 1837–39. Chapter 3 analyzes the settlers' understanding of communal relations based on local economic exchange by comparing their dealings with native peoples, the Ottawa and the Potawatomi, to litigation for debt in the township justice courts. Chapter 4 focuses on family farming, which was at once highly cooperative and driven by the desire to accumulate capital. Chapters 5 and 6 treat communal institutions as forums for the articulation of social order and status. Chapter 5 examines the settlers' demand for local control over their churches in the context of the collapse of the Plan of Union, the interdenominational Calvinist program for proselytization in the West. Chapter 6 describes the relationship between local officeholding and status after the arrival of party politics in the townships. The conclusion examines the rhetoric of speeches given at meetings of the Pioneers Society of Kalamazoo County as a way of understanding how the settlers themselves interpreted their experience.

# Those Desirous of Removing to the Kalamazoo

# 1

## THE DESIGNS OF SETTLEMENT

### Richland

On March 10, 1830, the *Northwestern Journal*, a Detroit newspaper, published a report of the Kalamazoo Emigration Society. The Hudson, Ohio, association announced that a party of eighteen teams was bound for Michigan Territory. Anyone "who cherish[ed] . . . temperance, morality, and religion" would be welcome in the new settlement.[1] The party's destination was Gull Prairie. Shaped "like an old-fashioned physician's saddlebags," the prairie had marked federal township 1 south, 10 west, as the second site of settlement in Kalamazoo County.[2] Gull extended over 4,400 acres—a little over a fifth of the township—and of the nine Kalamazoo prairies was second in size only to Big Prairie Ronde.

The area that was to become Richland Township contained all of the desirable attributes of a prairie settlement. Most of the land in the township was arable; three-fifths of it, including the prairie, was well suited to general farming, capable of sustaining high yields.[3] Besides the prairie, the township consisted mostly of rolling plains "timbered principally with oak," providing a ready supply of lumber.[4] Such plains were a characteristic feature of the southwestern Michigan landscape. Burned periodically by the Indians to make hunting easier, they were not heavily wooded but were, as many observers commented approvingly, "park-like."[5] Besides their aesthetic appeal, these "oak openings" were far simpler to drive a team through or to clear than forests. There was also ample water in township 1 south, 10 west—from the small lakes dotting the eastern half of the township and from Gull Lake in the northeastern corner—and water power for gristmills and sawmills—from outlets on Gull Lake and from Spring Brook, a tributary of the Kalamazoo River running along the western border of the township. Finally, Gull Prairie was strategically situated on an Indian trail that settlers seeking supplies could follow nine miles south and west to a ford in the Kalamazoo River, where a French-Canadian employee of the American Fur Company had a trading post, and on through the county to Prairie Ronde.[6] North of Gull Prairie, the trail led into Grand River country. The Kalamazoo Emigration Society had done well in selecting its new home in the wilderness.

Despite this astuteness, the society was a peculiar organization. Corporate ventures were not an unusual form of Yankee settlement in the two generations following the Revolution, and they owed much to the collective approach of colonial New Englanders to town founding. The impulse to settle by formal colony seems to have been strongest during the 1830s, the apparent result of land hunger and an equally fervent sectarianism aroused by the Second Great Awakening.[7] Most organized settlements in Michigan, such as the one at Vermontville, near Lansing, involved relocations of entire congregations, led by their clergymen. With their organic association of church and community, initial joint ownership of property in land, and nucleated villages, colonies like Vermontville seem today to be Puritan relics in the midwestern landscape.[8] But although such colonies were fairly common, they were not usual. Most settlements—no less Yankee—were founded by groups of families. The efforts of the Kalamazoo Emigration Society, however, differed from both the familial and the sectarian modes of settlement. With more pretensions than the former and less coherence than the latter, the society's venture was an awkward attempt to combine New England proprietary tradition with nineteenth-century voluntarism. In the society's organization and articulation of purpose, and in the aspirations of its leader, Colonel Isaac Barnes, old ends met new means in an uneasy alliance.

The society's second report to the *Northwestern Journal*, published later in March, contained its "articles of agreement," drafted in February at a public meeting held at the home of Dr. James Metcalf, a leading Hudson citizen and sponsor of "educational, religious, and benevolent enterprises." The articles were a curious cross between a formal charter and a promotional tract. They set no conditions for membership but promoted the Michigan venture as both an evangelical mission and a good business proposition. Article 1 was an urgent appeal: "[It is] of vast importance that new settlements be commenced under Christian principles." This sweeping statement evoked long-standing American fears of frontier barbarism that many antebellum Yankees translated into a belief that only New England ways could save the West.[9]

The five other articles enumerated these ways, thereby providing assurance of the society's success. Article 2 declared that the new settlement would be properly prospected. The society would not lead the faithful blindly into the wilderness. Article 3 asserted the society's commitment to social order, Congregational discipline, and evangelical preaching: "The injunctions of the gospel shall be adhered to generally. . . . A Congregational Church shall be organized, a gospel minister procured and supported." Article 4 not only stated a familiar principle but addressed a local interest: "Common schools and Sabbath schools shall be early established and supported, and if circumstances seem to require it, an academical institution." The society could promise schools because they could be established cheaply by the settlers themselves. By noting the possibility of creating an "academical institution," the society hoped to attract settlers like the contributors of the seed money for Western Reserve College, founded in Hudson in 1826.

Article 5 allied the society with the temperance movement that had swept the Western Reserve in the 1820s by forbidding "the use of ardent spirits . . . except as medicine." The society did not explain how or against whom it would enforce its ruling in the new community. It simply assumed that its supporters were abstemious and that if enough of them migrated to Michigan, the new settlement would be temperate as well. Thus, the society reiterated its call for Yankee frontiering as a moral mission.

The investiture of authority in shared principles, however, cost the society power as an organization. The final article revealed the tension between its aims and means: "Those desirous of removing to the Kalamazoo, having the good of their posterity, and of the community in general, at heart; being willing to assist and alleviate a fellow citizen in distress, which is considered obligatory; and to adhere to the rules of Christian morality and temperance . . . will receive the support and encouragement of this society." In this final statement, the society presented itself as a mutual self-help association. The evocation of "posterity" and "community" was double-edged, an appeal at once to the future as a perpetuation of the present and to the moral and material here and now. We will "support" and "encourage" one another, the society declared, because we want to promote what we have as individuals and as a community. We will do what is right because we know what right is.

The articles of agreement were a call to a community a scant generation out of the wilderness to replicate itself on yet another frontier. The society's faith in personal morality was not utopian but reflected the historical experience of Yankees in town founding. Its promise of a church with a settled minister and schools recalled the requirements of colonial assemblies that new towns found such communal institutions to enforce moral order. Historical experience shaped even more directly the aspirations of Isaac Barnes, the leader of the Gull Prairie venture. Much on his mind were economic and political aspects of town founding on which the articles were silent.

Barnes had been learning about town founding for most of his life. He was born in Litchfield, Connecticut, probably soon after the Revolution. In 1789, his father, Benjamin, moved the family to Paris, one of the earliest settlements in Oneida County, New York. At the first town meeting, Benjamin was elected assessor, a position that his older brothers and father had held in Litchfield. The Barnes family relocated less than a decade later to the nearby settlement of Camden, where Isaac's parents became charter members of the Congregational Church, as they had done in Paris.[10]

In 1818, Isaac, by this time married and the father of four sons, moved from Camden to Medina Township in the Western Reserve, Ohio, county of the same name and located in the settlement of Weymouth. The township was as yet unorganized; Barnes arrived only four years after the first permanent settler. Like his father, Isaac was a first-comer on the frontier. Moreover, he acted in Medina much as his father had acted nearly thirty years before in Paris and Camden. Shortly after his arrival, Barnes served as judge of the first township elections and was elected township clerk. The Medina Congregational Church organized in his home the following year.

Barnes also learned in Medina Township an object lesson in why some settlements flourished and others did not. When Barnes arrived, Weymouth was a town of some prospects. It contained a mill and a post office, and the main Wooster-to-Cleveland road ran through it. Nevertheless, the town of Medina in the southeastern corner of the township soon economically eclipsed Weymouth and eventually became the county seat. A county historian blamed Weymouth's stagnation on "those . . . [who] lacked sufficient public spirit to donate land for public buildings," but Medina's triumph clearly rested on its capture of the Cleveland-to-Columbus traffic.[11] The town's first permanent building was a tavern that became a stage coach stop.

By 1830, Weymouth was a backwater, and Isaac Barnes, corresponding secretary of the Kalamazoo Emigration Society and prospector of Gull Prairie, was ready for another frontier. Nearly fifty years old, he had accumulated experience and capital.[12] Barnes sought support for the Michigan venture not in Weymouth but in Hudson in adjacent Summit County. There lived his kinsmen, John B. and Orville Barnes, who would accompany him to Michigan. There also lived David Hudson, Esquire, proprietary patriarch, who, even more than Benjamin Barnes, served as a model for Isaac's aspirations.

In 1798, Hudson had bought with Birdseye and Nathaniel Norton a 26,000-acre tract in the Western Reserve. Hudson was the poor partner in the purchase. Birdseye, a wealthy merchant in Goshen, Connecticut, put up half of the capital; his brother, Nathaniel, a well-to-do farmer in Bloomfield, New York, contributed a quarter. Hudson exchanged his Goshen farm with Birdseye for the remaining share. Neither of the Nortons intended to move to the Western Reserve. Nathaniel sold his interest to three men equally uninterested in emigration, and Birdseye made Hudson agent for the sale of his portion. Thus, Hudson assumed control of three-quarters of the wilderness in which he had invested everything.[13]

Hudson visited the purchase in 1799, returning to Connecticut late in the year to gather supplies and settlers. He recruited a band of twenty-eight souls and bought tools, seeds, livestock, and a "good" dog on credit from Birdseye Norton. Hudson's careful preparations paid off. The settlement quickly took root, and Hudson Township was formally organized in 1802. Securing the settlement was only the beginning of Hudson's efforts. When the Connecticut Missionary Society organized a Congregational church in the township in 1803, he became a charter member and a deacon. He proved a strong defender of the Connecticut way. Offended by the erection in 1817 of a church open to communicants of all denominations, he oversaw the building of a proper Calvinist edifice. Hudson also directed the construction of roads and bridges, turned his home into the township's first tavern, and encouraged local enterprise. His seed money and the grindstones that he hauled from Connecticut enabled local milling as early as 1803. Late in life, Hudson presided over the incorporation of Western Reserve College, contributing $2,000 of the $7,000 raised for the college and donating a 160-acre site.

Hudson's controlling interest in the township that bore his name encouraged his exertions. His success as a real estate dealer depended upon convincing buyers that wild land could become a civilized place. To this end, he tried to ease the first settlers' journey to the tract and guaranteed their provisions once they arrived. Hudson then directed the development of the township. Such efforts as establishing a tavern and erecting a gristmill assured his centrality to the economic life of the township long after he had sold off much of his and Birdseye Norton's land. It was not that after the first years of settlement nothing happened in the township without Hudson's approval so much as that his imprimatur tended to make things happen. What Hudson did in his own interest was not readily distinguishable from his service to and leadership in the township. Personal eminence and communal prominence were one.

David Hudson and his township belong to the last generation of town planting under the colonial New England system of land distribution. Because the Western Reserve was a Connecticut province apart from the federal domain, settlement in the region proceeded much as it had in New England during the colonial period. "System" is perhaps too strong a word to apply to the colonial assemblies' apportionment of land for new towns. The Puritans' approach to the conversion of what they viewed as "waste," or wilderness, into civilized places was *sui generis*. Their vehicle for the planting of new towns was the land corporation, unrecognized by English law yet combining features of the borough and the joint-stock company.

For much of the seventeenth century, the New England assemblies made direct grants of land to corporate bodies that partitioned some of it among the shareholders and retained the rest in an undivided state. Some corporations created nucleated settlements by apportioning village lots and fields and by keeping much of the land in commons; others promoted dispersion by doing without lots and dividing more of the land at once. Dispersed settlement and large, initial divisions of the commons became the standard in new towns as the century wore on. Pressure for land from the sons of shareholders and from later-arriving settlers also promoted dispersion within established towns, sometimes almost immediately, sometimes after several generations.[14]

Membership in these land corporations was highly restricted. The shareholders were disinclined to water their stock in undivided lands by expanding their membership, and they wanted as business partners only reliable individuals who could bear the expenses of settlement. The exclusivity of the corporations, moreover, fit well with Puritan conceptions of social hierarchy. Indeed, as the recent work of John Frederick Martin has shown, seventeenth-century New England towns operated as land corporations. Only shareholders, called "inhabitants" or "commoners," had rights to common land. Only they had the right to vote, so town meetings were effectively gatherings of shareholders. The status of inhabitant did not depend upon residency; one might live in one town and be an inhabitant of another. "Sojourners," permanent residents who had been granted the right to live in a town, could not vote, and although they might acquire land by individual purchase, they could not share in the common land. Over time, as town populations and the pool of potential landowners increased, this fundamental inequality became even more stratified. Some residents were admitted as inhabitants with the right to vote but without land rights.[15]

Despite the control that land corporations exercised over their institutions, towns were not without public functions. If located near the frontier, they served as defense posts. They were charged by the assemblies with responsibilities for the provision of common schools and settled ministers. The creation of basic infrastructure, such as the assignment of mill rights and the laying out of roads, also fell within their purview. Leadership roles in the carrying out of the various responsibilities of a town tended to overlap. Just as the status of an inhabitant established his stake in the town—his share of the common land—so that stake signaled his role in the establishment and maintenance of town institutions. The larger the stake, the greater the inhabitant's responsibility, which in turn reinforced his status. The blurring of public and private created "inequality, not just between individuals, but between groups of individuals."[16]

Between 1680 and 1720, however, New Englanders were forced by the Crown to confront the peculiarity and, from an English point of view, illegality of their towns. As hybrid institutions, the towns had no legal means of holding or granting land and restricting the number of landholders. Nor were there any legal grounds for town meetings. And so, under Sir Edmund Andros, governor of the Dominion of New England during the few years of its existence in the 1680s, town meetings were abolished and the colonists were required to submit their land claims for royal confirmation and to pay quitrents. Although the overthrow of the Dominion and the confirmation of previous land grants to individuals and towns in the Massachusetts charter of 1692 relieved the immediate threat to the colonists' land titles, the shock of the Crown's challenge forced a wholesale reconsideration of the nature of New England towns. Over the next few decades, the "assemblies stripped towns and their inhabitants of their titles and bestowed ownership on proprietors."[17] Henceforth, towns and land corporations would be separate entities—the former public and the latter private. Shareholders in land corporations became known as "proprietors." "Inhabitant" came to mean a town resident, a status obtainable by virtually anyone except a newly arrived pauper. Voting privileges were awarded on the basis of property ownership, and only the enfranchised present at town meetings could vote. Armed with this new political power, resident nonproprietors forced land corporations to open their memberships and thereby grant access to undivided town lands.

The separation of land corporations from towns was the first major change in the New England system of land distribution. The second occurred in the second quarter of the eighteenth century when the provincial governments authorized a new method for the initial assignment of lands. No longer did corporate bodies petition for a grant of land; would-be proprietors, as individuals and as corporations, bought into towns at public auctions.[18] The auctions heralded a new relationship between the means of land distribution and the responsibility for the establishment of town institutions and infrastructure. Although the auctions created unprecedented speculative opportunities, the ultimate purpose of proprietorship was to encourage settlement by providing access to land. This might well entail the provision of town institutions and infrastructure, which, at the same time, took on new meanings. In the first place, official toleration and then disestablishment privatized the responsibility for founding churches in new towns. The settlers' interest was no longer in the creation of a single Congregational church for an entire community but in the establishment of institutions that suited their religious preferences. Second, dramatic economic growth spurred unprecedented concern for market connections—roads and later canals—and for the developmental prospects of new towns. Whereas villages in the colonial period, evenly spaced across the landscape, had contained little more in their centers than a church and a tavern, their counterparts in the early national period were now also devoted to the provision of the goods and services of a commercializing economy. These commercial villages, whether grafted onto older settlements or created on the frontier, were slowly embedded into an emerging central-place system.[19]

Commercialization gave proprietorship a potentially far greater developmental function than it had had for much of the colonial period. Would-be settlers did not wish to be left out of an expanding commercial network that favored some towns' prospects for growth over others. Large-scale proprietors, such as the great land companies that controlled much of central and western New York—the origin of so many of the settlers in Michigan Territory in the next generation—found that land sales depended upon their provision of infrastructure. Their record as developers was mixed. One of the more successful, the Holland Land Company, tried through its resident agent, Joseph Ellicott, to provide enough aid to settlers to encourage land sales but to avoid doing for the settlers what they could do for themselves. The company cherished none of the neofeudal ambitions of the Wadsworth family of the Pulteney Purchase in New York or of the great proprietors in

Maine. Nor did it operate as remotely from settlement as the Connecticut Land Company in the Western Reserve, which folded in 1810 when it could not secure enough return to pay the interest on its borrowed capital. Instead, Joseph Ellicott pursued a deliberate course of placing land gradually onto the market, adjusting credit rates to stimulate demand, and preventing large speculative purchases. He also tried to shape the regional development of the Holland Purchase by laying out major highways, platting key nodes of settlement, and subsidizing stores and mills.[20]

Concern for the developmental prospects of new towns also shaped the efforts of smaller-scale proprietors like David Hudson. The key to his behavior was the changed status of the proprietor in his community. For much of the colonial period, a direct relationship had existed between ownership of property in a place and position in the social order. In the seventeenth century, however, status in a sense preceded ownership of property. The hierarchical social order was presumed fixed. Elite status was equated with a larger stake in the community—a larger share of the common land and of the responsibility for the town's affairs—than that of most other residents. Early New England proprietorship did not distinguish between private business interests and the public good. Once land became available to the highest bidder, the situation was reversed. The social order remained hierarchical, but the proprietor's status now derived from his stake in the community instead of his stake deriving from his status. He had to demonstrate his commitment to the development of the new town. To demonstrate that commitment, he took on as a business risk responsibility for the community's welfare. David Hudson thus acted as an entrepreneur to succeed as a proprietor.

In the first generation after the Revolution, moreover, the role of the proprietor in his community itself began to change. Beyond securing the services essential to the survival of the settlement in its early years, he had to guide the community to its place in an as yet unelaborated regional commercial network. He had to ensure access to trade. Isaac Barnes understood these demands of proprietorship very well. He would attempt on the Michigan frontier what Hudson had done in the Western Reserve; he would try to personify settlement, to be all things to all men. Unlike David Hudson, who controlled land sales in his township, however, Barnes could not direct the alienation of Gull Prairie, and as the charter made clear, the Kalamazoo Emigration Society itself had no authority beyond moral and economic inducement. Barnes would arrive and compete with other settlers for land owned by the federal government and for the power to direct the development of the settlement. While Gull Prairie competed for its place among settlements in the Kalamazoo River valley, Isaac Barnes would compete for his status in the new community. He would act as an entrepreneur simply to be a proprietor, let alone to succeed as one.

The *Northwestern Journal* printed its last communication from the Kalamazoo Emigration Society late in June. Colonel Isaac Barnes reported the society's arrival on Gull Prairie. Barnes's designation of himself as a colonel asserted his superior status on Gull Prairie. The title was undoubtedly a legitimate Ohio militia rank; Barnes commanded southwestern Michigan volunteers the following year during the scare over the Black Hawk uprising. But Barnes's use of his colonelcy was more than military. He signed neither of his communications from Ohio as the society's corresponding secretary as "Colonel Barnes," yet on Gull Prairie he was always known as "the Colonel." To the *Journal*'s readers, the colonel announced that the new settlement was well supplied with mechanics and blessed with a "pious and respectable physician" but badly needed a blacksmith of "sober, industrious, and religious habits." He repeated the society's welcome to the similarly upstanding.[21]

Even without Colonel Barnes's promotional efforts, Gull Prairie would have quickly drawn settlers. The promise of the Kalamazoo prairies was well known by 1830. Sales were brisk in 1831 when the land office opened and were little affected by the cholera epidemic and the Black Hawk War, which temporarily slowed settlement in southwestern Michigan. Barnes's contingent was nearly outnumbered by the end of the first summer on Gull Prairie; only eight of the fifteen families in township 1 south, 10 west, were associated with the Kalamazoo Emigration Society. Three of these eight were related, and all of them had known one another in Ohio. Besides Barnes, his wife, and his four sons, society settlers included David Dillie and his family, Barnes's Hudson kinsmen, John B. and Orville Barnes, and Selden Norton from nearby Aurora. The pious and respectable physician was James Porter. Daniel Plummer, Cornelius Northrup, and their families were apparently also affiliated. The seven other families on the prairie apparently had no prior connection either to Barnes or to the society. Four came from western Connecticut, two from Vermont, and one from Massachusetts.[22]

By the end of the second summer on the prairie, unaffiliated settlers had outstripped society members. Notable among the new arrivals for the roles they were soon to play in the development of Richland Township were two groups of settlers whose unwritten bonds resembled those uniting the society. The first group appeared on Gull Prairie in May from Detroit and included Joseph and Philip Corey, Cyrus Lovell, Samuel Brown, Isaac Briggs, Philip Gray, and their families. The party had formed en route west.

Philip Gray and the Coreys may have known one another in Newport, Rhode Island, but the others set out for Michigan from homes throughout New England: Lovell from Vermont, Briggs from Cheshire County, New Hampshire, and Brown from Brimfield, Massachusetts. More than chance meeting, however, united the group. Like the Kalamazoo Emigration Society, it was composed of families: Joseph and Philip Corey were brothers; Samuel Brown had five adult sons with him; and Cyrus Lovell was probably an in-law of John F. Gilkey, already settled on the prairie. The party also had well-defined commercial and religious interests: Lovell and Gray were lawyers; Gray and Brown bought land speculatively; and Brown, Briggs, and Gray were deacons. The composition and orientation of the second group of settlers were similar. The Mills brothers arrived in July from Ann Arbor, where they had settled as early as 1826. Simeon, who had prospected Gull Prairie in the spring after sodbusting for wages in neighboring Calhoun County, returned, bringing with him Willard and Sylvester. Henry, Elihu, Augustus, Timothy, and their families followed. Like the first party, the Mills brothers were pious men of commerce: Simeon was a deacon; Willard and Sylvester were merchants; Timothy opened a tavern; and Henry and Simeon invested heavily in the local land market.[23]

The arrival of the Mills brothers and Brown, Briggs, and the others posed a challenge to Colonel Isaac Barnes's leadership on Gull Prairie. The early settlement was very much a case of like seeking like. Barnes got more than he bargained for when he welcomed the pious and respectable to the new settlement, for the prairie attracted men with proprietary instincts as keenly developed as his own. Not only was the society outnumbered, but as a small group of families and neighbors, it was unlikely to maintain a formal, corporate identity. Such authority as the Kalamazoo Emigration Society possessed reposed in the person of Isaac Barnes.

By the time the Mills brothers and the New England contingent made their way to Gull Prairie, the settlement's place in the emerging regional trade network had become evident. Territorial governor Lewis Cass had in April approved a commissioners' report delivered in January designating a tract owned by Titus Bronson, "at the great bend of the Kalamazoo River," as the site of the Kalamazoo County seat. The report shows the regional thinking that governed efforts to develop new settlements. Noting that prairies would be the loci of population in the county, the commissioners singled out three for special consideration: Prairie Ronde in the southwest, where "two hundred families reside on the border of this lake of land"; Grand Prairie, "four miles north west of the geographical centre of the county"; and Gull Prairie. The three prairies were nearly "in a direct line" and "about equi-distant" from one another. Titus Bronson's tract both fit the county population axis delineated by the three prairies and opened Kalamazoo to trade from all points. It was on the bank of the navigable Kalamazoo River, two miles west of Grand Prairie and in a direct line between Gull Prairie and Prairie Ronde. It was well located at a site convenient to roads "into any part of the county" and at the convergence of "four or five trails . . . to as many different places of importance on the St. Joseph and Grand river[s]." Finally, "the great Territorial Road passes through it."[24]

About Gull Prairie, the commissioners remarked, "[Its] settlement . . . has only commenced, but from the character of its present inhabitants, and local and other advantages it possesses, a heavy population may be reasonably anticipated." Prairie, timber, and water power were the "local" advantages of township 1 south, 10 west, and would make it a center of county population. Location, the township's "other" advantage, would make it a center of trade. The question for settlers on Gull Prairie was not which resources to exploit but who would control their development.

Isaac Barnes's particular interest in Gull Prairie was as a trading center. He was not directly involved in local milling, which was for good reason an early priority of the settlers. After the first grain was threshed on Gull Prairie in the summer of 1831, Simeon Mills's son hauled it fifty miles south to the nearest gristmill in White Pigeon. The mill was broken when he arrived, and he had to wait for repairs. On the way home, he found the Kalamazoo River so high that he had to "swim" his oxen and cross over himself with the grist in an Indian canoe. When the son finally returned to Gull Prairie after an absence of three weeks, the settlers had eaten the last of their flour and resifted the bran. The next season's harvest was ground at a mill in Comstock, on the Kalamazoo River, less than a quarter of the distance to White Pigeon. Volunteers from Gull Prairie had spent much of the summer helping to dig the millrace. Two years later, Isaac Barnes's brother, Tillotson, who had arrived on Gull Prairie in 1832, built a gristmill even closer to the settlement on an outlet of Gull Lake. Tillotson also built one of three sawmills operating in the township by the end of 1833.[25]

Because he had neither the backing nor sufficient capital of his own, Isaac Barnes also did not attempt, as others did, to buy federal land for resale to settlers. He bought only 240 acres of federal land in the township in the 1830s. By contrast, the largest township landowner, John F. Gilkey, in the same period acquired 910 acres. The assessed value of Barnes's real and personal property in 1839, the first year in which rates were set for Richland as an independent township, was $1,372, making him the fifteenth wealthiest of eighty taxpayers, for whom the mean holding was $1,080.99.[26] To be sure, by 1839 Barnes had invested some of his assets in pine lots in neighboring Allegan County, but so had other well-off Richland residents. Merritt Barrett, for example, who like Barnes acquired tracts in Wayland Township, owned property in Richland with an assessed value of $2,157. John F. Gilkey, who made extensive purchases of federal land in Kalamazoo County and elsewhere, led the list of taxpayers with a total holding of $6,647.[27]

With such limited resources, Barnes focused his ambitions on making the federal land he did buy, and by extension himself, the center of life on Gull Prairie. If he could not, like David Hudson, control the development of the township as a whole, he could establish Gull Prairie. Bisecting Barnes's tract in section 14 was a well-traveled Indian trail that extended from southwest to northeast across the county and connected the settlements at Prairie Ronde, Bronson (as the county seat was first named), and Gull Prairie. From Barnes's land, the trail headed due north into the Grand River valley. A second Indian trail branched north and west from Barnes's tract to follow the Kalamazoo River to Lake Michigan. Both of these trails were destined to become territorial roads, and thus migration axes, with a good deal of help from Isaac Barnes.

Michigan territorial law provided for two sorts of public ways—roads and highways. The establishment of both depended upon local initiative and was subject to local control. Designed to connect major settlements, roads were authorized by territorial enactments specifying starting, terminal, and sometimes middle points. The legislative council appointed several commissioners to lay out each road, empowering them to hire a surveyor, chain carriers, and other aides as necessary. In the choice of commissioners, territorial concerns merged with local politics and schemes for local development. The council tended to select men who were familiar with the country along a proposed route and therefore directly interested in how it would be laid out. Territorial law also gave commissioners considerable latitude, stating only that a road be "on the most direct route, where suitable ground can be found . . . always having regard for the intermediate points."[28]

Construction and maintenance of territorial roads were the responsibility of annually elected township highway commissioners, who organized work corvées on which every able-bodied male over twenty-one had to serve or pay a fine. The commissioners also laid out township highways, usually also constructed and maintained by work corvées along section lines, to connect individual farmsteads with territorial arteries. As townships grew in population, they were divided into highway districts, and district representatives were elected annually to oversee the upkeep of highways.[29]

Isaac Barnes was in an excellent position to benefit from the laying out of roads. Besides having located his claim at the junction of two Indian trails, he was, like his son, Carlos, a surveyor. He was also not slow to seize his advantage as first citizen of Gull Prairie by right of prior arrival. On June 18, 1832, he was appointed commissioner of a territorial road to "commence at a suitable point on the Territorial Road [now I-94] . . . thence running northwesterly . . . across Battle Creek near its mouth, through Gull prairie, and on either side of Kalamazoo river to its entrance into Lake Michigan."[30] The road that Barnes and his associates established is present-day M-89. It began a few miles east of the new settlement at the confluence of Battle Creek and the Kalamazoo River, where Gull Prairie men had earlier in the spring helped to build a bridge.[31] The road then snaked west across the northeasternmost and still largely uninhabited federal township in Kalamazoo County. From the eastern border of township 1 south, 10 west, the road followed the section line due west until it intersected with the north-south Indian trail. It joined this trail for a mile to the north and then picked up the second Indian trail to the north and west through the Kalamazoo River valley. Isaac Barnes's property was thus nicely nestled in the crook between the road he laid out and the trail into the Grand River country.

Shortly after commissioning the territorial road, the legislative council again acted in the general interest of the inhabitants of Gull Prairie and in the particular interest of Isaac Barnes. Again, it responded to local initiative. At a barn raising in the spring, "the inhabitants of the Gull Prairie region" had resolved to petition the legislative council for a new township in Kalamazoo County to be called Richland, an old place name promising a bright future.[32] The council's response was to create a civil township composed of the four northeastern federal townships in the county. The first Richland Township elections were scheduled for the first Monday in April of the following year.[33]

Territorial authorization of a road and a township put into gear Barnes's plans for himself and his property. In November, Carlos Barnes surveyed a town plat of three east-west and five north-south streets within a forty-acre parcel in section 14 owned by his father and James Porter, another society member. All of the streets were sixty-five feet wide except for Main Street, the major east-west route, which was eighty feet wide, and Broadway, which was "216 feet wide, and designed expressly for public buildings and other public uses." At the time of the survey, Broadway was a stretch of Indian trail running north into the Grand River valley. The only "public" building on it was Isaac Barnes's house at the junction of that trail and the road that he had laid out along the other trail into the Kalamazoo River valley. The house served as a resting place for travelers, much as David Hudson's home had done, and as the Gull Prairie post office—Isaac Barnes being the newly appointed postmaster. Carlos Barnes's plat was a map of his father's expectations. The prospective town was named "Geloster," after his sons, George, Carlos, and Lester.[34]

Isaac Barnes believed in Geloster's future, but his fellow settlers had other ideas. Within a few months after Carlos Barnes completed his work, township 1 south, 10 west, contained two more plats. One of these, called Bridgewater, was not intended as a trade center. It was laid out in section 19 on the western border of the township around a sawmill at the junction of Spring Brook and a feeder stream. The pretensions of the other plat, however, resembled those of Geloster, although it was smaller and lacked a great thoroughfare. Willard and Sylvester Mills platted the town of Richland around a village green. Then they opened a store and a tailor shop and, like Barnes, waited for buyers for their other lots.[35]

Richland's location in section 23 meant that despite Isaac Barnes's efforts, the township's transportation nexus was still unfixed. The plat lay about a half mile south of where Barnes's road first met the Grand River trail. The Mills brothers apparently platted Richland in February 1833 in relation to where they expected other roads to go. A little over a month later, the legislative council authorized two more territorial roads directly affecting the Gull Prairie settlement. One followed the Grand River trail and is today M-43 from Kalamazoo to Grand Rapids. The stretch from Kalamazoo to Richland is now called Gull Road, but in the nineteenth century it was known as the "diagonal road" because it cut resolutely across section lines from southwest to northeast until turning sharply north a mile east of the geographical center of Richland Township. The other road was to begin at the Indiana border and run north through White Pigeon to the junction of Isaac Barnes's and the diagonal roads. Had the road been built, it would have passed directly to the west of the Richland plat.[36]

The very desirability of the road helps to explain why it remained on paper. Settlers first entered the Kalamazoo River valley from the south, and they continued to do so long after the "great" Territorial Road from Detroit was laid out. It was easier to travel west on the more improved Chicago Road along the Indiana border and then head north into open country. The proposed road from White Pigeon through Kalamazoo County was intended to facilitate an already preferred route. This road, moreover, would have run through the village of Comstock, located on the Kalamazoo River just east of the county seat and vying with Bronson at the time for urban supremacy of Kalamazoo County. The upstart's proprietor, Horace H. Comstock, had even orchestrated a county vote in 1832 on moving the seat to his village. The vote failed, but competition between the two villages remained intense until 1837, by which time Bronson, now Kalamazoo, had acquired the land office, a bank, a newspaper, and a hotel. Comstock then joined the winning side by purchasing a quarter interest in the Kalamazoo plat.[37]

In the meantime, however, settlers on Gull Prairie took seriously the rivalry between Comstock and Bronson, as the Mills brothers' plat adjacent to the proposed road from White Pigeon attests. Comstock and Gull Prairie were as yet the only two settlements in Richland Township, and the inhabitants were used to working together—raising barns and building millraces. Comstock and Gull Prairie men predominated at the first township elections, which took place in Comstock a few days after the authorization of the road from the border. If Comstock village bested Bronson for county seat—and in 1833 many settlers thought it still might—then construction of the road from White Pigeon seemed assured.

Such calculations came to naught. In the end, the possibility of three territorial roads joining on Gull Prairie led to decisions about the location of villages that sounded the death knell for both Isaac Barnes's and the Mills brothers' schemes. Later in 1833, another Mills brother, Timothy, built a hotel near the new township "center," and the Presbyterian Church of Gull Prairie erected its first edifice nearby. Two years later, Mumford Eldred Jr. and John D. Batcheldor opened the township's first general store in what would soon be known as Gull Corners (later Richland Village).[38] The Millses' plat passed quietly into oblivion, but Isaac Barnes fought for Geloster until 1841, when he sold out and left the township. The struggle engaged not only his hopes for Geloster but his dream of founding a Congregational church and presiding over the township in the manner of David Hudson. His challengers were drawn from the two parties who had arrived on Gull Prairie in 1831 and, as evangelical, entrepreneurial groups of families, resembled the Kalamazoo Emigration Society. These men owned the land around the junction, and they were stout Presbyterians.

## Climax

Intense competition over the development of township resources and institutions characterized the early years of the Gull Prairie settlement. All townships, however, were not endowed with the potential of township 1 south, 10 west, nor did all settlers seek to realize local status and promote economic growth through commercial villages. The uncle of Mumford Eldred Jr., Gull Corners' first merchant, was, like Isaac Barnes, the founder of a settlement and in his own way every bit as ambitious. Like the colonel,

Judge Caleb Eldred came to Michigan with a title that helped to establish him in the territory. Barnes rallied the settlers during the Black Hawk scare, and Eldred was appointed a side judge of the Kalamazoo County court. Also like Barnes, Eldred's plans reflected concern for his adolescent and adult sons—Daniel B., Caleb Jr., Thomas B., Stephen, and Nelson. But the judge's aims in Climax Township were focused differently than Barnes's ambitions in Richland, thus shaping a distinct rural landscape.

Caleb Eldred's life before he came to Michigan reveals that he possessed a high degree of adaptability—not the stolid sort that makes the best of things as they are but the aggressive flexibility of a man who continually recasts his ambitions. Born in Pownal, Vermont, in 1781, Caleb worked as a young man in the cattle trade, driving herds from Vermont to Portsmouth, New Hampshire. He then ran a retail meat business in Green County, New York, with his older brother, Mumford. Mumford would follow Caleb to Michigan, settle briefly on Gull Prairie with his merchant namesake, and then locate permanently in Allegan County.[39]

Caleb did well enough as a drover and retailer to marry Phoebe Brownell of Pownal at the age of twenty-one and to buy, in 1803, a farm near the tiny frontier settlement of Laurens, New York, where earlier another brother, Daniel, had located. Daniel would later join Caleb in Climax Township. Caleb established himself as a figure of some authority in Otsego County, serving at various times as justice of the peace, township supervisor, president of the Otsego County Agricultural Society, and state representative. When his health, and probably his farm, failed sometime in the 1820s, however, he returned to his old life as a drover, plying the trade out of upstate New York to New York City and Baltimore. When acceptance of unredeemable notes again put his health and fortune in jeopardy, Caleb struck out for Michigan Territory.

On his prospecting tour in the summer of 1830, Eldred found a prime mill site on a feeder stream of the Kalamazoo River in what became Comstock Township. He marked a claim and returned to Buffalo to collect his family. When the Eldreds converged on their new tract in January, they found the claim jumped. There was no legal recourse. Before the land office opened, possession proved ownership. Eldred settled his family elsewhere on the stream and began to look for other land with prospects and without rivals. In the spring, he explored a prairie south and east of the Kalamazoo River near the county line in township 3 south, 9 west. He and his party spent their first evening on the prairie trying to name it. Basking in the glow of campfire and discovery, Eldred's son, Daniel B., proposed, "As this caps the climax of all prairies, I move we call it Climax."

The Eldreds' elation was well founded. Climax Prairie was not large; covering much of sections 1, 2, 3, and 10, it was less than half the size of Gull Prairie. But because Climax was well to the east of the southwest-northeast axis along which most of the prairies and early settlements in Kalamazoo County lay, it had escaped much notice. Climax Prairie was the highest ground in township 3 south, 9 west, and a summit of the watershed between the Saint Joseph and Kalamazoo River valleys. Five streams cut across the township, debouching into the rivers or Portage Creek. One of these, Beaver Creek, defined the township's topography and the prairie's place in it.

Beaver Creek flows from the higher elevation in the northeast, near the prairie, to the southwest. The creek cuts the township into two rough triangles, nearly equal in size. Above the creek lie oak opening and prairie soils; below it are heavy loams underlaid by clay. The township's principal topographical feature is this difference in drainage between the northern and southern triangles. Virtually all of the land in the township is of above average fertility, but the settlers found nearly half of it not readily suitable for general farming. The land of the southern triangle was heavily wooded, and much of it was too wet to plow without artificial drainage.[40]

The settlement of township 3 south, 9 west, consequently followed the drainage system. Beginning with the Eldreds, the settlers first claimed the small prairie in the northeast and then the oak openings in sections 3, 4, 9, 10, and parts of 15 and 16. From there, they made entries south and west above Beaver Creek. Only after these areas were taken did they locate in the southeastern portion of the township, and then they avoided the swamp, except to collect marsh grasses for winter hay. Most of the wetlands—extending from sections 12 and 13 on the Calhoun County border west to section 15 and south to Wakeshma Township—were turned over unsold by the federal government to the state of Michigan for disposal in the Swamp Land Act of 1850.

Township 3 south, 9 west, thus presented excellent prospects for the few who arrived early and more limited opportunities for the many who came later. The earliest of the favored few lost no time in locating their claims. In May 1831, Caleb Eldred plowed a 20-acre strip through the center of 160 acres of section 2, turning over sod in each quarter and sowing corn. The crop was not a success—gophers and sandhill cranes gobbled up the seedlings, and a Potawatomi band helped themselves to the ripe ears—but the claim was established, as were those of his sons, Stephen and Daniel B., who staked out three abutting quarter sections.[41] These 640 acres of prairie were the core of the Eldreds' investment in the township. By 1838, the family's holdings, not including the land owned by Caleb's brother, Daniel, and Daniel's sons, totaled over 1,400 acres.

Despite his haste to claim the prairie, Eldred did not hurry to move there. He by then had interests in the Comstock settlement that he used to gain control over the development of township 3 south, 9 west. Eldred's discovery of Climax Prairie coincided with Horace Comstock's arrival in Kalamazoo County, and he became party to Comstock's plan to wrest the county seat from Bronson for his settlement. As part of this campaign, he attempted to demonstrate that the water power at his village on the Kalamazoo River was superior to that at Bronson by building a gristmill in 1832. Comstock financed and had one-half interest in the enterprise; Samuel Percival served as millwright in exchange for a quarter interest; and Caleb and Stephen Eldred divided the remaining share, for which they contributed lumber, carpentry, and millstones hauled from Detroit.[42]

Even though the mill did not help Comstock to capture his prize, it was still of vital interest to settlers like the Gull Prairie men who worked on the millrace. It was also used for many years by settlers on Climax Prairie, which did not have good access to water power, until the township finally acquired a steam-powered mill in 1848. Caleb Eldred linked the development of Climax Prairie to the Comstock settlement in other, more direct, ways in 1832. He built a log home on his prairie holding and divided his family between Climax and Comstock, his wife and daughter, Phoebe, commuting between the two households. Eldred also became postmaster at Comstock and in March 1833 was appointed a commissioner of the proposed road from the Indiana border through Comstock to Gull Prairie that would upset Isaac Barnes's plans for Geloster. A few days after Eldred's appointment, the first Richland Township elections took place at his Comstock home.[43]

The judge was not elected to any township office, but he may not have sought one. His interest in Richland Township involved the relationship of Climax Prairie to Comstock. In December, Eldred sold his Comstock property and reunited his family on the prairie. The following March, the southern half of Richland was set off as Comstock Township. To Comstock was attached township 3 south, 9 west, formerly part of Brady Township, then the southern half of Kalamazoo County. A few days before the April election, the highway commissioners of the old Richland Township approved a December survey of a road that would ultimately connect Climax Prairie with Gull Prairie.[44]

Having so carefully laid the groundwork for their move to the prairie and as its first permanent inhabitants, the Eldreds easily dominated the first years of the new settlement. The only federal land alienated before 1835 in township 3 south, 9 west, lay in sections 1, 2, 3, 4, 9, and 10, encompassing the prairie and the surrounding oak openings. Sales began soon after the family staked its first claims in 1831, but some of the buyers, such as Titus Bronson, the proprietor of the county seat, and John F. Gilkey of Gull Prairie, were absentees. Others, such as C. W. Spaulding, actually lived on the prairie but sold out after a few years. The settlers who with the Eldreds became fixtures on the prairie—Isaac Davis, Isaac Pierce, and Willard Lovell—arrived within months after the judge consolidated households.

The judge did not attempt to build on the prairie a commercial village in the manner of Geloster. Comstock was the prairie settlement's village. The Eldreds' purchases instead constituted a family holding, and they treated their involvement in the provision of local services as an extension of the family's interests. Climax Corners simply grew as an accretion of buildings around the crossing of section lines in the center of the judge's property. The first permanent structure was a massive post-and-beam barn that the judge, aided by settlers from as far away as Gull Prairie and Battle Creek and by a "considerable number" of Potawatomi, raised in the summer of 1833 to house his and his neighbors' grain. Eldred ran the Climax post office from his home, his son, Stephen, fetching the weekly mail from Comstock. Another son, Daniel B., opened the first township store in 1837.[45]

Caleb Eldred also tended to treat such communal institutions as churches and schools, and the buildings that housed them, as his personal property. He was not in this regard unlike Isaac Barnes, who sought to derive his status on Gull Prairie, and thereby his communal leadership, from his stake in the settlement. But the balance between the personal eminence and communal prominence of the two men differed. From the beginning of the Kalamazoo Emigration Society's venture, Barnes had thought communally while attempting to achieve personal ends. For Eldred, communal institutions were instruments of his personal will. Perhaps not surprisingly, the judge was more successful at getting his own way than the colonel. But he met resistance from other prairie dwellers who also had claims to local leadership and who resented his heavy-handedness.

In both Richland and Climax Townships, then, assessments of the potential for local development had by 1835 merged with the proprietary aims of the settlements' founders to shape distinctive rural landscapes. Across Kalamazoo County in extreme northwestern township 1 south, 12 west, the process of landscape definition was just beginning and would lead to very different results.

# Alamo

Settlers passed over township 1 south, 12 west, in their search for prime land in Kalamazoo County. The township had no prairie and was otherwise lacking in superior agricultural land. Soil maps rate as supermarginal less than 1 percent of the township. Some areas, designated as locally supermarginal, are adaptable to truck and fruit farming. Over four-fifths of the township's lands, however, are marginal—fertile but requiring constant improvement for general farming.

Even more significant for the pattern of settlement in the township than the quality and quantity of arable land was its distribution. Township holdings in 1837, two years after the arrival of the first settlers, skirted a swatch of land running roughly from section 12 in the northeast through section 31 in the southwest. Composed of two parallel bands of soil unfriendly to husbandry, the swatch divided the township in two and fractured its settlement. The northern band is wet and sandy and descends in places into muck. By 1880, some of it had been drained and farmed. Gravelly, sandy loam, worthless for farming, makes up the hilly southern band. Below the sandhills in the southeast are primarily loams and sandy loams underlaid by clay. North of the band of wet sand, sandy loams and plains overlie sand and sandy gravel. Portions of sections 4, 5, and 6 in the northwest are a hodgepodge of fine sands, silts, clays, and wet and dry plains.[46]

Township 1 south, 12 west, thus presented settlers with a choice between underdrained and overdrained land of unremarkable fertility. Like their Climax counterparts, the settlers avoided the wetlands and generally selected the droughty plains and sandy loams in the northern portion of the township. Early residents clustered on a little over 1,100 acres in sections 1, 2, 3, 9, and 12 in the northeast and on 160 acres in the southeast. Farmsteads gradually stretched out from both nodes of settlement. From the southeast, they pushed north until blocked by the sandhills; from the northeast, they extended south into a crevice in sections 14 and 23 between the wet and dry sandy lands and west into the township's center. In the crevice and central portion of the township, the major landholders eventually located: Julius Hackley, James Tallman and his sons, and Nelson and Mahlon Everett in the center and Fletcher Ransom and his son in the crevice.

If topography gave settlement in township 1 south, 12 west, no "natural" center, early roads did not create one. One road was originally an Indian trail that ran from Paw Paw in Van Buren County to Otsego in Allegan County, where it joined the road that Isaac Barnes laid out following the Kalamazoo

River to Lake Michigan. Entering township 1 south, 12 west, in the southwest, it snaked north and east, roughly paralleling the bands of wet and dry sand. It was not well improved for many years, and today it is a bumpy county road. Another road was established by the highway commissioners of Kalamazoo Township (renamed from Arcadia in 1836), of which township 1 south, 12 west, was a part until 1837. The route was selected without consideration of settlement in the township, of which there was, in any event, very little in 1836. The road began at the southern township line between sections 31 and 36 and proceeded straight north to the county border.[47]

Whatever degree of spatial coherence that early settlement in township 1 south, 12 west, possessed derived from the inhabitants' reluctance to isolate themselves in the wilderness. The northeastern node was an extension of the settlement in Cooper Township to the east, to which township 1 south, 12 west, was attached for a year before it achieved independent status in 1838. Half of the eighty acres that the first settlers, William Finch and his five sons-in-law, bought in 1835 were in Cooper—of which they saw themselves as outlying residents and to which they looked for services. The first business that the new Alamo Township board addressed in 1838 was the improvement of a road connecting the Finch settlement, as it was called, to Cooper. Cooper by 1837 contained at least one general store and a sawmill. Alamo had neither as late as 1850.[48]

Thus, although it was the earliest and most densely populated portion of the township, the Finch settlement never became a center of life in Alamo. The less-than-wholehearted commitment of Finch's sons-in-law to the township was typical of settlers in the northeast. Finch himself died a few months after his arrival. Two sons-in-law, James Kendall and Henry Swartout, were listed as absentee landowners on the 1838 tax roll. Another, Jerome Thrasher, vanished from township records by 1840. Thomas Chamberlain probably died in Alamo in the mid-1840s. Only the fifth son-in-law, Solomon Case, remained in the township long enough to play a major role in local affairs. Before his departure in 1853, Case occupied many township offices, worked a 120-acre farm in section 1, and served as a land broker between absentee owners and newly arrived settlers.[49]

None of the Finch sons-in-law, except for Case, lived more than a few years in Alamo, and at least three were involved in local land speculation. This is another factor that, besides topography, explains the fractured pattern of township settlement. As the county history asserted: "Much of the land . . . was originally entered by parties for purposes of speculation, and this fact greatly retarded [Alamo's] growth."[50] This statement carefully

avoids the distinction scholars have long made between absentee speculators and resident settlers, a distinction that in Kalamazoo County in general
and Alamo Township in particular obscures the dynamic of federal land
alienation. Even before the district land office opened in 1831, settlers in
Kalamazoo County were speculating in unentered claims. Once federal land
became available for purchase, eastern speculators descended on Kalamazoo County, but settlers continued to dominate sales.[51] Many bought land in
several places and moved several times before settling permanently. For the
most part, the distinction between an absentee and a settler in Kalamazoo
County depended on the township in question. Richland settler John F.
Gilkey was a Climax absentee, as was Josiah Buel, who also owned land in
Alamo. One of Richland's largest absentee landowners was Horace Comstock, promoter of Bronson's rival for the county seat. When the land office
registrar declared in 1837 that the county's lands "were mostly taken up by
settlers," he could only have meant that most entrants listed Kalamazoo as
their residence.[52] They certainly did not occupy all the land they owned.
The receiver himself, who lived in Kalamazoo village, bought land in Climax
and Alamo Townships.

Most so-called absentee speculation in federal lands in Richland and
Climax, as well as in Alamo, occurred at the height of the land boom. In
1838 and 1839, absentees made a little over 60 percent of all government
land purchases in the two townships, acquiring nearly 32 percent of Richland's and close to 40 percent of Climax's lands. Although ultimately responsible for the alienation of slightly over half of the federal land in both
townships, absentees generally bought the poorer lands. Settlements on
Gull and Climax Prairies were securely established before the buying mania
began. Absentee holdings in 1837 hugged Richland's periphery—around,
but never on, the prairie. In Climax, they were concentrated on the wetlands
below Beaver Creek.

Alamo Township, however, was settled at the height of the land boom.
Precisely because it offered a choice between only marginal and unaccept-
able land, settlers bought into the township at the same time that absentee
buyers were most active. The line in Alamo between absentees and settlers
was thus exceedingly fine. The 1838 tax roll, which unfortunately contains
only names, is filled with shadowy figures like William Finch's sons-in-law;
seventy-five men are designated as absentees and thirty-two as resident
taxpayers.[53] Twelve of the absentees (16 percent) either eventually became
residents or were related to settlers living in the township in 1838. A little
under half of both resident and absentee taxpayers, moreover, did not actually own land in the township.[54] Who owned land or paid taxes in Alamo

had precious little to do with who lived there. Only eleven settlers (34.4 percent) of the resident taxpayers of 1838 appeared on the first complete surviving tax roll of 1845. By contrast, over 60 percent of Richland's resident taxpayers in 1839 and Climax's in 1838 remained in the townships through 1845.

Speculation characterized Alamo's settlement. The land gave it no focus; the settlers floated in and out of the township. Nevertheless, a few came to stay before 1840, and their stories are instructive. Unlike William Finch and his sons-in-law, who clung to the amenities of Cooper, Julius Hackley and Mahlon and Nelson Everett plunged into the wilderness. The gamble paid off for Hackley but not for the Everett brothers. Hackley first came to Michigan from Livingstone County, New York, on a prospecting tour in 1835, during which he bought a quarter section in section 17 that included the only superior land in township 1 south, 12 west. He returned to Michigan the following year and made extensive speculative purchases, amounting by the summer of 1837 to over 1,700 acres in and around Alamo. He then went back to New York, married, and in the autumn brought his wife to his holding in section 17. The Hackleys' isolation was nearly complete. They were occasionally visited by mission Indians who bought meals from Mrs. Hackley, but their nearest white neighbors, the Everetts, lived over six miles away in section 29.

Yet Hackley's choice of land over neighbors and services paid off. He appears to have informally operated as a land agent in the township. For example, he probably had a lien on absentee William R. Churchill's Alamo holdings. Churchill and Hackley had traveled to Michigan and prospected Alamo and the nearby countryside together in 1835. Hackley lent his friend money to help pay for land in Allegan County but later acquired the parcel when Churchill could not make up the purchase price. Through such activities, Hackley over time managed to consolidate and improve a 640-acre holding in sections 17 and 18. In 1860, his farmstead was the largest in Alamo.

Nelson and Mahlon Everett did not fare as well as Hackley. The brothers also came from Livingstone County in 1836 and selected a 240-acre tract. The site was not as promising as Hackley's, however. Section 29 contains the usual Alamo mix of overdrained and underdrained soils, primarily sandy loams and muck. The Everetts, moreover, probably did not have the assets to speculate in federal lands like Hackley. Both brothers left the township in the mid-1850s. In explaining his departure, however, Mahlon blamed not the inadequacy of his farmstead but speculation. Absentee holdings "prevented improvements in the neighborhood and retarded greatly the progress of school interests."[55]

Mahlon Everett's complaint was factually correct. By the end of 1839, absentees owned over 75 percent of the land in Alamo, and the brothers' farm remained surrounded by absentees' holdings for over ten years. Land speculation promoted and sustained a fractured rural landscape. In Everett's view, the extreme dispersion of settlement in Alamo resulted in laggard economic development and crippled communal institutions. The first of these charges speaks to Everett's disgruntlement over having to wait until the 1850s for his "unearned increment," what Paul Wallace Gates called a rise in land values due to someone else's improvements.

The second charge was equally personal. The Alamo township board found it difficult to represent fairly such a scattered citizenry. To make it easier for the settlers to vote, for example, the board held elections over two days in two locations.[56] It made some equally awkward decisions about Alamo school districts. Local governments in the Upper Midwest generally tried to make districts congruent with neighborhoods and to locate schools within districts on cheap, more or less centrally located lots.[57] But sometimes, as in Alamo, natural boundaries of neighborhoods were not obvious, and there was no location for a school convenient for everyone. Part of the price that Everett paid for a farm surrounded by absentee landholders was borne by his daughter, who walked four miles daily to and from school.[58]

Everett's complaints are instructive. The formative effect of the land boom of the 1830s was to reinforce Richland's, Climax's, and Alamo's varying prospects for development. These prospects represented the settlers' assessments of the value of local resources—soil, water power, and the likelihood of transportation routes—and they determined who bought federal land, where, and for what purpose. In the end, these assessments proved to be self-fulfilling prophesies. The greater the amount of land in absentee hands, the harder the struggle of township residents to develop local infrastructure over the generation of settlement. Everett's retrospective bitterness also attests to another, equally serious, effect of the land boom: it shaped the settlers' expectations for the future. In the words of Malcolm Rohrbough, "Michigan entered the Union [as] the child of the land office business," and the ruling concern of the state legislature when it met for the first time in 1837 was to perpetuate boom times.[59]

# This Walking before Creeping Will Never Answer

THE NECESSARY MARKET

## Boom Times

On July 9, 1836, the office of the Kalamazoo Land District at Bronson closed its doors, turning away an ever-changing, never-diminishing crowd of applicants. For months, this crowd had lined up nightly for the few beds available in village inns or settlers' homes, crawled into tents, or curled up on piles of straw in barns. They had arisen each morning before dawn to await the opening of the land office. Now they were forced to break their vigil. Inside the land office, the June days passed in a state of siege as the registrar, Abraham Edwards, the receiver, Thomas C. Sheldon, and a small staff of clerks prepared to enforce the specie circular, scheduled to take effect on September 1, and attempted to catch up on a backlog of some 1,500 applications.[1]

The specie circular was the Jackson administration's attempt to brake a runaway national inflation it had itself helped to fuel. After vetoing the recharter of the Second Bank of the United States in 1832, Jackson determined to destroy the bank before its charter expired in 1836 by removing its federal deposits and placing them in so-called pet banks. The decision encouraged the chartering of new banks throughout the nation that, unimpeded by the Bank of the United States, pumped great quantities of paper money into the economy and vastly extended easy credit. Sales of public lands boomed. Poorly capitalized new banks readily issued loans in notes, payable to bearers in specie, to borrowers who used them to purchase government land, which they quickly resold as land prices soared. The specie circular was intended to curb the inflationary spiral by requiring that purchasers of government land pay in specie. Bona fide settlers were allowed until December 15 to acquire up to 320 acres with bank notes.[2]

In any event, the specie circular did little to slow sales of public lands, and the closing of the Kalamazoo District Land Office in June provided only a respite from but no solution to the backlog of applications for the weary staff. The office had closed once before in April, after total sales for the first quarter of 1836 topped $467,000. During the hiatus, the registrar yielded to demands that he continue to take applications and mark tracts as sold on office maps. The decision immediately prompted speculators to apply for land they neither wanted nor intended to pay for and then to auction their entries, the top bidders to purchase their parcels when the office reopened. Business for the latter half of April and May, however, exceeded $720,000, an increase of over 50 percent from the first three months of the year. In the crush, the office staff found it impossible to keep track of the unpaid-for parcels and continued to list many of them as sold.

But the worst—or best—was yet to come, for when the land office reopened after its June recess, it took in over $550,000 in sales. Again the office closed, this time for most of August and all of September and October until November 10. In total, the Kalamazoo District Land Office was open only 169 days in 1836, yet it took in $2,043,866.87; as the editor of the *Kalamazoo Gazette* marveled, "The *average* amount of daily sales was the upward of TWELVE THOUSAND DOLLARS; but sales to the unparalleled amount of SEVENTY THOUSAND DOLLARS have been made in this office in a single day."[3] He had every reason to marvel, for the receipts of the office at Bronson exceeded those of any other land office in the United States in 1836. Michigan was a locus of the great land boom of the 1830s, and the Kalamazoo Land District was the center of the territorial buying frenzy of 1836, the peak year of the boom. Acreage sold in Michigan in 1836 comprised slightly under 20 percent of the public domain transferred to private hands in that year. Nearly 6 percent of the alienated government land lay in the Kalamazoo Land District, the area south of the baseline and west of the principal meridian.[4]

By 1836, absentee speculators like New York City banker Arthur Bronson and his associate Charles Butler, soon to be major owners of real estate in an infant Chicago, and Baltimore lawyer and banker John Montgomery Gordon had descended upon the Kalamazoo Land District. Gordon, who much admired prairie land, passed through Gull Prairie on his way to Grand River country in late October 1836, but he declined to buy land in the township. He was interested in large tracts, unencumbered with settlers, and Gull Prairie was "in most respects exactly similar to those [prairies] we have seen before"—owned, occupied, and selling for ten times the government standard of $1.25 per acre. First settled in 1830, Gull Prairie was, according to Gordon, home to "old farmers" in 1836.[5] His judgment confirms a cardinal principle of the land boom, to which the pattern of purchasing in Richland, Climax, and Alamo also attests: the best land sold first to resident buyers.

In 1836, however, few Michigan residents were pondering the distinction between local and absentee speculation in federal lands. Like the editor of the *Kalamazoo Gazette*, most simply celebrated the extraordinary volume of sales, convinced that it augured the rapid development of Michigan Territory. Such optimism pervaded the first meeting of the state legislature early in 1837. To perpetuate the boom, the legislature authorized the implementation of a system of free banking and a program of internal improvements. The timing of these inherently flawed schemes, enacted on the eve of the panic of 1837–39, guaranteed a peculiarly harsh end to the boom.

Intended to make paper cheap and credit easy, free banking had the effect of destroying Michigan banking for the better part of the 1840s. When the land boom began, a single bank, the Bank of Michigan, established in 1817, served the territory. By the end of 1836, the territorial legislature had authorized nineteen banks, yet still the clamor intensified for more of these institutional pumps of the land boom. Free banking was designed to satisfy this demand. The General Banking Law of March 15, 1837, enabled any twelve landowners to form a banking association on application to a county treasurer or clerk. To guarantee security, the new banks were required to have a capital stock of at least $150,000, 30 percent in specie, a small portion of which was to be deposited in a state safety fund.

Of the forty-nine banks rapidly organized under the General Banking Law, the forty that opened for business went to great lengths to avoid paying any specie into their capital funds—showing the banking inspector strongboxes filled with nails topped by a layer of gold and silver coins or lending one another the requisite hard money in advance of the inspector's visit. For a time, the getting was good for "wildcat" banking. Sales of government land in Michigan, although far below the record set in 1836, remained strong in 1837, comprising nearly 14 percent of all federal land alienated in the United States. The Kalamazoo Land District's share of these sales actually increased slightly from 5.5 to 5.7 percent. When the second financial contraction of the panic came in 1839, however, the wildcats collapsed, dragging down the older banks with them, and their issue, derisively known as "shin plasters," found a new use as wallpaper for drafty cabins.[6]

The state legislature knew that cheap paper and easy credit could not by themselves perpetuate the boom times in Michigan. Continued prosperity also depended upon establishing a market connection with the East. Five days after the passage of the General Banking Law, the legislature approved an internal improvements bill designed to provide the lower peninsula with a comprehensive transportation network. The bill authorized the construction of three railroads at a time when only one of twenty chartered lines in the state was in operation. The Erie & Kalamazoo had completed thirty-nine miles of track between Adrian, in the southeastern corner of the state, and Port Lawrence (present-day Toledo). Nevertheless, the bill envisioned the simultaneous survey and construction of a line through the southern-most tier of counties from Lake Erie to Lake Michigan; another line through the second tier of counties from Detroit to Saint Joseph; and a third, northern line from Saint Clair (present-day Palmer) on the Saint Clair River to the Grand River at Grand Rapids or to its mouth at Grand Haven. The bill also authorized two canals—one to benefit the third tier of counties by connecting the eastern Clinton with the western Kalamazoo Rivers and the other to border the northern reaches of settlement by linking Saginaw, at the base of the lower peninsula's thumb, with the Grand River. To finance this extraordinarily ambitious program, the legislature empowered the governor, Stevens Mason, to negotiate a $5,000,000 loan from the sale of state bonds.[7]

Unfortunately, 1837 was not a good year to enter the stressed eastern financial markets, and Mason was not a good representative of the state's interests. Unable to find a buyer for the bonds until July 1838, the governor agreed to the Morris Canal and Banking Company's demand for a commission that reduced the proceeds from the bonds below par despite the legislature's stipulation that they be sold at full value. Mason initially deposited $1,300,000 in bonds with the company on the understanding that the state would receive payment as they were sold. In November, however, the company offered to buy only a quarter of the bonds, the rest to be acquired by the Bank of the United States, now operating under a Pennsylvania charter. The state would receive quarterly payments of $250,000. Mason delivered the remaining $3,700,000 in bonds to the company, and the legislature did not object to the new agreement when it learned of it in the spring of 1839. Throughout 1839, as the surveys were completed and construction of the rail lines and canals began, the state received its payments on time.

But the full effect of the panic had reached Michigan by that time. In April 1840, the Morris Canal and Banking Company defaulted on its payments. The following year, the former Bank of the United States went bankrupt. When the legislature demanded that the companies return the as yet unpaid-for bonds, it discovered that they had been deposited in England as security for the companies' own loans. Michigan was now obligated to repay loans for which it had received no payment. In the end, after much acrimony in the legislature between proponents of full payment and advocates of partial repudiation, the state paid about a third of the face value of the unsold bonds and interest and principal on those for which it had received full value.

This resolution did not, of course, undo the damage long since done. Michigan's internal improvements program had been thoroughly blasted, and no attempt would be made to salvage even a portion of it with state funds. Only a few miles of canal were ever dug. The northern railroad was abandoned stillborn. The legislature stopped construction of the southern line at Hillsdale in 1843 and funded the central line only to Kalamazoo, which the line reached in 1846. It then sold both companies to private corporations. Not until 1852 did the Michigan Central reach Chicago; two years later, the completion of the Great Western Railway to Windsor provided the link across Canada between the Michigan line and New York at Niagara.[8]

The cumulative effect of the land boom, which fueled the speculative mania; the wildcat banking, which destroyed Michigan currency; and the $5,000,000 loan, which ruined the state's credit and crippled the creation of a transportation network—all epiphenomena of the panic and the ensuing years of depression—was to arrest Michigan's economic development until the Civil War. Asserting that "Michigan society in 1860 resembled that of 1837 in all essentials," Ronald Formisano points to the steep decline in the rate of population growth after the 1830s, when Michigan grew faster than any other state or territory, and to farm values in 1860 that remained far below those of New York, Ohio, and the New England states.[9] On the eve of the Civil War, Michigan continued to be overwhelmingly rural, its population concentrated on farms and in small villages in the southern two tiers of counties. And despite the eventual success of the Michigan Central and Southern Railroads, farmers still relied on roads and rivers to get their crops to market. The state contained only a little under 800 miles of track in 1860, "less than the mileage built in any other state in the Middle West during the preceding decade except for Iowa."[10]

Because Kalamazoo, in the second tier of counties, obtained a rail link in

1846, Richland, Climax, and Alamo were more fortunate than many other localities. Before the coming of the railroad, however, the settlers, like all white inhabitants of southwestern Michigan, participated in a frontier economy characterized by dependence on a precarious river trade and lack of reliable currency. Boom, panic, and depression had little effect on the structure of this economy. The settlers were as bereft of cash and a viable, long-distance market in the midst of the boom as they would be a decade later.

Boom, panic, and depression, however, had a powerful effect on the settlers' expectations for frontier farm making. The boom encouraged extensive investment in federal land and concentration on wheat production on the assumption that a market connection with the East would rapidly develop. The panic and long years of depression taught two sobering lessons. Life on the frontier, the settlers learned, meant economic and perhaps psychological marginalization. Inconveniences that had seemed temporary during the boom became semipermanent with its end. The second lesson derived from the first. Farm making predicated on long-distance market participation, however desirable, was risky. Safety lay in a strategy of diversified commodity production.

## Life on the Margin

Throughout the 1830s and much of the 1840s, the settlers looked to water transport to convey such goods as they could to market. In so doing, they adapted themselves to a pattern of trade established in western Michigan with the opening of the fur trade in 1806. Critical to this trade was the physical geography of the region. Three rivers—the Grand, the Kalamazoo, and the Saint Joseph—originating close to one another near the center of the state, enclose a rough triangle whose base rests at Lake Michigan. The Grand is the northern river, the Saint Joseph is the southern, and the Kalamazoo bisects the triangle. All three of the rivers were navigable by small craft such as bateaux, keelboats, and "arks"—"long flat-bottomed boats of planks"—and could accommodate steam-powered vessels for some miles inland.[11]

Of the three rivers, the Grand was clearly the best suited for transport. It was navigable by steam-powered vessels 40 miles inland to the falls at what became Grand Rapids. Construction of a canal around the falls in the late 1830s extended safe passage to steamboats 50 miles further inland. The Saint Joseph, which followed a far more circuitous course and had a much more erratic current, was navigable by small steamboats to Niles and by small craft to Three Rivers, a distance of 103 miles. The gentlest of the rivers, the Kalamazoo, had enough volume to permit steamboats to travel 38 miles upriver to Allegan and in wet season an additional 37 miles to Kalamazoo.[12] Richland, Climax, and Alamo settlers apparently availed themselves of both the Kalamazoo, on which a flatboat line began operations from Kalamazoo village in 1841, and the Grand, to which they hauled flour via the Grand River road.[13]

Use of the rivers for transport, however, was hampered by the limited harbors on Lake Michigan into which they debouched. The costs of transport around the lakes required ships of sufficient tonnage to make the effort pay, yet south of Grand Traverse Bay, none of the harbors on the eastern shore of the lake, clogged as they were by sandbars, could readily accommodate larger vessels. In his 1839 *Gazetteer of the State of Michigan*, John T. Blois put the best face on the matter by calling "the mouth of the Grand River . . . a superior port to any on this coast" but allowed that "the harbor at St. Joseph," while "good at times . . . requires improving." He termed the harbor at the mouth of the Kalamazoo "commodious" and declared that the tiny settlement of Newark (later Saugatuck) had a "prospect of . . . becoming a place of importance." Far less optimistic was James L. Barton, who in the mid-1840s wrote two pamphlets on the lake trade intended to curry support in the U.S. House of Representatives for federal subsidies for harbor improvements: "So far as steamboats are concerned, owing to the entire want of harbors around Lake Michigan to afford their protection, their whole business is now confined to the western shore of that lake."[14]

The difference in perspective between Blois and Barton reflects more than Blois's boosterism and Barton's awareness of the rapid increase in traffic through the western ports on Lake Michigan, particularly Chicago and Milwaukee. At the time Blois wrote his gazetteer, the Michigan legislature had just passed its massive internal improvements bill, which included plans, summarized in some detail by Blois, for the removal of obstructions in the Grand, Kalamazoo, and Saint Joseph Rivers, the regulation of their flow with dams and locks, and the dredging of their harbors. None of these plans, of course, was realized any more fully than the canal-building program authorized by the same bill, but they indicate the extent to which state boosters in the late 1830s saw the future of Michigan's internal improvements system as dependent on a partnership of water transport and railroads.

In the absence of railroads, water transport for the settlers of western Michigan was the only link, however imperfect, to the eastern market. As physically inadequate as they were, the ports at Saint Joseph, Newark, and Grand Haven at the mouth of the Grand River handled a vital traffic. Indeed, the grain trade at Saint Joseph surpassed that of Chicago until 1843, and its volume increased steadily until 1847, when the Michigan Central extended far enough west of Kalamazoo to cut into its hinterland. The year before, nearly 13 percent of Michigan's lake commerce passed through Saint Joseph, making it the third busiest port in the state after Detroit and Monroe, both of which were fed by railroads. Grand Haven ranked fourth, handling about 4 percent of all exports.[15]

As critical as the river and lake trade was in the 1830s and much of the 1840s to settlers in southwestern Michigan, however, it was also precarious. Early merchants lived from boatload to boatload of cobbled-together goods. The difficulty was partly logistical; loaded downriver with the settlers' produce or freighted upstream with goods to sell to them, the small craft navigated the rivers as obstacle courses. E. Lakin Brown, a Schoolcraft merchant on Big Prairie Ronde in southwestern Kalamazoo County, for example, recalled an ill-fated expedition on the Saint Joseph when the crew of his firm's wheat-laden ark tied up to collect a barrel of whiskey. The ark broke up in the current, and all of the wheat was lost. Indeed, Brown so tired of the Saint Joseph's swift current that he decided to try the Paw Paw, a much smaller river south of the Kalamazoo that empties into Lake Michigan with the Saint Joseph.

The trip went wrong from the beginning. The channels of the Paw Paw proved so twisting that Brown and his partner often poled for several hours only to find themselves back where they had begun. After unloading their wheat at Saint Joseph and filling their boat with goods "as deep as prudent," the men had to fight through a snowstorm to return safely upchannel. The alternative was to wait out the storm and risk their boat's being dashed to pieces at the wharf. Upriver, the men encountered the rapids at present-day Watervliet, through which they could not pole without the loan of a team of oxen. Finally, Brown and his partner reached the mouth of Brush Creek, a feeder stream a few miles below present-day Paw Paw. In the wake of the storm, the river was unnavigable. The men tied up the boat and walked home to Schoolcraft, leaving the goods unprotected. Brown later sent a wagon to collect his cargo. His voyage on the Paw Paw had taken two weeks.[16]

Even an uneventful trip downriver did not guarantee Brown a profitable return on his cargo. Accumulated shipping charges might equal or even exceed the price produce brought once it reached the New York market. Merchants like Brown were consequently "subject to constant losses which could be endured only by the high price at which goods sold." But Brown's ability to sell his goods at premium prices and satisfy his eastern creditors in turn depended upon the settlers' ability to pay promptly with reliable currency. Never plentiful, cash became especially scarce after the collapse of the land boom and wildcat banking in the late 1830s. While in Detroit serving as a state representative in 1841, Brown grew worried that his firm would be unable to satisfy its debts, "the notes of the Bank of Michigan," to which his firm remitted funds for payment to eastern creditors, "having become of doubtful value, 'wild-cat' issue valueless, and other money either scarce or worse than the old bank's notes." He wrote to his partner, instructing him to collect as many outstanding debts as possible and with this "considerable sum" to obtain from the Bank of Michigan drafts to the firm's New York creditors. The drafts were "either received at a large discount or returned to us." When the Bank of Michigan went bankrupt, Brown's firm received a share of the settlement in notes and mortgages to cover its losses.[17]

Such uncertainty was characteristic of Brown's business in trade goods. Indeed, he would have preferred to deal exclusively in goods on consignment or, better still, to market his own produce. One year he and his partner rented a farm and raised a large crop of wheat that they hauled to Paw Paw, "floured," and "boated" downriver to Saint Joseph for transshipment. "Prices were low and profits light but better than the goods business." But Brown could not afford to specialize as a merchant; his business consisted of buying and selling what he could when he could. Nor could he afford to be simply a merchant. Brown's partners changed continually during the 1830s and early 1840s, and his investments, like theirs, whether in real estate, milling, banking, or merchandising, were in constant flux.

From the perspective of settlers attempting to wrest a living from half-broken land, the lack of reliable currency was equally frustrating and perhaps cut even closer to the bone. Throughout the 1830s and much of the 1840s, the settlers lived in communities so lacking in cash that in 1843, when the Alamo highway commissioners reviewed their ready money, they reported only a suspect $20 "Illinois Bk bill" and $45.15 in state scrip, legally acceptable for payment of taxes but otherwise valueless.[18] Like their dependence upon the river trade, scarcity of cash was for the settlers a constant fact of economic life. Dependence on the river trade, however, rested on another unchanging fact: the lack of an alternate means of transport. By contrast, the reasons for the settlers' cashlessness changed repeatedly, as reports of clergymen to the New York office of the American Home Missionary Society (AHMS) make clear. The society underwrote the maintenance of newly organized Presbyterian and Congregational churches with the understanding that the congregations would contribute to the support of their ministers. More often than not, the settlers offered produce in lieu of cash. Why they did so changed with the fortunes of the frontier economy.

As the Reverend William Jones reported from Geloster (Gull Prairie) early in the land boom, the costs of acquiring land and of basic farm making quickly exhausted funds brought from home. It took time, moreover, for the first hastily plowed acres to produce more than the simplest provisions. In January 1833, the settlers anticipated in the coming year their first reliable harvest of wheat for bread.[19] A little over three years later, Silas Woodbury surveyed from Bronson a countryside swept by "land fever." Those with any money were certainly not using it to support the good work of the society. Some had lent their cash at interest rates that Woodbury estimated between 50 and 100 percent. Others had heeded the exhortation of the *Kalamazoo Gazette* to put as much land as possible into production as quickly as possible. "Turn farmer," the editor cried to mechanics and laborers on their way to Michigan; "produce commands a high price and a ready market will be found for all that you can raise."[20]

The editor's optimistic view of a ready market was based on a combination of happily perceived present and rosily anticipated future. The ready market in southwestern Michigan was composed of newly arrived settlers and merchants involved in the river trade like E. Lakin Brown, who would pay only a fraction of what the produce was worth on the eastern market. Like the Michigan legislature a year later, the editor of the *Gazette* assumed that the system of internal improvements designed to forge direct market ties with the East would perpetuate the boom. Indeed, few people in 1837 seem to have considered the possibility that declining land sales and hard times in the East foretold the end of the boom. As a Yorkville settler, giddy with boomer fever, reported to his hometown newspaper in Salem, Massachusetts, "Many who came here five or six years ago with barely enough to buy a single 80 acre lot are now worth $50,000 to $200,000."[21]

Some, however, could read even then the signs of systemic disorder. In November, the Reverend George N. Smith wrote the American Home Missionary Society from Plainfield (later Plainwell). The settlers, he reported, were destitute; they could not sell enough grain even to meet current expenses. Since June, he and his family had lived on donated provisions. Circumstances had not improved with the harvest, although grain and potatoes were now plentiful.[22]

The following September, "A Farmer" laid out the problem for readers of the *Gazette*. Rapid expansion of agriculture as a strategy for perpetuating the boom had backfired: "The absence of pecuniary means cannot be supplied even by the great surplus of grain." At least three-quarters of the farmers, he estimated, were in debt—some to merchants, themselves pressed by eastern creditors, some for stock, and some for farm mortgages held by "speculators" anxious to rid themselves of paper "drawing only 7 per cent, whereas money is worth perhaps 25 percent." Still others owed for improvements on their farms. "Yet we are 'hooted at' (and in some instances almost threatened with Mr. *Lynch*), when we civilly propose to pay them in grain, being the only means in our possession."[23]

Sale of the county's surplus of grain, which "A Farmer" estimated included 150,000 bushels of wheat, was the only solution. Such marketing required cheap, efficient transport to the East. Poling grain down the Kalamazoo River by flatboat to Lake Michigan was neither cheap nor efficient, and eastern grain prices were low. "A Farmer" knew whereof he wrote. Wheat prices on the New York market reached a high for the decade of $2.12 per bushel in 1836. By the time "A Farmer" wrote, they had plummeted to $1.25 and would dip below $1.00 by 1840. They would not reach the levels of 1836 again until 1854.[24]

In the absence of a viable external market, "A Farmer" argued, the alternative was to sell wheat locally for perhaps 50 cents per bushel. Here, again, he did not exaggerate. At the height of the land boom in 1836, wheat prices in Kalamazoo ranged between $1.00 and $1.50 per bushel. A year later, they had fallen by 50 cents, and they continued to fall until hitting bottom at about 44 cents per bushel in the early 1840s.[25] "A Farmer" had done his sums. He estimated the cost on twenty acres of land of breaking, harrowing, sowing, harvesting, and threshing, of seed, and of incidental crop loss from vermin at $255. Twenty acres of wheat at eighteen bushels per acre yielded 360 bushels. At 50 cents per bushel, the farmer's return was $180, or a loss of $75.

Although their accuracy cannot be gauged precisely, these figures nevertheless represented a plausible scenario for Kalamazoo farmers in the late 1830s. The highest costs, according to "A Farmer," were for breaking wild land to the plow at $5.00 per acre, or $100, and for harvesting, including stacking, at $2.00 per acre, or $40. Comparison of his estimates with those of contemporaries and modern scholars shows, at the very least, that "A Farmer" did not inflate his figures to make his point. Historian David Schob concluded from a survey of accounts from several midwestern states in the 1830s and 1840s that breaking prairie cost on average between $1.50 and $3.00 per acre and up to $5.00 per acre in new, isolated settlements. George N. Fuller's survey for Michigan in the same period, however, placed the cost considerably higher—at $10 per acre for prairie, $10 to $12 for oak openings, and $15 for timberland, figures that were corroborated by James H. Lanman in his 1839 *History of Michigan*. Blois, in his *Gazetteer* of the same year, reckoned the cost of clearing timberland somewhat lower, at

$10 to $12 per acre. "A Farmer's" estimate was modest but well within the range of plausibility.[26]

Until reapers came into widespread use in the 1850s, grain was cut with a scythe. A cradler working with two binders could harvest about two acres a day. Schob estimates wages in Michigan in the 1830s and 1840s as between $1.00 and $1.25 per day. Economists Jeremy Atack and Fred Bateman have placed Michigan wages in 1859 at $1.38 per day, a figure they see as representing a decrease in wages over previous years that reflects "an easing of demand for harvest labor with the passing of the wheat boom, the labor-saving effects of the reaper, and the unexceptional nature of the 1859 crop."[27] Schob's estimates would mean that a cradler and two binders, each working for $1.25 per day, could harvest twenty acres of wheat in ten days for $37.50. Atack and Bateman's would place the laborers' combined wages at $41.40. "A Farmer's" calculation of $40 was therefore entirely reasonable.

"A Farmer" demonstrated a similar perspicacity in his estimate of crop yields. Atack and Bateman have shown that antebellum midwestern reports of yields were often optimistic, a species of boomerism designed to attract prospective settlers. "A Farmer's" figure of eighteen bushels per acre, however, was fairly modest, below Lanman's estimate of twenty to thirty-five bushels and at the lower end of the commissioner of patents' reckoning of twelve to thirty bushels per acre for Michigan farms between 1843 and 1856. Atack and Bateman's own estimate for Michigan in 1859 is considerably lower—10.4 bushels—although their sample for the state includes none of the high-yielding prairie counties.[28] Decreasing "A Farmer's" estimated wheat yield, however, only strengthens his case for the severe effect of the boom's end on the settlers' agricultural prospects. At his yield of eighteen bushels of wheat per acre, a settler needed to sell wheat grown on newly broken land at 71 cents per bushel—21 cents above "A Farmer's" going price—to break even. Under these circumstances, few settlers were likely to put additional land into production, and the prospects for new arrivals attempting to build farms on wild land were bleak. If a settler had amassed enough improved acreage before the end of the boom to produce a reasonable crop, he could just manage to ride out the bad times. To break even, he had to receive 44 cents per bushel—the going local price for wheat in the early 1840s.

Scraping by left little room for the unexpected. A scheme by two Richland merchants in 1841 to grind, barrel, and ship east local wheat was so plagued by unanticipated costs that it halved the settlers' return to 22 cents per bushel.[29] The exceptionally severe winter of 1842–43 was proof to those who needed none that their economy was precariously balanced. An extreme report came from the Reverend L. M. S. Smith at Lyons on the Grand River: "Farmers to pay their debts, had sold their wheat until they had scarcely enough for their families, designing to eke out their breadstuffs with coarser grains. But their fodder grew short, and they resorted to the woods and browsed their cattle. But this was poor living and they began to feed them coarse grains sparingly. But week after week winter held in all its rigor. The grain was all consumed, and the cattle . . . wasted away . . . and starved to death." By spring, Smith concluded grimly, the settlers were without bread, meat, and potatoes. One man paid "$1 per hundred [weight] for *bran* for his family."[30]

To "A Farmer," such marginality was intolerable. "This home exchange," he exclaimed, "carries with it no lasting benefit; it is the foreign exchange that is the great agricultural regulator." Such marginality also appeared insolvable. "Gentlemen," he lamented, "in the absence of money, in the absence of a demand for grain, and in the absence of a means of transportation—what are we to do?" If the correspondence of the laborers for the American Home Missionary Society is any indication, the answer was no more apparent to most of "A Farmer's" readers than it was to him. "Do not think me extravagant," pleaded John Dudley in 1838; "I could easier support my family in the city of New York on six hundred doll. than here at the *enormous* price of everything." Dudley spoke metaphorically. Six hundred dollars, as Jeanne Boydston has shown, was the annual cost of subsistence commonly reckoned by contemporary observers for an urban, working-class family, and it was calculated without the wife's contribution of paid and unpaid labor. What Dudley meant was that he and his family could live on his congregation's contributions, but they could not live well: "Potatoes, bread, & just a log house, now & then a piece of butter. . . . I have never been able to get a cow or anything nearer a bureau for my dear wife than Indian baskets, etc."[31]

His comments were echoed two years later by Sylvester Cochrane: "Money indeed scarcely exists in this western country. I have received but one five dollar bill for ministerial services since I came to Mich. (2½ years ago) except what I have received from you [the American Home Missionary Society] and now and then a wedding fee. . . . We do not find any difficulty in procuring the necessaries for our table, but to procure the means of purchasing clothing, paying postage, and a multitude of other little items is impossible."[32] Cochrane's means of living had not changed since his arrival in Michigan, yet he had experienced boom, panic, and depression. It was less the structure of the economy that had changed than the settlers' expectations of it. As the Reverend Hiram Smith put it: "A few years ago, people here were in a rage to get rich; now the chief concern of many is how shall we get a living." His colleague, Justin Marsh, gave a poignant example of the conjoined psychological and material effects of the boom's collapse on the settlers. Investigating a slackening of attendance at Sabbath services, he discovered that members of his congregation were reluctant to attend unless respectably dressed. "Clothing is cash here, and many cannot obtain cash to buy it."[33]

Most telling in the clergymen's comments are not the tales of genuine deprivation—of starving cattle and hollow-eyed families grinding their teeth on bran—but the sense that the supposedly temporary inconveniences of frontier life had become permanent. In this thinking, economic marginality perhaps merged with psychological liminality. The Reverend John Dudley's wife had only Indian baskets in which to store her linens. Her husband was not grateful that his family's subsistence was secure; on the contrary, like the Reverend Hiram Smith's congregation, he was embarrassed by his lot. He did not consider how he would have felt if his wife had neither bureau nor Indian baskets. If the latter was only a poor substitute for the former, the lack of both was unthinkable.

## Toward a Strategy of Diversification

In the midst of such demoralization, some settlers nevertheless attempted to solve "A Farmer's" dilemma: the "absence of money, demand for grain, and . . . means of transportation." The answer was not to wait indefinitely for the arrival of the railroad and prosperity but to find a commodity without the disadvantages of wheat, with its high transportation costs relative to its market value. In 1839, therefore, settlers in the Kalamazoo area debated planting mulberry trees for the raising of silkworms. In the wake of the panic, however, investment in the silk business seemed to many downright silly, if not immoral. By all means, let us plant mulberry trees, wrote "A Farmer," "but *first* let us raise the flax and wool and make our own clothes, and our butter and cheese, and the necessaries of life, and then, if we choose, will be time enough to go into the silk and such *extras*. I think we had better wait till we get our logging done, and til we have grubbed out the bushes, and put in the timothy and clover, and fenced our pastures in; because I don't think silk would answer very well to log in, and if we don't grub out the bushes we might be liable to tear our silk breeches going after cows." Another writer saw the silkworm scheme as another example of the dangers of boom psychology: "This walking before creeping will never answer, and the people of this state begin to find it out too. We never stopt to creep, but commenced by taking lofty strides, and now we find ourselves prostrate."[34]

To its critics, the silkworm business was a metaphor for what was wrong with the settlers' approach to frontier farming. In their concentration on a market connection with the East, on "walking before creeping," the settlers had rendered themselves vulnerable to panic and depression. The critics' objection was not to the market per se but to the nature of the settlers' relationship with it. The settlers' ability to develop their farms—to break wild land, fence improved fields, sustain and increase their livestock, and convert crude dwellings into civilized homes—rested largely on the sale of their wheat on the eastern market. They had focused on producing a marketable surplus without securing the basis of subsistence, the "necessaries of life." Or rather, for the settlers, the marketable surplus had become the basis of subsistence. If they could not sell their wheat, they were reduced to scraping by on potatoes and bran.

The critics of the silkworm business spoke to a real problem, but their judgment of their fellow settlers was harsh. It took time and money to develop a diversified farming regime that would allow the settlers to reap the benefits of the market and insulate them from its uncertainties. Richland, Climax, and Alamo farmers did concentrate on grain production in their first years in the townships, but in retrospect, it is difficult to determine what else they might have done. John Montgomery Gordon to the contrary, the oldest "old farmers" in the townships had been resident for less than a decade, and most for only a few years, when the panic struck. Where would the funds to develop frontier farms come from if not ultimately from the sale of a cash crop? Although the evidence will not allow a full analysis of the settlers' early farming strategies, it suggests the limited possibilities of production.

The sole record of local production before 1850 is found in the state census of 1837, which simply lists by household for Climax and Alamo and by township for Richland the quantities of crops raised and the number of livestock owned.[35] Moreover, each township was indiscriminately enumerated with an adjacent one—Richland with Ross, Climax with Comstock, and Alamo with Cooper. These couplings of more and less developed townships mean that intertownship comparisons are not very useful. The size of farms and the proportion of their acreage that was improved are unknown, so it is impossible to determine how much land the settlers devoted to wheat. Because the census for Richland does not list production by household, it cannot be compared to tax rolls that do record improved acreage. No tax rolls survive from the 1830s for Climax and Alamo.

Despite these limitations, however, the census shows clearly that the settlers' farms were hardly balanced operations that weighed home consumption against market production and wheat against other commodities. Except for a negligible amount of flax raised in Climax and Comstock Townships, all production was in grain, 46.8 percent of which was wheat. The settlers raised a considerable amount of oats (38.6 percent of production) and a much smaller amount of Indian corn (12.2 percent) for both household and livestock consumption as well as small amounts of rye and buckwheat. Some portion of their fields was undoubtedly also given over to potatoes, a staple of the settlers' diet, but potatoes were not listed as a commodity in the census.[36]

Livestock were mostly intended for home consumption and use. Hogs were the most common source of meat because they could forage for themselves and reproduce rapidly, averaging six per household, or slightly over one per capita, figures consistent with production for home consumption. The census did not distinguish between dairy cows and other cattle but grouped them together as "meat stock." The animals were raised for both meat and milk with the result that they produced large quantities of neither. "Meat stock" also presumably included oxen because there were not enough horses (an average of .9 per household) in the townships for most households to make up teams. The average of six head of meat stock per household, then, probably comprised a team of oxen and several head of cattle, at least one of which gave some milk.[37] Finally, the settlers were hardly more invested in wool than they were in flax production. Sheep were few and far between in the townships, averaging .9 per household.

Thus, the critics of the silkworm business had a point. The settlers were producing little that was marketable besides wheat, and if they could not sell their wheat, they were thrown back on a meager subsistence. The solution to the dilemma, the critics insisted, was to diversify production for both home use and for the market. Such a strategy was gradually put into place in the 1840s and 1850s. To supplement wheat production, the settlers branched out into livestock raising. With the exception of sheep, which they came to raise both for their wool and for their sale as blooded stock, the settlers' venture into animal husbandry was not highly specialized. Their small herds of hogs, cattle, and milk cows were intended to provide subsistence plus a margin of marketable surplus sufficient to lessen their reliance on wheat. Other sources of surplus included home manufactures and orchard and garden produce.

Diversification reduced the settlers' dependence upon but not their involvement in the market for wheat. Indeed, after the arrival of the railroad in

1846, Kalamazoo wheat found its way to Detroit, the principal entrepôt of the grain trade for counties along the Michigan Central line. Shipments from Detroit helped to make Michigan the second largest exporter of western wheat after Ohio until the Civil War. Thereafter, Michigan's market share was steadily reduced by competition from wheat-producing states further west. The late 1840s and the 1850s were the glory days for Michigan wheat. As the editor of the *Kalamazoo Gazette* crowed in 1849 upon reviewing samples of wheat and flour at the county fair, "Already our breads are sought with an avidity awarded only to the famed Genesee; and Kalamazoo flour is destined ere long to be known as widely, and take as high a mark as the former."[38]

Responding to the demand for western wheat, Richland, Climax, and Alamo farmers markedly increased their acreages devoted to the crop. According to the agricultural censuses, improved acreages more than doubled in Richland and Climax and nearly quadrupled in Alamo between 1850 and 1860. Wheat not only absorbed the newly improved acreage but took over older fields that had previously produced other grain crops. As in 1837, the largest grain crops after wheat remained Indian corn and oats. Indian corn was as universally grown as wheat, but between 1850 and 1860, the average output per farm decreased by nearly half in Richland and by almost a fifth in Climax, while increasing only modestly (10.2 percent) in Alamo. At the same time, the number of farms growing oats declined from over eight to less than seven in ten in Richland and from nearly six to less than three in ten in Alamo, while remaining constant in Climax. The more dramatic jumps in grain and wheat production in Alamo reflect the slowness of settlement in the township in the 1830s and 1840s, followed by a decade of rapid farm making and improvement. Indeed, percentages of improved acreage planted in grain and of grain lands planted in wheat show a striking convergence of crop mixes in the townships by 1860. In that year, Richland and Climax farmers devoted over 60 percent of their improved acreage to grain, over two-thirds of which was in wheat. In Alamo, grain production commanded over half of the improved acreage, of which over 60 percent was planted in wheat.[39]

Livestock, however, played a key role in the expansion of township farms in the 1850s. Farm values rose dramatically over the decade—climbing at a rate of 56.7 percent in Climax and 157 percent in Richland. Much of this increase was obviously a function of newly improved acreage and attendant fencing and outbuildings, but it was also a result of an increase in the value of livestock, which jumped by two-thirds in Richland and Climax and more than doubled in Alamo. In contrast, the value of farm implements remained constant in Richland and Climax at an average of slightly over $145. The mean value of farm implements in Alamo did increase, from just under $100 to nearly $140, but this simply indicates that farmers in all three townships sought to provide themselves with a minimum of equipment and eschewed expensive machinery.[40]

The increased value of livestock was partially a result of farmers' acquisition for home use of animals that had formerly been in short supply. During the early years of settlement, for example, township farmers had few horses at their disposal and relied instead on oxen. Cheaper and better suited to breaking wild land, especially tough prairie sod, oxen were the preeminent frontier draft animal. They were, however, considerably slower and less versatile than horses.[41] A shift from oxen to horses in the townships was under way by 1850; the majority of township farms had at least one team of horses. Ten years later, more than two-thirds of all farms were so equipped, while fewer than one-third still used oxen.

For most other livestock, the agricultural censuses show clearly that although herds had certainly increased since the late 1830s, they had not become so numerous as to indicate production for a specialized market except on the largest farms. This does not mean, of course, that township farmers did not slaughter cattle or swine for sale but rather that the animals so disposed of represented a surplus beyond home consumption and a supplement to the income generated by the wheat crop. As we will see, moreover, surplus livestock were by no means the only potential sources of additional income. In fact, Richland, Climax, and Alamo farmers balanced wheat production against the production of an assortment of crops and animals intended both for home use and as a safeguard against the vicissitudes of the wheat market.

As the historian John G. Clark has shown, despite the dominance of wheat as a grain crop, antebellum farmers in Michigan were "less committed to wheat farming" than their counterparts in northern Illinois and southern Wisconsin. From the travails of the late 1830s and early 1840s, the settlers learned to avoid the risks of farming by diversifying production. Grain traffic over the Michigan Central, the market route for Richland, Climax, and Alamo farmers, grew steadily in the 1840s and peaked in 1849, the year of the *Gazette* editor's salute to Kalamazoo wheat and flour. Thereafter, the proportion of wheat and flour relative to other provisions carried by the line declined in response to a leveling off of foreign demand and competition from cheaper wheat grown further west. The process of diversification was well under way on Michigan farms in the 1850s, although it was temporarily halted by a surge in foreign demand in 1860 and 1861.[42]

The move toward diversification was readily apparent on Richland, Climax, and Alamo farms in the 1850s, although the exact mix of alternatives to wheat varied within and across townships. Many factors affected what township farmers chose to raise, including soil type, microclimate, and neighborly example as well as capital resources and labor supply, which in turn depended on the age structure of the farming family. Such complexity underscores Allan Bogue's point that even in a region as highly oriented toward commodity production for market as the Iowa and Illinois corn belt of the 1880s, farming operations varied enormously and were not limited to universally raised, specialized crops and stock.[43] It also raises the issue of the extent to which the scale of farming operations in the townships reflected the settlers' options for diversification.

Richland, Climax, and Alamo farms varied in size from fewer than 30 to more than 320 acres. They were distributed on a bell-shaped curve: roughly 66 percent of the farms ranged between 40 and 160 acres; about 40 percent contained between 60 and 120 acres. One might expect diversity of production to rise steadily from the smallest farms, whose size limited their operators' options, to the largest, but such was not entirely the case. The smallest farms were the least diversified, but, beginning with forty-acre spreads, the scale of production options was in proportion to the number of farms in each category of size. What did change, although not consistently from the smaller to the larger farms, was the amount of any one kind of produce grown or livestock raised. Clearly, if the measure of specialization was the restriction of crop and stock options for market, large-scale township farmers were no more specialized than their neighbors on smaller farms. Instead, larger farms gave their operators a better opportunity to hedge a greater amount of surplus produce and livestock against their wheat.

The majority of township farms had cattle, and virtually all of them raised hogs in the 1850s. Neither animal, however, was raised in great numbers. Herds on most farms averaged five or fewer head of cattle and ten or fewer head of swine. Except in Climax, where farms as small as 80 acres or more sustained average herds as large as twenty head by 1860, only farms of 320 acres or more contained more than ten head of cattle. Only in Richland in 1850 were there mean herds in excess of ten hogs on farms as small as 80 acres; otherwise herds of this size could be found only on farms larger than 160 acres.[44]

Sheep were less universally raised but far more directly targeted for the long-distance market. Thirteen years after the state census had recorded a near absence of the animals in the township, the Kalamazoo area had become a major sheep-raising region. In taking up sheep, Richland, Climax, and Alamo settlers, like their counterparts elsewhere in Michigan and in Ohio and Illinois, followed the lead of farmers in northern New England. For twenty years after the War of 1812, Yankees had built up large flocks and labored to improve them by importing blooded stock from Europe. By the 1840s, however, cheap western wool, produced from large, indifferently bred flocks, had cut into the market for the New England product. Yankees responded by reducing the size of their flocks and intensifying their efforts to improve the weight and quality of their fleeces through selective breeding. Vermont sheep in 1850 outproduced all others in the nation, with an average clip of 3.3 pounds. Michigan sheep ranked third after New York, with an average fleece of 2.7 pounds.[45] Mean clips in Richland, Climax, and Alamo mirrored the state average, at 2.6, 2.3, and 2.7 pounds, respectively.

Kalamazoo-area farmers, however, did not rest content with low-quality wool. Fletcher Ransom, a well-to-do Alamo settler, explained his decision to acquire blooded animals to the editor of the *Gazette* at the county fair in 1850: "It was of little use to attempt to make money out of common stock, for it would not pay—the outlay for keeping far overbalancing the avails. . . . None but blooded stock . . . would throw the balance on the credit side of the ledger." Ransom sought "the sheep that would produce the most wool, for the least keep," and pointed proudly to the results of his efforts. His flock of 155 sheep now yielded an average clip of over four pounds per sheep. Duly impressed, the editor doubted whether many flocks in Michigan could match Ransom's.[46]

Many, of course, could not compete with Ransom, but he was by no means the only Kalamazoo wool grower in 1850 involved in stockbreeding. Across the county in Climax Township, the Lovell brothers, George and Lafayette W., were winning prizes for their merinos at the county fair, as was John F. Gilkey of Richland Township for his blooded stock. Indeed, within a decade, the Kalamazoo area would become well known to flockmasters as far west as central Iowa as a leading supplier of well-bred animals outside New England. Nor were breeding programs confined to large, well-capitalized farms like those of Ransom, the Lovells, and Gilkey. By 1860, the average township clip had risen a full pound to 3.5 in Richland, 3.3 in Climax, and 3.7 in Alamo.[47]

Average weights of fleeces, however, tell little about the dimensions of sheep raising in Richland, Climax, and Alamo: who raised sheep, how many sheep they raised, and the effect of breeding programs on the scale of production. Because sheep raising required extensive pasturage, it occurred most commonly on larger farms. Over 70 percent of township farms with flocks in the 1850s exceeded eighty acres. This tendency strengthened over the decade as the number of farms without sheep increased between 1850 and 1860 from roughly 25 percent to over 33 percent in Richland and Climax and from 40 percent to over 66 percent in Alamo. The size of flocks, however, varied over time and by township. The number of flocks of fifty or more sheep between 1850 and 1860 declined in Richland from 60.5 to 49 percent but rose in Climax from 41.1 to 50.2 percent and in Alamo from 4.5 to 9.4 percent. These figures suggest, first, a convergence in Richland and Climax in optimal flock size. Second, the relative paucity of sheep in Alamo compared to the other townships reinforces the point that livestock raising for other than home use was associated with better developed farms.

To assess the role of sheep raising in township agricultural regimes, it is useful to compare the sizes of flocks and output per sheep in Richland, Climax, and Alamo with Hal Barron's figures from Chelsea, Vermont, for the same years.[48] Sheep were far less commonly raised in the Michigan townships than in the New England town, where slightly under four out of five farmers maintained flocks. Those who raised sheep in Richland and Climax, however, did so on a far larger scale.[49] More than a quarter of Richland and Climax farmers maintained flocks of more than fifty sheep compared to less than one-fifth of their Vermont counterparts.

Moreover, despite over a decade of stockbreeding in the townships, Chelsea sheep still outproduced Richland, Climax, and Alamo sheep. The average clip in Chelsea was 4.1 pounds, considerably better than the best township mean of 3.7 pounds in Alamo. Nevertheless, breeding programs in Richland, Climax, and Alamo had produced an effect. Not only had average township clips risen over the decade at a rate comparable to that in Vermont, but in Richland, as in Chelsea, more than one in five sheep raisers produced average clips of five or more pounds. These comparisons indicate, again, that township sheep raising, unlike production in Vermont, was embedded in a mixed farming regime. Farmers weighed the clip against other uses for their land—the most wool for the least keep, as Fletcher Ransom put it. Sheep raising was one option among several for farmers seeking a balance between grain and other forms of production.

Another option was dairying, although never on a large scale. Only farms larger than 160 acres in Richland and 320 acres in Climax in 1850 and larger than 160 acres in Climax and 320 acres in Alamo a decade later maintained more than an average of five milk cows. Still, virtually all township farms had milk cows. As Atack and Bateman have shown, although the number of milk cows on antebellum northern farms tended to rise with farm size, even fairly small farms were capable of producing surplus cheese and butter.[50] All township farms larger than thirty acres produced surpluses of butter in 1850 and 1860. Butter production on farms of eighty or more acres was considerably greater than on smaller spreads. This increase reflected the difference between farms averaging between two and three and three or more cows. In contrast, relatively few farms—a high of 25.5 percent in Richland in 1850 compared to a low of 7.4 percent in Alamo in 1860—made cheese, little of which was for other than home consumption.

Scholars have identified dairying as part of women's farm labor, although Lee A. Craig and Nancy Grey Osterud have demonstrated in different ways the difficulty in making strict correlations between gender and type of farm labor. Craig has shown that antebellum farming families on the frontier tended to apportion labor according to the needs of farm building. In her examination of relations between farm husbands and wives in a dairying region in upstate New York in the latter half of the nineteenth century, Osterud has revealed the important role that personal preference played in determining work patterns.[51] Despite this evidence of variations in work allocated by gender, however, it is likely that Richland, Climax, and Alamo women played a considerable role in dairying and that this role increased with the decline of home manufacturing in the townships.

Certainly the editor of the *Gazette* held women responsible for both dairying and home manufactures. As he complained after viewing the fruits of women's labor at the county fair in 1851, "It would have pleased us better to have met a full display of domestic flannels, good woolen stockings, socks, mittens, drawers, shawls, etc., as well as specimens from the dairies of our countrywomen. These have to do with the substantial comforts of everyday life."[52] The relationship, of course, between what women produced and what they exhibited at fairs was hardly direct, and the editor's comment spoke more to what he thought women ought to be doing than to what they actually did in the townships. Although most farms were involved in dairying, most were not engaged in home manufacturing, and markedly fewer produced home manufactures as the decade wore on.

The trend in the townships, moreover, was away from home manufacturing and toward dairying. Surpluses of butter increased greatly in the 1850s—by 66 percent in Richland, nearly 80 percent in Climax, and more than 20 percent in Alamo. By contrast, the number of farms engaged in home manufacturing and the value of goods thereby produced declined substantially. In 1850, 10 percent of farms in Richland and less than 25 percent in Climax and Alamo produced home manufactures with an average value of $27.80, $17.32, and $17.77, respectively. A decade later, fewer than 10 percent of all township farms did so, and the mean value of goods ranged from $13.90 in Climax to $9.07 in Alamo. These declines were part of a larger trend away from home manufacturing on northern farms in the decade before the Civil War. Most township farms on which this activity continued were larger than 120 acres, and the average value of the goods they produced was comparable to that of other midwestern farms of similar size. These, as Atack and Bateman have shown, remained the most committed to home manufacturing of all northern farms.[53] Hence, for a certain kind of township farm, home manufacturing remained a viable form of production.

Farm women probably also contributed to the cultivation of fruit and garden vegetables in the townships, neither of which appeared on the 1850 agricultural census. By 1860, about half of the farms in Richland and Climax and over a third in Alamo maintained orchards. Fruit cultivation occurred most frequently on larger farms, which could better afford the land, time, and care necessary for nurturing young trees into production. By contrast, market gardening required a far smaller outlay of capital and was therefore practiced on nearly four-fifths of Richland and on over half of Climax farms regardless of size. A final source of saleable surplus in the 1850s depended on having the right kind of woodlot. One in three farms in Climax and one in ten in Alamo produced maple sugar.[54]

Maple sugar, fruit, vegetables, home manufactures, butter, meat, and wool—these were the complements to grain-based production on township farms. By establishing diversified agricultural regimes, farming households in Richland, Climax, and Alamo had by 1860 secured the "necessaries of life." They had acquired the means of surplus beyond subsistence to allow them to participate in the market for wheat without depending on it. Having learned to creep, they could now walk. Their success, however, did not come easily, and many families on frontier farms in the 1830s left the townships without achieving such security. The great irony is that those who did stay were helped through the transition by native peoples whose displacement the settlers had mistakenly assumed their arrival would effect.

# The Unhallowed Dicker Traffic

## THE NECESSARY NEIGHBORS

On November 4, 1843, one Paris Fletcher appeared before Richland Township justice of the peace, Mumford Eldred Jr., in response to a warrant issued on the complaint of Chauncey W. Calkins. Five witnesses gave testimony. The defendant then signed a confession, drafted by Eldred, admitting his "violation of . . . an act to provide for the protection of the Indians. . . . A[p]proved April 9th 1841." Fletcher was fined $20 as mandated for first-offense violations of the state statute. He was also charged a hefty $5.07 in court costs, for the Richland justice of the peace court had expended considerable time and effort in bringing him to trial. Meticulously, Eldred recorded the costs of a warrant and two subpoenas, the constables' fees for their delivery, as well as the costs of Calkins's affidavit, Eldred's judgment, and payments to the witnesses. All in all, Fletcher's trial had involved a fairly elaborate and expensive procedure for a legal forum in which most defendants either responded readily to a summons and confessed their guilt in person or admitted it by failing to appear.[1]

Fletcher's case was unusual for another reason. The principal business of the Richland justice court was the litigation of petty debts. In the first state statutory code of 1837–38, Michigan justice courts acquired original and exclusive jurisdiction in all civil suits brought for debt or damages of less than $100, excluding real actions and actions for disturbance of easements, replevin, libel or slander, malicious prosecutions, and probate.[2] Criminal actions were not initially within the purview of the justices, and such powers as they gained over the next two decades were limited to cases involving first-offense larceny of property worth less than $25, malicious damage to highway markers, land, or livestock (the last not to exceed $100), and trespass of under $50 in damages.[3] Under these circumstances, it is no surprise that debt cases in the Richland dockets constituted a little over four-fifths of all suits.

Fletcher, however, was no delinquent debtor. He was brought to the Richland justice court on an action of debt in accordance with procedures specified by the 1841 statute, but he was convicted of selling liquor to the Ottawa who lived at a Baptist mission founded in 1836 just across the township border in Barry County. The suit was brought in the name of the people of Michigan by Calkins, a white settler, but the five witnesses against Fletcher were all Indians, including a woman named "Rachel." Fletcher's case thus appears curiously out of place among the dockets of the Richland justice court. It is surrounded by suit after suit for failure to pay within a specified period—usually months and less than a year—for goods received, services rendered, or cash loaned.

In October 1842, for example, William Lewis declared himself in assumpsit; that is, he was owed a debt for a note signed by John C. Stonehouse in September 1841 in which Stonehouse promised delivery in January 1842 of three tons of "good ground plaster of Paris" (gypsum, commonly used for fertilizer) worth $35. Other debts were for goods purchased and services on account. Township merchants appeared in court to press claims against patrons whose tabs had run too high. Laborers who had waited too long for their pay brought suit against their employers. William Stone worked for John T. Lake in the summer of 1842 for two weeks for $5 and for one and a half days for 75 cents a day. In December 1843, Stone declared himself in assumpsit for his labor. In contrast to such cases, the 1841 act barred all dealings with Indians involving liquor, making it illegal to "sell, exchange or give, barter or dispose of any spirituous liquor, wine, mixed liquor, or other intoxicating drink to any Indian or Indians, male or female." Violation of contractual relations was irrelevant in suits brought under the act.

In other ways, however, Fletcher's case was of a piece with the fabric of economic life revealed in part by the debt litigation in the Richland justice court. Like most other cases in the dockets, his trial brought together neighbors, for justice courts were truly local institutions: justices were local men, as were the litigants who appeared before them. Residents of each Michigan township elected four justices to four-year, rotating terms. To bring suit in a justice court, one of the parties had to live in the township of venue or an adjacent township.[4] In Richland, the estimated ratio of resident to nonresident litigants was a little over three to one, and most of the latter came from townships, like Richland, in the northern tier of Kalamazoo County.[5]

Moreover, although the trial of Paris Fletcher is the only known instance of Indians appearing before the Richland justice court, it may not have been a unique event. The case was recorded in the only surviving docket book of four kept by township justices between 1841 and 1859. Each justice was legally required to keep a single-volume record of his work and to pass it to his successor when his term ended. The docket book contains two other prosecutions of illegal sales of liquor to Indians, both brought by the Reverend Leonard Slater, who ran the Baptist mission. Neither, however, involved witnesses.

As sparse as the details of Fletcher's case are, they nevertheless open a window on a complex, highly personalized interaction between Yankee settlers and native peoples in western Michigan in the three decades before the Civil War. Who Fletcher himself was is unknown, except that he was a Barry County resident. The timing of the charges against him, however, suggests that he attempted to sell liquor to the Indians at the Slater Mission when they had money to pay for it; that is, in late September or early October, shortly after the yearly disbursement of treaty annuity monies in silver half-dollars. As part of their payment for ceding their lands to the federal government in 1836, the Ottawa people received annually $18,000. From this sum, each person received $7 to $8—not a large amount, but in a period in which hard cash was in short supply and most paper currency was of dubious value, it was enough to make violation of the law prohibiting the sale of liquor to the Indians worth the risk.[6] And it was risky because many of the Yankee settlers were ardent advocates of temperance. Richland Township had been dry since the arrival of the Kalamazoo Emigration Society. By the early 1840s, moreover, many of the Ottawa were themselves eager to suppress the traffic in liquor, as the presence of Indian witnesses at Fletcher's trial attests. Clearly, temperance was one issue on which at least some Indians and settlers could agree.[7]

But Fletcher's case was not merely, or even primarily, about the shared moral climate at Richland and the Slater Mission. Indians served as witnesses, not complainants, in Fletcher's case, even though under the 1841 statute they were "capable of suing and being sued" in any Michigan court and "entitled to all judicial rights and privileges of other inhabitants." The suit came about at the behest of two white men, and although it is possible that they acted at the request of the Ottawa, as Slater and other settlers are known to have done, neither was a disinterested or even simply a morally righteous participant. In the first place, Chauncey W. Calkins, the complainant, had a direct financial interest in the outcome of the suit, for he was entitled to half of Fletcher's $20 fine—considerably more than the 49 cents that each of the five Ottawa received for their testimony. Mumford Eldred Jr., the presiding justice, received $1.01 in court fees.

More important is who Calkins and Eldred were. Eldred was the owner of the only general merchandise store in Richland; Calkins was his clerk and soon-to-be brother-in-law.[8] The merchant was in all likelihood as much the complainant in Fletcher's case as his clerk. The suit may well have originated when Indians from the Slater Mission, drunk on Fletcher's liquor, created a disturbance in Eldred's store. The Ottawa were long accustomed to doing business with Eldred, and he was undoubtedly as interested in collecting their silver half-dollars as was Fletcher, particularly if, like other merchants in western Michigan, he was used to extending credit to the Indians.[9] The amount the Ottawa spent on Fletcher's liquor reduced the cash available to Eldred to pay his own creditors. His recourse when white customers failed to settle with him was to sue them in the township justice court. Indeed, debt collection through litigation was for Eldred a standard business practice. Eldred, along with Richland's other principal merchants between 1841 and 1859—Calkins, who took over Eldred's store in 1845, and Elnathan Judson, who owned a shop and a boardinghouse—participated in one out of six debt cases brought before Richland justices for which records survive. The case against Fletcher was a means of removing the competition for the Ottawa's trade. The suit was not so different from the debt cases litigated in the township justice court after all—with one exception: the peripheral role of the Ottawa. There is no record in the dockets that, despite the act of 1841, Indians ever participated in suits on their own behalf. Mumford Eldred Jr. apparently did not sue his Ottawa customers, and they in turn did not sue white settlers, as the latter readily did to one another.

Fletcher's violation of the "act to protect the Indians" thus points to a sustained interaction between Yankee settlers and native peoples predicated upon economic exchanges, the value of which each understood in congruent, if ultimately dissimilar, ways. The very date of the suit suggests the peculiar circumstances that made possible these relations. Fletcher was brought before the Richland justice court seven years after the Ottawa ceded their lands in western Michigan to the federal government and two years after the removal of the Indians west of the Mississippi River was supposed to occur. Had it not been for the failure of federal Indian policy, the timing and geography of white settlement, and the economic crisis of the late 1830s—the panic and ensuing depression—Paris Fletcher would have found some other means of earning a living, and Yankee merchants like Mumford Eldred Jr. would not have counted Indians among their valued customers.

## "Our Country Cousins"

Richland, Climax, and Alamo are townships of the Kalamazoo River valley. In the early nineteenth century, the river was the traditional boundary between the Potawatomi and their neighbors to the north, the Ottawa.[10] Both Richland and Climax were the sites of Indian encampments long before the arrival of white settlers. Climax was visited every spring by a band of Potawatomi who gathered sap and made sugar in township maple groves. The Indians probably also did some planting on the prairie.[11] According to Isaac Barnes, the Kalamazoo Emigration Society found a band of "harmless" Potawatomi ensconced on Gull Prairie when it arrived in 1830. Although they were undoubtedly harmless, the band may also have included some Ottawa. *The Kalamazoo County History* declares that the "remnant" of the "once powerful tribe of *Pottawatomies*" was led by "old chief Noonday," who is later in the *History* correctly named as the leader of the Ottawa at the Slater Mission. Gull Prairie was also the site of a well-known winter Indian encampment regularly visited by fur traders.[12]

In theory, the settlers' encounter with the Indians should have been brief. In 1833, the Potawatomi ceded the last of their claims to land in western Michigan after negotiations that extended over twelve years and six treaties. The total area ceded included lands between the Kalamazoo and the Grand Rivers that were actually inhabited by the Ottawa. Three years later, the Ottawa gave up their lands in the lower peninsula between the Grand River and the Mackinac Straits.[13] Indian lands thus became public domain, and with the authority of the federal government behind them, the settlers brooked no interference from the former owners, now mere occupants, in their conversion of the domain into private property. In Climax Township, for example, Caleb Eldred's son, Stephen, made clear to the Potawatomi that they now shared the prairie on sufferance from white settlers. When the settlers shot some of the Indians' dogs for killing their hogs, the dogs' owners demanded compensation of between $20 and $30 per dead canine. Eldred put an end to these "annoyances" by telling the Potawatomi that "he would report them to the Indian agent at Detroit, and they would receive no more presents from the federal government"; that is, he threatened the Potawatomi with the loss of their annuity monies and goods established by treaty.[14]

This story is revealing for several reasons. The first is that the settlers' hogs, like the Indians' dogs, were free-ranging, and the former were, in their own way, as destructive as the latter. The settlers were accustomed to paying for livestock depredations to crops, but only if it could be proved before a justice of the peace that the animals had broken into a well-fenced field.[15] The Potawatomi may well have set their dogs on the settlers' hogs because the swine were uprooting the Indians' unfenced fields, and they may have set the damages as high as they did to compensate not only for the dead animals but also for the loss of their crops. Eldred, however, did not recognize the legitimacy of the Potawatomi's claims. If the Indians did not fence their fields, he undoubtedly reasoned, they deserved the damage, and in any event, they could not fence what they did not own. No right of preemption protected the Potawatomi's fields. They were squatting on federal land soon to become the property of a white settler. Eldred saw no need to arbitrate informally the dispute with the Potawatomi. He simply summoned the authority of the federal government.

As this episode attests, Indian land cessions in western Michigan coincided with and were prompted by the massive land boom of the 1830s. As early as 1821, the year that the Potawatomi made their first cession of land in the Treaty of Chicago, federal negotiators had considered how white settlers would enter and take possession of the region. The treaty authorized the creation of the Chicago Road, which ran west from Detroit, skirting the Indiana border. A decade later, Yankee settlers, who had arrived at Detroit via the Erie Canal and Lake Erie, drove wagons west along the road. Approaching western Michigan from the south, they occupied in succession the Saint Joseph and Kalamazoo River valleys and entered the Grand River valley on the eve of the panic of 1837–39.

The federal government thus saw as its twin goals quieting Indian land claims and removing the Potawatomi and the Ottawa from western Michigan in advance of white settlement.[16] It was successful in the first objective but failed in the second. Although subjected to a brutal, military-style roundup in 1838, many of the Potawatomi managed to escape deportation. Only 600 of the estimated 2,500 Potawatomi living in Michigan in 1837 were forcibly relocated west of the Mississippi River. Of the rest, a small band of Catholic Potawatomi, the Pokagons, was granted exemption from removal under the 1836 treaty. Others fled to Canada, from which a number later returned, or moved north to live among the Ottawa, with whom they were already inter-married. As for the Ottawa, they were assigned five tracts on which they were to live for five years, pending removal. The Grand River Ottawa were expected to relocate to a reserve near present-day Manistee. Few actually did so, and there the matter rested for twenty years, the federal government being unwilling either to prosecute its program of removal or to assign permanent lands to the Ottawa.[17]

The federal government's plan to remove the Ottawa failed for a number of reasons. In the first place, the panic of 1837–39 and the ensuing depression effectively curtailed federal land buying and reduced white settlement to a trickle until well into the 1840s. The federal government, therefore, was under little pressure from newly arrived migrants to decide the fate of the Ottawa. Even in the area between the Kalamazoo and Grand Rivers, the lands last occupied by white settlers before the panic, much of the federal domain remained unpurchased, allowing Yankees and the Ottawa to coexist for a number of years. Under the terms of the 1836 treaty, the Indians were permitted to continue hunting and planting on lands not taken up by white settlers.[18]

Moreover, decentralized Ottawa political organization frustrated the attempts of federal negotiators to achieve agreement among the Indians on a new location outside Michigan. The two divisions of the Ottawa, the Grand River and the L'Arbre Croche, disagreed frequently with each other. They were in accord only in their determination to avoid removal. Within each division, the Ottawa lived in small, autonomous bands that seemed to white settlers to pose little threat. Finally, the Ottawa themselves worked aggressively to demonstrate their ability to live among Anglo-Americans. To this end, they sought white allies not only among the Indian traders, who were deeply interested in the Ottawa's annuity monies, but also among the Yankee settlers.

As evangelical Protestants, many of the settlers saw assisting the Ottawa as an exercise in benevolence, as a way of encouraging the Indians on the path to "civilization." The Ottawa understood well the real and symbolic value of land in fee simple in their resistance to removal. Although wards of the federal government, as landowners, and thereby state and local taxpayers, they demonstrated their adaptation to Anglo-American ways. Hence, they enlisted the settlers' help in purchasing land with their annuity monies. All three of the Ottawa's permanent bases between the Kalamazoo and the Grand Rivers after the treaty of 1836 were Protestant missions, and all three resulted from Ottawa purchases of federal land with the assistance of white allies: the Episcopalian Griswold Mission in Allegan County, the Congregational Old Wing Colony near present-day Holland, and the Baptist Slater Mission, whose inhabitants did business in Mumford Eldred Jr.'s store and appeared before the Richland justice of the peace court.[19]

Despite the settlers' support of the Ottawa's efforts to avoid removal, however, Yankee and Indian views of the role of the missions differed. Yankees saw the missions as an opportunity for the Ottawa to obtain the rudiments of white civilization: Protestant Christianity, reading and writing in English, male techniques of settled agriculture, and female domestic skills. The Reverend George N. Smith proudly concluded when the Ottawa band at Old Wing bid successfully on a county road contract that the band was striving to act like a "company of white men."[20] But the Ottawa were far less interested in becoming like a company of white men than in learning to live as Indians in the midst of white settlement. For them, the missions were less cradles of civilization than bases from which to pursue a seasonally migratory economy.

The Indian economy of western Michigan combined horticulture—the cultivation of corn, beans, and squash—with hunting, fishing, and collecting wild plant foods. Villages attained their largest populations during the planting and harvesting seasons, then split up for winter hunting, followed by visits to maple groves for sugar making, to rapids for spring fish runs, and to trading posts. Contact with whites, beginning in western Michigan in the latter half of the eighteenth century, introduced new technology, such as guns and traps, and new domestic plants and animals but did not fundamentally alter the subsistence economy. The Ottawa, for example, acquired seeds from the French for apple and peach orchards, and the Grand River valley became a provisioning ground for traders and military personnel at the Mackinac Straits.[21] The record of the Ottawa at Old Wing shows the continuing adaptation of white ways to the seasonally migratory economy. The Indians may have owned private property, with fenced fields worked by oxen and plows, but they refused to live on their farms year-round. The missionary Smith's efforts to preach and teach were regularly interrupted when the band left Old Wing to hunt, fish, gather cranberries, or carry their harvest to Kalamazoo, Saint Joseph, or Chicago to exchange it for such Anglo-American provisions as white flour.[22]

Thus, the Ottawa clung stubbornly to a way of life that in the eyes of their white allies marked them as uncivilized. It is therefore deeply ironic that the Indians' seasonally migratory economy complemented and, indeed, supported the settlers' frontier economy. The settlers lived in a world in which long-distance trade was tenuous, and local exchanges were transacted with little cash. To survive, they were forced to adapt to a complex, multifaceted trade in which the Potawatomi and particularly the Ottawa had long proved adept. First, in the absence of a more viable means of transport, the settlers poled their produce down the Saint Joseph, Kalamazoo, and Grand Rivers for transshipment around the lakes to the East. In pursuing the riverine trade, they followed the course of the fur trade as it had evolved in western Michigan since 1806, when the previously untapped region was opened to fur gathering. The American Fur Company consolidated, extended, and intensified the fur trade in 1821 by establishing the Grand River outfit, with posts as far south as the Kalamazoo River. By the time that significant white settlement advanced into western Michigan, the heyday of the American Fur Company had nearly passed. In 1834, John Jacob Astor sold out of the company; two years later, the Grand River outfit was abandoned, the head of the outfit, Rix Robinson, receiving a hefty claim in the Treaty of Washington, which he had helped to negotiate.[23]

The fur trade continued into the early 1850s in less valuable pelts and skins such as muskrat, deer, and raccoon under the aegis of highly competitive private individuals formerly controlled by the American Fur Company. As the travels of the Ottawa band at Old Wing make clear, moreover, furs were not the Indians' only merchantable commodity in this late phase of the trade. Barrels of cranberries and huckleberries were shipped to Buffalo from Lake Michigan ports at the mouths of the Saint Joseph, Kalamazoo, and Grand Rivers. Maple sugar, consigned to merchants in Boston and New York, was "packed in 'mokirks' (also 'mococks') which were small baskets or boxes . . . weighing from one to sixty pounds. The small 'mokirks' were often elaborately decorated by squaws with fancy beadwork." There was also a small trade in beaded moccasins.[24]

Yankee merchants entered readily into the trade in furs, berries, and maple sugar and into competition with other traders, accustomed to dealing only with Indians. Disgruntled, some of the Indian traders attempted to monopolize their clientele by stocking goods attractive to Indian but not white customers.[25] Yankee merchants, however, quickly discovered that the Indians themselves were uninterested in such exclusivity, and Indian commodities soon took their place alongside white produce poled downriver on flatboats. Unlike many whites, moreover, at least some of the merchants' Indian customers could pay cash, "always in silver half dollars," for goods. It is, of course, well known that much of the government annuities went directly to Indian traders, squandered in liquor or in payment of inflated debts for goods.[26] But not all of the silver half-dollars were captured in this manner, as the case against Paris Fletcher in the Richland justice of the peace court attests.[27]

How valuable the Indian trade in commodities and coin was for the Yankee merchants of western Michigan is difficult to determine. Certainly Mumford Eldred Jr.'s role in Fletcher's conviction indicates that he found dealing with the Ottawa worth his while. The importance of this trade in his overall business scheme, however, is unknown. Moreover, the few surviving firsthand accounts of other Yankee merchants are retrospective, reminiscences of old pioneers. Still, as precariously situated as these men were, the availability of Indian commodities surely had a stabilizing effect on their operations. Similarly, although there is no way of knowing how many of the Indians' silver half-dollars went into circulation, any source of coin in this economy was welcome.

The merchants' reminiscences suggest that the value of the trade depended on the standard applied—an absolute monetary reckoning or an evaluation of the role of the trade in the frontier economy. A. H. Scott of Bronson (later Kalamazoo), for example, flatly asserted that the Indians' "trade was of little value." His sometime partner E. Lakin Brown remembered otherwise: the Indians were of "some importance to the business of the early traders." After receiving their government payments, they "sometimes had considerable sums of money, always in silver half dollars, which they paid for goods. The fur trade was of considerable value at Bronson."[28]

Despite this problem of perspective, the merchants' recollections do provide clear evidence that they and their Indian customers applied different standards of value to their transactions. The fact that the merchants grudgingly tolerated the discrepancy supports the notion that the trade was valuable to them both on their own and on the Indians' terms. Scott remembered that

the trade . . . [was] mainly an exchange (or as they called it, "swap") of their furs, venison, berries, dressed deer skins, moccasins, blackberries, cranberries, etc. for flour, salt, tobacco, powder, lead, sugar, and all the articles the Indians used to clothe themselves. I never knew an Indian to sell to white people any part of the carcass of a deer except the ham. The price . . . was always two shillings. . . . Whenever we sold a squaw any goods that had to be made up into any of their garments a needle and a thread for each garment must be given; only goods for one garment could be bought or swapped at a time. It required a good knowledge of their ways and much patience to be a successful trader with the Indians. We frequently sold them goods on credit and found them about the same kind of paymasters as the white men; some paid promptly, some after a long time, and some never paid.[29]

What puzzled Scott was the Indians' insistence on fixed values for the goods they exchanged. Some of these values were the result of the fur trade, which operated with standardized prices by weight and quality for pelts and skins.[30] Scott did not comment, however, on how his involvement in the fur trade shaped his business practices. Instead, he found it curious that the Indians were not in a strict sense his customers: he could not set prices for his goods in accordance with market demand. Nor did the Indians behave as maximizing trading partners. They did not try to sell many cuts of deer or adjust the price of the hams they did sell. They did not bargain to acquire more goods than they needed (additional cloth, needles, thread) in a single transaction.

Scott concluded from such behavior that Indians lacked business acumen. Although he saw them as no more or less honest than white settlers, they seemed ill-prepared to participate in a market economy. In making this judgment, however, he ignored the extent to which his trade with Indians resembled his dealings with whites. He could not demand prompt cash payment from his white customers, and he often had to accept from them goods that he did not want on terms detrimental to relations with his own creditors. Moreover, as much as Scott, a Vermont emigrant, deplored this awkward way of doing business, it could not have been a new experience for him. Although such conditions were the unanticipated result of the peculiarities of the frontier economy, they were hardly unique to western Michigan.

Scott's business relations were not unlike those of local merchants in New England in the early decades of the nineteenth century. Customers treated merchants as they did their neighbors, with whom they engaged in a endless round of exchanges of goods, services, and small amounts of cash. Exchanges were face-to-face and reciprocal, although years often passed before accounts were settled. These exchanges not only satisfied mutual economic need, allowing farming communities to maintain a high degree of self-sufficiency and independence from the external market, but also structured social relations. As Christopher Clark has argued, local exchanges were guided by a morality that "emphasized restraint, caution, and consideration of the debtors' ability to pay." Terms of payment were therefore always negotiated, often between individuals who kept book accounts only of the obligations owed to them, which rarely bore interest. In contrast, merchants involved in long-distance trade, who dealt frequently with individuals they did not know, conducted their affairs by different rules: "Promptness and system were essential to commercial morality." But poised as they were between two different ways of doing business, merchants were forced to conform their local dealings to the rules of local exchange.[31]

By the generation before the Civil War, however, market integration had sufficiently advanced in the northeastern United States to allow merchants to gain the upper hand over their customers, as signaled by refusals to extend long-term credit, unwillingness to accept certain goods in lieu of cash, and demands for prompt cash payment. The commercial ethic began to compete locally with the customary neighborly one. Yankee settlers brought both sets of values with them to the Michigan frontier. Their behavior in farm building was predicated on the assumption of the rapid profitability of commercial agriculture, but they learned quickly to defer their expectations of market integration. Under these circumstances, they could complain, like Scott, of the uncertainties of trade and at the same time reassert the older ethic they called "neighborliness."

The settlers were in many ways intolerant of Indian culture, hostile, like Stephen Eldred, to any perceived infringement on their absolute right to private property. But they did understand neighborly economic exchange, and "neighborly" was their highest praise for the Indians. As Mrs. L. W. Lovell, Stephen Eldred's sister, recalled, "We could not have done without the Indians. They were our market men and women. They brought us venison, huckleberries, maple sugar, and many other things that we in a new settlement needed." The Indians, she continued, "were friends and very kind neighbors to the early settlers. They treated us so much like kith and kin, that we called them our 'country cousins.' Although extremely *backwoodish* in habit and mode of living, yet we could not wish for kinder, more accommodating neighbors. . . . The Indians were often a great help at raisings; a log house or barn could not, at times, have been raised without their aid."[32]

Mrs. Lovell's use of a familial metaphor—"kith and kin," "country cousins"—to describe the special quality of the Indians' neighborliness is telling. Algonquian peoples had long incorporated outsiders, Indian and white, into their local political and economic orders on the basis of both fictive and adoptive kinship relationships. Reciprocal exchanges of political allegiance and worldly goods cemented the relationships and supported tribal society.[33] It was on this point that white and Indian understandings of the value of economic exchanges between them converged, although they did not meet. Both whites and Indians understood exchanges as the satisfaction of mutual economic needs. Both understood that they exchanged equivalencies of value unmediated by market demand. And both understood that economic exchanges structured social relationships. But Yankees did not view these exchanges as expressions of an intense loyalty and reciprocity that went far beyond the exchanges themselves. Neighborly exchanges did not create familial relationships. Many exchanges did, of course, occur among members of Yankee families, but they were like those between unrelated parties. Communal self-sufficiency served the ideal of independent farming households.

Mrs. Lovell's reminiscences make clear that the Indians' involvement in local exchanges was as vital to the frontier economy as their participation in the long-distance trade. The Indians themselves apparently did not distinguish between the two forms of transaction. Yankees, however, did see a difference between local exchange and long-distance trade, as the comments of A. H. Scott and Mrs. Lovell attest. The local exchange that the merchant disparaged, the settler applauded; what he reluctantly accepted as a poor substitute for long-distance trade, she embraced. But local exchange and long-distance trade were not operationally separable. If local exchange shielded settlers from the uncertainties of the external market, it also forced merchants like Scott to adopt business practices that exacerbated those uncertainties. From one vantage point, local exchange was part of what was wrong with the frontier economy because, as the editor of the *Kalamazoo Gazette* explained, it prevented men from "calculat[ing] with some certainty their progress in business, and mak[ing] their calculations on a reliable basis."[34] From another, local exchange was a form of "neighborliness," a critical means of communal support.

But no community on the Michigan frontier was truly self-sufficient. Local exchange and long-distance trade coexisted in unhappy mutual dependency. Merchants could not avoid dealing as neighbors, and settlers could not so immerse themselves in local exchange as to be free from all reliance on the external market. In contrast to the inclusivity and consistency of the Indians' trading relations, moreover, the settlers understood that local exchange and long-distance trade rested on different kinds of social relationships. Participation in local exchange attested to one's place in a network of communal relationships. Failure to secure that place, to become a neighbor in more ways than geographical propinquity, meant far greater reliance on debt instruments characteristic of the long-distance trade, as litigation among Yankees in the Richland justice of the peace court demonstrates.

## "On a Writ of Assumpsit"

The chief concern of the Richland justice of the peace court of the 1840s was the mediation of connections between the local economy and the external market. The nature of this work needs to be carefully stated. Most petty debts contracted in Richland did not become subjects of lawsuits. Not all debtors were delinquent. Not all delinquent debtors were sued for debt. The justice of the peace dockets represent the portion of township indebtedness that could not be resolved between parties, or the debts that failed.

These debts resulted from the settlers' inability to pay for day-to-day farming expenses. Even when the dockets do not state a cause of indebtedness, it is unlikely that the debts could have been for anything else. They were clearly not for capital investments. The suits involved sums well below the $100 limit for actions within the purview of the justices. Nearly three-quarters of all claims were for less than $30; nearly a quarter for less than $10.[35] Thirty dollars would not buy even one ox and would pay for breaking only a few acres of land, but it would purchase hired labor, seed grain, or a loan of storage space.[36]

The settlers suffered most from cash shortages during the growing season. By plowing time, crop returns from the previous year were sunk into improvements for the farm or spent paying off accumulated debts. Debt contraction and litigation in Richland conformed to this annual cycle of cash shortage and availability. A comparison of the due dates of promissory notes, the most common debt instrument in the dockets, with the dates of the hearings on them demonstrates that litigation for debt followed indebtedness as harvest followed cultivation and cash inflow followed cash shortage.[37] The seasonal pattern is clearest for 1841–45. A little over 70 percent of the notes were drafted between April and September and litigated between October and March. The seasonal pattern of litigation for all debt cases between 1841 and 1845 provides additional proof of the annual debt cycle. Nearly 78 percent of the suits were brought in the fall and winter months.[38]

The busiest time for the justices was in the late fall and early winter. Nearly four out of five suits involving promissory notes between 1841 and 1845 occurred between the last weeks of October and early January.[39] Thus, the timing of litigation was closely connected to the settlers' decisions about when to sell their crops. As Clarence Danhof has pointed out, a number of factors could be brought to bear on these decisions. Although farmers preferred to avoid marketing immediately after harvest because produce prices tended to be low at that time, for example, many had to sell quickly to repay short-term loans, which essentially functioned as crop liens, accumulated during the growing season.[40] The exact relationship between litigation and marketing is unclear, but the fact that few of the debt cases involved security, which postponed payment on debts brought to judgment, is suggestive. Had Richland farmers wanted or been able to wait for higher prices, surely more of them would have delayed payment in this way. Instead, only slightly over one in four of all debts brought to judgment between 1841 and 1859 were secured.[41]

Richland creditors went to court to assure themselves a share of the harvest. The intervals between the dates of the litigated notes, routinely made for three, six, or nine months and seldom for over a year, and the dates on which the holders brought suit are so regular that creditors could have wasted little time in pressing their claims. This promptness signals a second characteristic of the litigated debts: they were cash debts. Lending that resulted in delinquent, litigated debts may have occurred among neighbors, but it was not "neighborly." Lending was not a communal sharing of scarce resources, nor was it intended to enable debtors to pay when they were best able. Lending generated cash as much as it redistributed it. Lending made money. The debts bore interest, and they were assignable.

Over 60 percent of all debt cases in the dockets indicate interest charges. In suits involving promissory notes, the justices documented the terms of indebtedness with such phrases as the amount "due on a note," "payable with use," and "with interest." A comparison of the amount of indebtedness stated by the plaintiff in his plea or by the defendant in his confession with the amounts awarded in judgment and collected by the constable leaves little doubt that other debts also bore interest. The litigated debts potentially carried three interest rates. The first was the legal rate of 7 percent a year on the notes themselves. The second was the interest at the legal rate that Michigan law allowed a debt brought to judgment to accumulate until paid.[42] The third was the discount or hidden interest that handlers of notes charged against the papers' mature value.

Discounting was a function of the assignability of debts involving promissory notes. These debt instruments were legally treated as bills of exchange; that is, they were assignable by law.[43] Richland creditors acted upon the legal presumption of assignability. Plaintiffs in nearly 40 percent of the cases involving promissory notes were not the original promisees. This figure undoubtedly underestimates the amount of turnover because in many cases the record simply states that the plaintiff declared on a note of hand signed by the defendant. Moreover, turnover could also occur after the notes came due. Part of a creditor's incentive to litigate promptly on overdue notes was that judgment renewed assignability by providing assurance of payment. Plaintiffs in eighteen (12.6 percent) of the cases brought to verdict in the Richland justice court between 1841 and 1859, all but three involving promissory notes, assigned recovery to a third party.

The assignability of promissory notes did not make them fully negotiable.

An innocent purchaser did not have a perfect claim regardless of what had passed between promisor and promisee. If the promisor had rendered his obligation in full to the promisee without the knowledge of the third-party acceptor, that bona fide purchaser could not extract payment from the promisor. Obligations were contingent upon performance: neither buyer nor seller could profit from inexplicit liabilities. Thus, the circulation—the assignment—of a promissory note depended on whether all parties had equal knowledge of obligations incurred by a note's transfer.[44]

Because promissory notes could circulate without full negotiability, they could also do so without endorsement. The point is a critical one because some historians of the American rural economy during the late eighteenth and early nineteenth centuries have confused endorsement with assignment, assuming that a note did not circulate unless it bore the promisor's signature. They have thus concluded that unendorsed promissory notes are evidence of "use-values," not cash exchanges.[45] In reality, endorsement was as much an indication of the limits of a note's assignability as proof that it had been turned over. Acceptance of any paper, banknote or personal note, in the antebellum period involved risk, and endorsement was one way of limiting the risk of accepting the latter. Endorsement allowed a third party to bring suit against a promisee should he fail to get satisfaction from the promisor.[46] It also provided evidence of payment for the promisee should an unscrupulous holder attempt to collect a debt twice—by demanding payment from the promisor while denying that the note liquidated the promisee's debt. More importantly, endorsement meant that for whatever reason—that he had better knowledge of the promisor or that his need to dissolve his own debt outweighed the risk of litigation—the promisee was less risk-averse than the party to whom he passed the note.

The dockets indicate that few Richland promisees signed notes before passing them. Only three cases give evidence of a note's endorsement. In October 1843, for example, William C. Mitchell confessed to owing Henry L. Mills $8.40 on a note given to him by Henry Edgcomb. The note, dated in September 1842, was for $15 and was payable in oats at the market price in January 1843. Clearly, Mitchell had passed only part of Edgcomb's debt on to Mills: Edgcomb may have partly paid, Mitchell may have retained some of it, or Mills may have refused to accept the entire amount. Edgcomb may not even have been the original promisor. But Mills's successful recovery meant that Mitchell's signature was on the note.

A suit like Henry L. Mills's against William C. Mitchell was a rare event. If endorsed notes had circulated in any quantity, cases in which a third party sued a promisee for a promisor's debt should have turned up more often in the dockets. Richland Township seems to have been an optimal environment for the circulation of personal paper. It is surely no accident that the other two cases of litigation over endorsed notes in the surviving dockets involved parties who were not local residents. In such a small community, parties knew one another personally; what their property was worth, the extent of their indebtedness, and their success at farming were common knowledge. In such circumstances, third-party holders of promissory notes had every reason to be less rick-averse than if they had been unacquainted with either promisor or promisee.

Who, then, were these "unneighborly" neighbors who treated the township justice court as a combination debt collection agency and money market? They were a distinct element in the community. Much of the litigation was the work of a small group of creditors and debtors. Litigants who appeared in court three or more times in five years—slightly over 16 percent of all litigants—were party to over 40 percent of the suits brought.[47] Repeated litigants were not, with a few notable exceptions, distinguished by their wealth but by their behavior in court. They owned real property with an average assessed value of $244 and personal property worth $70.[48] Roughly two in five Richland taxpayers in 1844 and 1845 owned real property valued at less than $250; three-quarters of taxpayers owned less than $100 in personal property. In court, repeated litigants were either consistent plaintiffs or defendants, the latter outnumbering the former by a ratio of three to two. Plaintiff-creditors, however, were more litigious than defendant-debtors. Five of the seven most frequent litigants—those who appeared in six or more cases—were creditors.

Three of the frequent creditors—Nelson P. Bowen, Francis Holden, and Henry L. Mills—were neither better nor worse off financially than most repeated litigants.[49] Why they should have initiated suits while Darwin W. Hooker and Henry Wells, the two frequent debtors, appeared as defendants is not clear. The debtors were somewhat but not significantly less well off than the creditors.[50] Hooker and Wells may simply not have been as financially adept as Bowen, Holden, and Mills and, having revealed their vulnerability in court, became easy targets of other lawsuits. It is also possible that the creditors had financial resources not reflected in their tax assessments that the debtors did not have. Neither Hooker nor Wells, for example, participated as extensively in the local land market as Bowen, Holden, or Mills.

Bowen, Holden, and Mills, however, were small fry. The two other frequent creditors were Richland's preeminent men of commerce: Mumford Eldred Jr., the merchant and justice of the peace who had enforced the act to protect the Indians, and Elnathan Judson, owner of a shop and a boarding-house. Nearly as litigious as Eldred and Judson after he became a merchant in his own right was Chauncey W. Calkins, Eldred's clerk. Judson and especially Eldred were exceptionally active in the township land market in the 1830s.[51] Eldred was one of the wealthiest men in Richland; Judson's holdings and Calkins's after 1850 consistently placed them in the top 5 to 10 percent of the taxpaying population. By virtue of their large estates and their positions as suppliers of much of the goods purchased by the farming community, they were the ultimate township lenders.

Thus, the Richland dockets reveal a township credit structure shaped like a pyramid. Settlers with little direct access to sources of financing outside the township were linked to local commercial types—men like Holden, Mills, and Bowen—who made the passage of personal paper their business. Holden and the others drew their line of credit from the township merchants—Eldred, Judson, and Calkins—who in turn drew upon such creditors from the outside as consignment merchants in Kalamazoo, Battle Creek, and Detroit. Litigation in the township justice court stabilized the credit structure. The temporal pattern of their suits indicates that creditors went to court when they themselves had to pay. Six of Eldred's nine suits occurred in one year, as did four of Calkins's five. Seven of Judson's eleven suits took place over a twenty-month period. In contrast, the court appearances of the most sued debtors were spread out over several years. Darwin W. Hooker was a defendant twice in 1841, twice in 1842, once in 1845, and once in 1846. Henry Wells felt the creditor's bite once in 1841, three times in 1842, once in 1844, and once again in 1845.

When the balance between money borrowed and money lent in Richland was upset, a round of litigation somewhat analogous to a run on a bank followed. Runs made by Nelson P. Bowen and Elnathan Judson in the winter of 1843–44 show clearly the transferal of obligations from an absentee creditor to a large number of township residents. Bowen struck first in December 1843 with suits against Samuel Griffin for a debt of $19.16 and against Philip Corey for $8.24, the amount due on a note dated in June of that year. Both defendants confessed their indebtedness, and both secured their debts to put off payment for three months. Several weeks later, Bowen obtained judgments against Elisha B. Seeley for $6.14 on a note dated in July 1843 and against James H. Calkin for another July note worth $8.86. In less than a month, Bowen had assembled a total recovery of $42.40, but he would not receive payment for any of it for at least four months.

The day after Bowen took Seeley and Calkin to court, Elnathan Judson brought suit against Bowen on a book account for $12 in board (presumably meals at Judson's boardinghouse) and stovepipe and $2.13 worth of hay and four and a half bushels of oats at $3 a bushel for Bowen's horse. Bowen's total indebtedness: $27.63. Judgments owed him would have more than covered this debt, but recovery was not immediately forthcoming. Bowen got security for his debt to Judson and went back to court. In January, he brought four more suits: against James Henry for a note worth $18.43 dated in October 1843, Henry Wells for $33.44 on a note dated in June 1843, William Stone for a note of January 1843 valued at $12.22, and, finally, William A. Ward for a note worth $9.89 dated in April 1843. Bowen's recovery for January came to $73.98, and the entire judgment for two months of litigation came to $116.38. But except for Henry Wells, who paid his debt with interest that month, Bowen got no return for his efforts in January until June.

Bowen did not use the money he got from Wells to pay Judson. Presumably, his cash supply was sufficiently low that he could not afford to pay immediately, and in any event, he had until March to pay Judson. In February, Bowen went back to court. This time, William Cook confessed his debt of $25.07 on a note for $23.76, dated May 1843, that he had given to Simon Howe, who had transferred it to Bowen. Days before his stay expired, Bowen assigned this judgment to Elnathan Judson. He now owed $2.56, surely a small enough sum to pay out-of-pocket. But on March 19, Bowen assigned all of William A. Ward's debt of $9.89 to Judson. Eleven days later, Philip Corey paid Bowen $6 of the $8.86 that he owed. Bowen got no more from his debtors until May. In the meantime, he had overpaid a debt of $27.63 by $7.33 and had actually collected only $39.44 of the $141.65 owed to him.

Bowen brought suit nine times before he satisfied his debt to Judson, and when he did, he overpaid with assigned judgments. His actions confirm that plaintiffs brought suit soon after the notes they held expired because they were themselves debtors. Judgment increased the chances that the debt would be collected but did not enable a plaintiff to pay his own debt right away. Judgment also, however, assured the debt's assignability because interest legally accrued upon it until payment, regardless of whether the debt had from the beginning borne interest. If a plaintiff could not wait the long months until payment—eight months on average for unbacked debts and a year for unsecured ones—he could accept payment in cash for the judgment from a third party and use it to pay his creditor; or like Bowen, he could convert it into outright payment.[52]

Assignment of judgment, whether to the plaintiff's creditor or to a third party, occurred at a discount. The $7.33 that Bowen overpaid was the price that Judson charged for having to wait for his money. Even if Judson had accepted the judgments at par value, however, Bowen would still have lost the interest that accrued on them until they were paid. When Judson received the cash is unknown, but he probably waited at least six months. Six months' interest on $34.96 at 7 percent a year is $1.22. Judson actually discounted Bowen's judgments by at least $8.55—30.9 percent of the original debt—not a bad return on an account of seventeen days in the autumn of 1843 for board and room for man and horse.

Judson put his creditor's screws to Bowen because he was himself under pressure to assemble a large recovery. Judson's own run on the Richland credit bank began two months before Bowen made himself a semipermanent fixture in the justice court when he brought suit against Lyman I. Earl for a note of $10.12 plus interest signed by the defendant in August 1843. There is no record of when Judson received payment for this debt. On December 30, he brought his action against Bowen, for which he eventually received at least $36.18 in assigned judgments, and another action against Leman Bendle for $72.50 that Bendle had endorsed in June on a Kalamazoo note of $137.10 dated in July 1841. Judson would never recover from Bendle. Writs of execution were issued in January, March, and May 1844, the last of which was returned marked "unsatisfied for want of property." Nevertheless, on New Year's Day 1844, Judson had assembled a total proved credit of at least $118.80.

By February, the first of the executions against Bendle had already failed, and Judson went back to court. William C. Mitchell confessed his indebtedness of $7.54 to Judson for a note dated in November 1843 that he had given to John Daubney. Again no record of payment exists. Three days after receiving judgment against Mitchell, Judson sued Asa Davis for a debt of $15.33. He collected part of this debt in June. By the end of February, Judson's recovery stood at $141.67.

On March 23, twelve days after the constable's second trip to Bendle's door, the reason for Judson's litigiousness became evident. Thomas and Luther B. Case, Kalamazoo County agents for Charles North and Hoag, merchants, brought suit against Judson for $118.47 on account. A little less than three months later, William L. Granger sued Judson for $40.70, the amount due on a note dated in November 1843. Judson had borrowed cash to see him through the season of litigation. As of July 1844, Judson's proved indebtedness was $159.17. Against it, he had received in cash for his winter's efforts $7.72, partial payment for Davis's debt.

Elnathan Judson did not go back to court until 1848. How he managed to pay Granger and North and Hoag is unknown. The record of his court appearances is probably incomplete, and he undoubtedly had other lines of credit on which he could draw without recourse to litigation. Judson could not have been too happy about Bendle's defalcation, but he could, and did, absorb the loss. Most lenders who resorted to litigation to collect their debts operated much closer to the margin. Indeed, most litigants in the Richland justice court borrowed or lent cash on the basis of remarkably little capital. Why did they take the risk when the cost of failure was so high?

Consider the fourteen men against whom Bowen and Judson brought suit in the winter of 1843–44. The pyramid-shaped credit structure revealed by litigation in the justice court stands out sharply. The litigants included one ultimate creditor, Judson, two other frequent litigants, a debtor and a creditor—Wells and Bowen—and three repeated litigants, all debtors—Stone, Mitchell, and Davis. The other men only appeared in the dockets as defendants in one or two cases. As clearly defined as their positions in the township credit structure were, it ought to be possible to locate the litigants economically in Richland. And yet what is most striking about these men is how little record of themselves they left in the township. One of the litigants was a sometime resident of Alamo Township, two are unidentifiable, and three are known only from the census or county history as living in Richland in the early 1840s. The other eight litigants all appeared on at least one tax roll, but of these, only two were listed for the entire decade of the 1840s.

The mobility of the men Bowen and Judson took to court was characteristic of Richland litigants generally, and it made them a discrete element of the adult male population of the township. Of the 144 litigants between 1841 and 1845 (80.9 percent of 178 in the dockets), 93 (64.6 percent) were identifiable as Richland residents through the tax rolls, the census of 1840, or the county history. Seventeen (11.8 percent) were identified as living in other townships. Of the Richland residents, 71 (76.3 percent) appeared on at least one tax roll in the years 1837–39 and 1844–45. The rolls for the intervening years have been lost. Forty-three (60.6 percent) were listed on a pre-1840 roll; 53 (74.6 percent) on at least one of the later rolls. Only 21 (29.6 percent) paid taxes in both the 1830s and 1840s.[53] Thus, less than a quarter (22.6 percent) of the litigants were resident in Richland for the entire period. The number is even smaller if one estimates conservatively that half of the 34 litigants between 1841 and 1845 whose residence is unknown really lived in the township. The percentage of persistent litigants is thereby reduced to 19.1 percent (21 of 110). Nearly 47 percent of all taxpayers in 1837 appeared on the 1844 roll. Richland litigants were thus more than twice as mobile as the taxpaying population as a whole.

The mobility of the Richland litigants was not a function of their wealth per se. Assessed real and personal property holdings of litigants and other taxpayers were similar, regardless of the frequency of the litigants' appearances in court. Most litigants were somewhat but not remarkably less well off than most taxpayers. Like most taxpayers, most litigants were assessed for less than $200 in personal property in the years 1837–39 (61.9 percent and 66.7 percent, respectively) and less than $50 in 1844 and 1845 (54.3 percent and 50 percent, respectively). Nearly 67 percent of the litigants, compared to 57.3 percent of all taxpayers, were assessed for less than $500 worth of real property between 1837 and 1839; 48.1 percent of the litigants, compared to 52.8 percent of all taxpayers, were taxed for less than $250 in 1844 and 1845. The mean assessed holdings of repeated litigants closely resembled those of other litigants and taxpayers. The one variation was the somewhat higher percentage of repeated litigants (69.3 percent) taxed for real property worth less than $500 in 1837–39. The decline in property values from the 1830s to the 1840s for all taxpayers, litigious or not, resulted from deflation combined with underassessment during the depression of the 1840s.[54]

The chief difference in wealth distribution between the litigants and all taxpayers was at the very bottom of the scale. Nineteen percent and 25 percent of all litigants (23.1 percent and 20 percent of repeated litigants) declared no real or personal property in 1837–39 and 1844–45, compared to 31.7 percent and 42.5 percent of all taxpayers, respectively. These findings do not mean that among the litigants fewer individuals lacked real or personal property than among the taxpaying population as a whole. As we will see in the next chapter, declarations that an individual was without one kind of property usually meant that he was splitting his taxes with someone else, which in turn signaled that he was farming cooperatively with other members of his family. Brothers or fathers and sons commonly divided taxes among themselves as a way of maximizing familial resources. Cooperative family farming, moreover, was positively associated with family persistence in Richland. The increase in the percentage of taxpayers not assessed for real or personal property from the late 1830s to the mid-1840s reflects both the farming community's emergence from the period of initial occupancy and family strategies designed to spread the burden of tax payments during the depression years.

Thus, litigants were mobile because they were not connected by family ties in the township, and their mobility in turn explains why they borrowed at such cost. They were, to use a phrase commonly associated with colonial New England towns, in the community but not of it. The litigants were not so much excluded from communal networks of borrowing and lending as they were incompletely incorporated within them. The important fact about the litigated debts is that they represented only a fraction of the economic exchanges in the township; they were the cash debts that failed. The men most at risk for such failures were those most likely to borrow at interest because they had the fewest alternate resources. This is not to say that township lenders anticipated which borrowers were liable to default or that men who did not go to court did not borrow at interest. The point is that the borrowers who came before the justice of the peace had no safety net, no way of resolving their indebtedness other than litigation.

For the men who appeared as debtors in the Richland justice court, then, the rules of long-distance trade applied locally. Such had not always been the case. As David Konig, Bruce Mann, and Christopher Clark have shown, litigation for debt in New England, from the seventeenth through the early decades of the nineteenth century, was the recourse of trading partners who did not know each other. Law, in a sense, helped to assure the vitality of highly personal social and economic relationships by providing a stable means of resolving extralocal associations.[55] In the midst of the depression of the 1840s, however, neighbor began to sue neighbor. Clark has argued that these suits represented a step in the long process by which the rules of long-distance trade transformed local exchange. Litigation among neighbors declined in the following decade as merchants refused credit to all but the most favored customers. The poor, compelled to deal exclusively in cash, were thereby rendered even more vulnerable to the fluctuations of the market.[56]

The same kind of pattern seems to have obtained in western Michigan. Although only one of the Richland docket books has survived, that for 1841–59, the vast majority of the cases in it occurred in the early 1840s, during the worst years of the depression. Thereafter, the number of suits declined, except for a flurry between 1857 and 1859, another period of economic hardship.[57] By the early 1850s, moreover, signs in the region indicated that the rules of long-distance trade were firmly in place. In 1851, the editor of the *Kalamazoo Gazette* happily reported the belated arrival of the capitalist order: "One of the most gratifying symptoms in the business transactions in our village is that the unhallowed 'dicker' traffic is in great measure going out of use. There is scarcely any produce which the Farmer now brings to market, but that he can readily exchange it for cash." "There is not one evil," he declared, "which can afflict a community in a business point of view more calamitously than the 'swap and dicker' operations which have reigned among us for the last twelve years." Thus "swap and dicker," which had characterized the frontier economy of western Michigan from the beginning, and whose roots extended still deeper into the settlers' past, was reduced to a temporary distortion of normal business relations. A man of the future, the editor had a short historical memory. Still, he recognized the magnitude of the change: the settlers were no longer suspended between two economic worlds.[58]

By the early 1850s, too, the sustained interaction between Yankee settlers and Indians in western Michigan was drawing to a close. The flow of white settlement had resumed, and the countryside in which the Indians hunted was being carved into fenced farmsteads. A few weeks after his pronouncement on the improved climate for business in Kalamazoo, the editor of the *Gazette* commented inadvertently on what the change would mean for the Indians who had played such a large role in the dicker traffic. Great quantities of venison were available for sale that winter. One man reported that he had killed sixty deer in a little over a month. This crucial element in the Indians' economy had been under assault for some years. In the 1840s, for example, a glove factory operating near the Slater Mission was supplied by settlers who ruthlessly killed deer for their hides and abandoned the carcasses. But the editor did not remark on the passage of a way of life; he mourned for the deer. "Such wholesale slaughter," he intoned, "must soon depopulate our forest of this noble animal."[59]

Faced with such pressures, the Indians finally abandoned the Kalamazoo and Grand River valleys. The Old Wing Mission had already moved north to Grand Traverse Bay in 1848; the Slater Mission closed in 1852. Three years later, the federal government set aside a tract of land considerably north of the valley for the Grand River Ottawa, allocating in anticipation of the Dawes Act eighty-acre parcels for heads of household and forty-acre portions for individuals. The emigration of the Ottawa began in 1857.

The order of white settlement, economic circumstances, the vagaries of federal Indian policy, and mutually congruent if ultimately dissimilar understandings of the value of economic exchanges had kept native peoples and Yankee settlers in close contact for a generation. The Ottawa had managed to avoid removal west of the Mississippi, to postpone any relocation for nearly thirty years, and to give the lie to the proposition that, at least under certain circumstances, white and Indian societies were incompatible. As for the Yankee settlers, the interaction had clearly been beneficial. They could afford to wax nostalgic in their reminiscences. The continuing presence of Indians in western Michigan had subsidized white settlement. In the meantime, the settlers would implement their own conception of familial relations in the townships, predicated not on local exchange but on family farming.

# Spoiling the Whole

FAMILIES AND FARMING

### The Barretts of Richland Township

In 1831, Hildah Barrett and his family left the state of New York for Michigan Territory and settled in Jackson, the second county to the east of Kalamazoo.[1] In 1833, Barrett bought twenty acres of land in section 28 of Richland Township from a settler. When he brought his family to the tract the following year, he was fifty years old and his second wife, Elizabeth, was thirty-six. His three children by his first wife ranged in age from Merritt, who was twenty-two, to fifteen-year-old Marvin. The middle child appears in the township record only as a member of his father's household in 1840. Since her marriage to Hildah, Elizabeth Barrett had borne at least three children in less than five years: Eliza, John M., Wright L., and possibly another son. Seven years separated Marvin and his half-sister, Eliza, born in 1826. Her youngest child, Wright L., was four years old when the Barretts settled in Richland.

As sparse as these details of the family are, they make clear that Hildah's purchase of land in section 28 capped a period of considerable dislocation for the Barretts. In less than a decade, Hildah had acquired a new wife, more than doubled the size of his family, and moved the entire brood twice. Barrett's bit of land held his family's future. Abutting the property of his father-in-law, Benjamin Cummings, the parcel affirmed his new familial relations.[2] It was the first in a series of acquisitions on which Barrett and his sons would all establish farmsteads. Revenue generated by the family's holding would give the Barrett sons their starts in life and provide their parents with economic security in their old age. And the consequences of Hildah's purchase extended beyond his lifetime: one of his sons would see the turn of the century in Richland.

## Merritt

Merritt, the eldest son, took the lead in establishing the family holding when, shortly after the Barretts' arrival in Richland, he bought 40 acres of federal land that, combined with his father's abutting parcel, would constitute Hildah's farmstead. Two years later, Merritt began to assemble his own farm when he acquired 160 acres in three purchases from other settlers in section 32, to which he added in 1839 an adjacent 18 acres in section 33. How Merritt was able to afford these properties is unknown: he may have been in partnership with his younger, unnamed brother; his father may have backed the purchases or settled on him part of the proceeds from the sale of a farm in New York; or he may have accrued some cash on his own before coming to Richland. Whatever the explanation, Merritt's 178 acres became his farmstead, distinguishable from any other land owned by the Barretts in the township.

Having become a farm owner, Merritt married and set up a separate household, but he did not yet sever his ties to Hildah. The son's farmstead was part of the larger family holding, as the tenure arrangements between Merritt and his father attest. Hildah made only two other purchases of township land in the 1830s—an additional 10 acres in section 28 from a settler and 40 acres in section 22. Until the mid-1840s, the focus of the Barretts' efforts lay in the 70 acres in section 28, of which Merritt owned 40, and in Merritt's 178 acres in sections 32 and 33: two farmsteads, one holding. Merritt paid the taxes on all of the family's properties in the 1830s.

## Marvin

The appearance in 1844 of three Barretts on the assessment roll marked a new phase in the tenure of the family holding. Hildah and Merritt paid taxes on their respective farmsteads. Merritt was also assessed for Hildah's 40 acres in section 22, and he remained the owner of 40 acres of his father's 70-acre spread. Twenty-five-year-old Marvin was assessed for $77 in personal property.[3] His assessment indicates that he was beginning to accumulate the capital to acquire his own farm. Marvin probably took this first step toward farm ownership as his father's hired hand, for the census of 1840 lists him in Hildah's household.

The following year, Marvin began to work land on his own account, as signaled by his payment of taxes on 40 acres of land in section 27 that were probably a recent acquisition of Hildah's.[4] Marvin broke Hildah's wild land in exchange for the proceeds of the crops he then raised on it. The cash thereby accrued enabled Marvin to purchase 80 acres in section 22 and to marry and set up an independent household in 1848. For the next several years, his erratic tax assessments reflected two related concerns: his struggle to create a working farm out of wild land and his partnership with Newell Barber, the husband of his sister, Eliza. Unable or unwilling to clear his 80-acre farmstead in 1848 unassisted, Marvin rented half of it. Having been his father's tenant, he now acquired one of his own. Three years later, Marvin took complete control of the property and then went into partnership with Barber. Marvin paid no real property taxes in 1854 because his brother-in-law paid them for him. The Barrett-Barber partnership was struck for the same reason that Marvin became Hildah's tenant in 1845: Barber needed capital to buy land; Marvin needed labor to work it. The arrangement ended in 1856 when Barber acquired his own farm—80 acres in section 32—from an absentee landowner.

### The Widow

Barber's 80 acres abutted the farmstead under the care of his sister-in-law, Hannah E., the widow of Merritt Barrett. When the eldest Barrett son died, apparently intestate, in 1852, his property descended equally on his three children, all minors. As legal guardian of William, Mary E., and Josephine, Hannah became responsible for the management of their inheritance from Merritt until they obtained their majorities.[5] Hannah was also linked to her husband's estate by her dower, the use for life of one-third of Merritt's real property, and by her right to share equally in his personalty with the heirs. For six years after Merritt's death, Hannah paid the property taxes on her husband's estate as head of a Barrett household. Then she remarried, and her relationship to the Barrett family became problematic.

If the treatment the family later accorded Merritt's widow and children is any indication, Hannah's new husband did not command much respect from the Barretts. Indeed, the marriage was probably seen as tainted with scandal. James Spencer was fourteen years younger than Hannah, and he brought no obvious resources to the marriage except his youth. When he assumed his wife's place on the 1859 tax roll, the assessments remained the same as they had been the previous year. He apparently had no family living in Richland; no Spencers predate him on any township record. If he arrived in the township much before his marriage to Hannah, he must have worked as an impecunious laborer because he paid no taxes before 1859. The Widow Barrett may well have married her former hired hand.

When James Spencer took another man's wife, he seemingly also acquired his household and farmstead. The agricultural census of 1860 lists him as the operator of Merritt's farm. The population census shows the twenty-five-year-old as head of a household consisting of his wife, age thirty-nine, an infant daughter, and William and Josephine Barrett, ages nineteen and eleven. The elder Barrett daughter, Mary E., had probably died. She was not listed in any township household, and since she would have been only fifteen in 1860, she was too young to have married. James Spencer's position on the censuses as head of household and farm operator, however, creates a false impression of his legal and economic relationship to the surviving Barrett children and their father's estate. Spencer did not have, nor did he ever obtain, a right in the Barrett property. His sole connection to all matters pertaining to the Barrett family was through his wife.

Hannah's remarriage legally ended her guardianship of her children. The identity of the children's new guardian is unknown, but another member of the Barrett family probably assumed the responsibility. The family apparently arranged with James and Hannah Spencer to postpone the settlement of Merritt's estate for as long as possible. Although under no legal constraint to do so, Spencer brought William and Josephine under his roof, thereby creating an obligation to see to their maintenance and welfare, even though that roof had once been Merritt's and would ultimately belong to the children. Hannah could have legally demanded her dower by outright settlement, but she chose to occupy the farmstead with the heirs.[6]

Personal considerations aside, Spencer, Hannah, and the Barretts had good reason to delay the settlement. Apportionment would depreciate its value by dividing consolidated working capital into liquid assets. Had Hannah insisted upon the assignment of her dower, a court mindful of the detriment to the farmstead might have awarded her one-third of the estate's revenues for life instead of the use of real property.[7] This solution would not have satisfied any of the parties interested in Merritt's estate. It would have placed Spencer and Hannah in a financially precarious position, for her portion would not have been sufficient to establish easily a new farm and household. It might have forced the guardian of the Barrett children to sell the farmstead because there was not enough cash in the estate to keep the farm going and compensate Hannah. The alternative to immediate apportionment was far more practical: to maintain the farmstead, and perhaps increase its value, against the day when the settlement of the estate was unavoidable.

The reckoning came in 1869. Directly involved in the settlement were Merritt's brother, John M., and brother-in-law, Newell Barber. The two bought out the interests of the Barrett children in their father's farmstead and then swapped farms, John M. exchanging his 160 acres in section 27 for Newell's 80 in section 32 abutting Merritt's property. John M. then assumed title to his brother's land, thereby creating a farmstead of nearly 260 acres. Presumably, Hannah received a cash settlement in lieu of her one-third share for life of the rents, interests, and profits from Merritt's old farmstead. What became of her and her husband is unknown; they do not appear on the 1870 census, and the county atlas of 1873 shows no Spencer farmstead.

The Barrett children fared little better in the settlement than their mother and her husband apparently did. The year before the division of her father's estate, Josephine, the wife of R. W. Lonsbery, died in Richland at the age of nineteen. Since by state law women retained title to all property they brought into a marriage or acquired during it, Josephine's inheritance passed to her next of kin by lineal descent.[8] Since she apparently died childless, her brother, William, became Merritt's sole heir. Like his mother, William accepted a cash settlement. Unlike her, he was able to acquire a 40-acre farm in section 34.[9] Unlike his calculating uncles, however, William failed to prosper as a township farmer. At thirty-nine, he was listed on the 1880 census as living in Richland Village with a wife and four children, whom he supported as a laborer.

## John M. and Wright L.

When John M. Barrett acquired the properties of his brother, Merritt, and brother-in-law, Newell Barber, he became one of the most substantial landowners of the township.[10] No one else in his family in nineteenth-century Richland was ever associated with a farm larger than 180 acres. Such an achievement could not have been predicted for John M. when he and his younger brother, Wright L., began their progress toward farm ownership. Then twenty and eighteen years old, Hildah's youngest sons first appeared on the township tax roll in 1848, when they were jointly assessed for the same 40 acres in section 27 on which Marvin had once paid taxes. As Hildah shifted his attention from his older children to help his sons by Elizabeth Cummings to obtain farms before his retirement from active farming in 1855, the tenure arrangements within the Barrett family holding changed accordingly. During this period, Hildah had no dealings with Marvin, and his single transaction with Merritt was directly related to his impending retirement and activities on behalf of Wright L. Shortly before his death, Merritt deeded to his father the 40 acres in section 28 that had for nearly twenty years comprised a portion of Hildah's farmstead.

For the next four years, John M. and Wright L. together worked and paid taxes on land in section 27 owned by Hildah. Unfortunately, the record of patents for this property is incomplete, so although it is clear that Barretts owned the parcels for which Barretts were assessed, which Barrett owned what land when is unknown. It is clear that the third farmstead of a Barrett son appeared on the tax roll in 1853 when newly married John M. was assessed for 120 acres in section 27. Two years later, he was taxed for an entire quarter, or 160 acres. In the meantime, the Barrett family holding yielded a fourth farmstead, much of it originally Hildah's own. Wright L. acquired by quitclaim and began to pay taxes on 120 acres in section 27 and 40 acres formerly belonging to Merritt in section 28. The sole parcel remaining in Hildah's name was 40 acres in section 22 adjacent to Marvin's farmstead. Hildah deeded the property to Marvin in 1860.

Although rapidly acquired, the brothers' quarter section farms came with strings attached. Faced with the same problem of breaking wild land that Marvin had confronted, John M. must have seen the opportunity to wrest control of Merritt's better-developed farm as heaven-sent. Wright L. took over a working farm, but he was obliged to care for his parents in their retirement. The son remained under his father's directive until the old man's death. In 1860, the seventy-six-year-old Hildah listed himself as a farm operator on the agricultural census, while the unmarried Wright L., although called a farmer on the population census, lived in his father's household. Hildah died soon after the enumerations. Elizabeth survived until 1867. Nine years later, Wright L., now married, sold his farm, left the township, and became a Methodist Episcopal minister.

And so it happened that of all of Hildah's children, only John M. remained in Richland to subscribe for a handsome tribute to himself in the 1892 *Portrait and Biographical Record of Kalamazoo, Allegan, and Van Buren Counties, Michigan*. Newell and Eliza left Richland before 1880; Marvin died in the township in 1884. In reciting the conventional pieties required of such works, however, the anonymous editor of the *Record* strayed from the truth. A "self made man" with only a "log school education," Barrett had "redeemed two hundred and forty acres of timberland."[11] "Family-made man" was more like it. John M. owed his good fortune to four men: his father, from whom he had obtained his capital start; his younger brother, Wright L., with whom he had worked Hildah's land; his older brother, Merritt, who had actually "redeemed" much of John M.'s 240 acres; and his brother-in-law, who had helped him to secure Merritt's farmstead. John M. had simply capitalized on the opportunities his family, for better or worse, had provided.

In this, he was hardly unique. Certain themes link the story of the Barretts to those of other Yankee farming families in the nineteenth-century Upper Midwest. Theirs was a version of a tale that can be told again and again about the settler-families of Richland, Climax, and Alamo. The tale centers on the family holding: the land owned, or on which taxes were paid, by individual members. Parcels making up a family holding nearly always abutted. Farmsteads that were set apart like Merritt's were extremely rare, and in his case, the lack of contiguity was neither permanent nor complete. Newell Barber eventually acquired land adjacent to his brother-in-law's property, and Merritt owned a portion of his father's farm. Contiguity made economic sense, for it enabled a family to maximize its resources. The settlers valued it so highly that some rented out parcels they actually owned and rented others adjacent to property worked by their families. Consider, for example, how George W. and Sheldon Reynolds organized their holding in Alamo Township in 1850. The brothers operated two adjacent 100-acre farms in section 34, all of which they rented. George W. actually owned but rented out 40 acres in section 27.

Contiguity, however, meant more to farming families than economic efficiency. A consolidated holding was emblematic of the family's conception of itself as a single unit, founded upon a bond between parents and children. That bond involved the exchange of patrimony for filial obedience. Several points need emphasis here. First, in the relationship between parents and children over the family's life cycle, the roles of fathers and sons were determinative. The roles of mothers, wives, and daughters are harder to trace because women generally benefited only indirectly from patrimony. Patrimony was intended to give sons and, in some cases, sons-in-law the opportunity to build a capital stake. Hildah Barrett probably settled a dowry in movable goods on his daughter Eliza, and before her marriage to Newell Barber he may have allowed her to work as a hired girl and to keep her wages—one of the very few opportunities for paid employment for women on the frontier. But if Eliza's experience was at all typical of that of young, unmarried women in the townships, she spent her adolescence in preparation for a life of domesticity. In the cold light of property relations, her marriage set in motion an exchange between her husband and her father and brothers: when Newell Barber assumed Eliza's maintenance, he also acquired access to capital through his male in-laws.

Second, the law and practice of inheritance, construed as the posthumous distribution of an estate, constituted only one aspect of the relationship between parents and children. The purpose of the family holding was to generate capital stakes for sons and to secure retirement portions for parents. Except for Wright L., who took over the family farm on the condition that he care for his aged parents, none of the Barrett sons obtained a farm from their father. Instead, they received the opportunity to work portions of the holding for themselves in order to raise the capital to invest in farmsteads of their own. Hildah apportioned capital, not land, among his sons. Neither he, Merritt, Marvin, John M., nor Wright L. treated the family holding as parcels accumulated by the father for distribution to his sons.

Hildah could not, in any event, have bestowed more than one farm of the optimal size in the townships of about 160 acres, and he made no attempt to add to his property so that he could bequeath others. His behavior was not idiosyncratic. The Barrett holding was the foundation of a commercial farming operation. Hildah distributed to his sons capital shares in the holding while preserving—indeed, increasing by their labor—its economic viability. In the words of an eighteenth-century Massachusetts statute, he was unwilling to "spoil the whole." The colonial law referred to intestate cases in which the division of an estate threatened its value by allowing the decedent's eldest son to take possession of the entirety and compensate the other heirs for their shares.[12] The law of inheritance in antebellum Michigan contained the same provision.[13] The statute, of course, did not apply in Hildah's case because he divested himself of real property before he died. But the idea of spoiling the whole was much broader and much older than the law itself.

## "Spoiling the Whole"

Spoiling the whole presumed the possibility of farming for market, meaning that holdings were large enough to produce surpluses for sale. The notion arose out of the adjustment of inheritance practices to the advent of a market economy in seventeenth-century England. In areas where partible inheritance was customary, transmission of the holding intact to one son with compensation in cash for the others, as opposed to the traditional division of real property, became prevalent among families with sufficient land to farm for market. Since the revenue generated by commercial farming made possible the cash compensations, the frequency of such bequests serves as an index of market relations. It has also been suggested that primogeniture, which took hold in England at the same time, was a legal variant of the same consideration: preservation of an estate's commercial value. The practice did not, as was once thought, deny younger sons a share of their fathers' estates but settled money on them instead of land.[14] The unsettled question in these findings is whether compensatory cash portions were considered as good as land, for the equation of land with cash caused land to lose its symbolic ability to confer status on the family in its community.

The fundamental social reality of the early modern world was the rural community. Place in the social order depended upon attachment to property in a place. In this sense, all status was local status. Thus, distribution of a landed patrimony in situ was a transmission of both a family's property and its status in the community. The effect of manorial relations on these conceptions of family and status is not a consideration here; regardless of the conditions of their tenure, families used their holdings to support themselves from one generation to the next. With the rise in the seventeenth century of a market economy, however, there began a detachment of social place from a place on the land and, concomitantly, a redefinition of patrimony. When a family, to protect the commercial value of its holding, bequeathed the property to a single heir, it also restricted transmission of the family's status in the community to that heir. The compensatory cash portions contributed to the growth of a commercial class of men whose status did not depend upon an association with family land.

The notion of spoiling the whole was perceived in seventeenth-century England as connected to a problem of land scarcity, for the enlargement of holdings for commercial farming occurred in combination with soaring rates of population growth. Contemporary legal commentators, arguing for the appropriateness of primogeniture for English conditions, for example, were at pains to show that the abundance of land in the colonies made partible inheritance possible there.[15] The commentators were only the first to make such a claim. Since then, countless perorations on the distinctiveness of American society and character have celebrated the failure of primogeniture to take root in wide, open space. Alexis de Tocqueville, to name a celebrated case, places partible inheritance at the heart of his analysis in *Democracy in America*.[16] Such thinking is true as far as it goes: ownership of property in land was far more widespread in the colonies than in England. It is also misleading. It is based upon a comparison of the English law of primogeniture with the colonial practice of partible inheritance without consideration of the blurred line between the practice of both in seventeenth-century

England. It is also based upon an estimation of the abundance of land in the colonies derived from maps. Thus, it begs the question of why the notion of spoiling the whole should have crossed the Atlantic. The evolution of inheritance law and practice in colonial New England tells the story.

The Massachusetts law of inheritance, derived primarily from the customary law of partibility in England, served as the archetype for the other New England colonies. The Bay Colony law was promulgated in the Body of Laws & Liberties in 1641, incorporated substantially intact into the second Massachusetts charter in 1692, and thereafter only slightly revised until the time of the Revolution. Its central feature was equal partibility by lineal degree with a double portion for the eldest son.[17] Although the law was directed toward cases of intestacy, seventeenth-century wills show clearly the principle of partibility in practice. What is remarkable about the bequests of the first and second generation of Puritans was the ability of fathers to provide property in land for each of their sons.[18] The notion of spoiling the whole—the transmission of holdings intact to one son with compensatory cash portions for the others—is not in evidence.

The development of this pattern of inheritance was the result of the frontier economy: the settlers were land-rich and cash-poor. Commercial opportunities were limited; the output of early Puritan farms was on a level with that of medieval English holdings.[19] But the Puritans had not simply reverted to older practices. The size of the bequests and the fact that they were in fee simple distinguished them from English inheritances before the rise of the market economy in the seventeenth century. A man did not need to be particularly well placed in the social order, and thereby entitled to generous grants of town land, to leave his sons 100 acres apiece—an inheritance large enough to inspire envy in the well-off English yeoman, owner of about 50 acres.[20] Thus, transplanted Englishmen expanded their landed expectations without adjusting their conception of rural community life— with one exception: every man could aspire to the status of yeoman. The landed patrimony of early Puritan fathers satisfied notions of family and status by conferring place within a place, but the bequests were on a scale that in England would have earmarked them for commercial farming.

By the early eighteenth century, however, little ungranted land remained in the older towns, and fathers found it increasingly difficult to acquire sufficient local property to establish their sons in anything like the manner of previous generations. To furnish landed patrimony in situ, some moved their families to the frontier, while others speculated in western lands to provide the capital to buy land in home communities. Such efforts were not always availing. Until after the Revolution, poor transportation and the threat of Indian attack stymied the expansion of New England settlement. The limited number of new towns that were planted was incommensurate with the demand for land. Long-settled communities stagnated as holdings were reduced in size and depleted from repeated croppings. At the same time, the thriving trade in the coastal towns began to orient the regional economy away from agriculture and toward commerce.[21]

The result was a pronounced change in patterns of inheritance. Whereas seventeenth-century Puritan fathers had withheld patrimony until they were near death or conferred it posthumously by will so that sons often remained legally landless until middle age, their descendants distributed property while their sons were still young men. Moreover, these inter vivos transmissions were made with deeds of sale, not with deeds of gift as the Puritans had done. Because they could no longer exchange farms for lifelong filial obedience, fathers had no reason to delay the distribution of patrimony until they lay dying. At this point, the notion of spoiling the whole, born of economic conditions in seventeenth-century England not dissimilar from those in eighteenth-century New England—namely, land scarcity and commercialization—surfaced in the colonists' inheritance practices. Reluctant to divide their holdings beyond a point of economic viability, fathers increasingly substituted cash or apprenticeships for landed bequests. By the time of the Revolution, a de facto primogeniture was in evidence in wills, a conveyance usually associated with the disposition of large estates.[22]

A great deal has been made of the anxiety of eighteenth-century fathers over their inability to provide for their sons and their loss of parental control. It has been suggested that straitened circumstances and the availability of economic opportunities elsewhere for their sons forced some fathers into a position of *sauve qui peut*. These men felt so badly about their powerlessness that they let the law of intestacy distribute their estates for them.[23] This psychological argument, however, can easily be turned on its head: whether a father chose to divide his estate beyond the point of economic viability or refused to spoil the whole depended on whether the whole was worth saving. The decision rested on the best way of realizing the estate's capital value.

A fundamental change occurred over the course of the eighteenth century in how land was valued in New England. As land scarcity made landed patrimonies increasingly problematic and as commercialization enlarged economic opportunities outside an agrarian existence, access to property in a particular place ceased to be the sole means of securing a position in the social order. The detachment of patrimonially conferred land from status happened much as it had in England a century earlier. It was not that land acquired value as a commodity but that as it lost the exclusive power to determine status, it became property like any other. Ultimately, this loss of power shifted the conception of patrimony from land to capital. Changes in the inheritances of daughters following the Revolution marked the transformation. As Toby Ditz has shown in her study of inheritance patterns in eastern Connecticut, daughters' shares in the mid-eighteenth century were nearly always in movable property—cash and household furnishings—and worth less than their brothers' shares. By the early nineteenth century, this was still the case in upland and interior towns. In the commercial port town of Wethersfield, however, daughters inherited land as readily as movable property, and their patrimonial shares had increased.[24]

What completed the detachment of land from status and the transformation of patrimony from land to capital was the dramatic expansion of the American economy and the opening of the trans-Appalachian West to settlement after the Revolution. By the end of the eighteenth and the beginning of the nineteenth century, young men could aspire to becoming farmers without benefit of land from their fathers. Patrimony in capital would serve their ambitions as well as land because land was also a form of capital. Writing in the 1820s, James Kent, a leading legal commentator, drew an explicit connection between the post-Revolutionary rationalization of inheritance law to equal partibility by lineal degree and the opening of the trans-Appalachian West. He argued that the de facto primogeniture in evidence in long-settled, land-scarce areas in the East was unlikely to become prevalent in the United States. The availability of western land militated against the practice.[25]

Thus, by the time that Hildah Barrett brought his family to Richland, the value of land was price, not place. He and his fellow settlers were less concerned with the status attached to owning property than with the market value of a property. They were oriented toward the profits of cash crops and the capital gains realizable from farm improvements. The function of the family farm was no longer to transmit a landed patrimony but to generate capital to provide sons with starts in life and parents with retirement portions. Nevertheless, the family, as represented by its farm, remained the fundamental form of communal order in the townships. The settlers discarded neither the idea of an economic bond between fathers and sons, founded on the distribution of patrimony, nor the idea of a family holding. On the contrary, bond and holding enabled their commitment to the rapid development of their properties.

Bond and holding were social and economic reference points for township populations in a constant state of flux. Mobility was a fact of life for the settlers. Over half of all taxpayers in 1850, for example, no longer lived in Richland, Climax, and Alamo a decade later. Over half of those who persisted, however, had family in the townships, whereas three-quarters of the taxpayers without family left. Family farming tied individuals to communities.[26]

## The Calculus of Family Farming

It is appropriate to pause at this point to consider the effects on the family holding of women as property holders. In light of Ditz's evidence that commercialization made women more likely to inherit property in land and the passage of the Michigan married women's property act of 1844, one would expect to find some women exercising influence as landowners over the management of the family holding. A review of all property transactions in the three townships suggests otherwise. Richland, Climax, and Alamo women participated in less than 4 percent of all transactions. Some daughters received real property in the posthumous settlement of an estate, but they tended to sell it quickly to a male family member. The few identifiable cases of widows, like Hannah Barrett, entering into property transactions involved dower rights. In a handful of instances, a husband and a wife each owned portions of a farmstead, but the distribution to sons of capital stakes from it proceeded as though the husband had complete control. Women may have had more legal access to the ownership of real property than they had enjoyed a generation earlier, but it did not interfere with the management of the family holding—the economic bond between fathers and sons. This may perhaps help to explain why only a few years later so many single women rushed to claim homesteads in the trans-Mississippi West. Homesteading may have been a way around an inheritance system predicated upon an economic bond between fathers and sons.[27]

Despite such strong arguments for this bond, it is nevertheless true that, of the families constituting between 30 and 45 percent of all landholding farmers in Richland, Climax, and Alamo, less than half were composed of fathers and sons. The others were either made up of brothers or composed of family members whose exact relation was unidentifiable but who were probably also siblings.[28] Brothers farmed cooperatively no less than fathers and sons, and their consolidated holdings were no less generators of capital. Furthermore, fraternal associations were, in a loose sense, extensions of the paternal relation. Merritt Barrett's relationship with his family benefited his younger brothers; the temporary partnership between John M. and Wright L. was a function of Hildah's patrimony. Tenure relations among the Eldred brothers of Climax Township as their father, the judge, approached retirement are another case in point.

By 1850, Caleb Eldred Sr. was no longer farming actively, and he had distributed his real property among his five sons, who ranged in age from twenty-eight to forty-six years old. One of his sons, Daniel B., had completely removed himself from the family holding. Another, Caleb Jr., was not listed as a farm operator, although he was enmeshed in tenure arrangements with Thomas B. and Nelson. The fifth son, Stephen, independently owned, paid taxes on, and operated a 400-acre farm. Thomas worked a farm of 250 acres that he owned. He was taxed, however, for 305 acres, of which he owned 120, the difference being 185 acres owned by Caleb Jr. Nelson operated a farm of 308 acres, of which he owned 160. He was taxed for 196 acres, of which he owned 100; the rest belonged to his brother-in-law, Daniel Lawrence. The remainder of Nelson's farmstead, a little over 100 acres, was owned by Caleb Jr., but Caleb Sr. paid the taxes on it.

Ten years later, Caleb Jr., the youngest son, had become a farm operator, Caleb Sr. neither owned land nor paid taxes, and the brothers independently worked farms ranging in size from 270 to 400 acres. They continued to rent and rent out land, but they did not deal within the family, with one exception: Stephen Eldred paid taxes on 120 acres owned by George Sheldon, his brother-in-law. As was true for the Barretts, the purpose of the Eldreds' tenure arrangements was to secure farmsteads for each of the brothers. Once the object had been achieved, cooperation among them ceased to be reflected in their tenure.

The other significant point about the tenure relations among the Barretts and the Eldreds is that, regardless of the complexity of the arrangements, none of the families' properties was jointly owned. John M. and Wright L. Barrett split the taxes on a parcel, but Hildah owned it. Partnerships like that of Hugh and Thomas Kirkland were rare.[29] The brothers came from Scotland to Richland with their parents in 1834. The father died soon after the family's arrival, the mother a few years later. Hugh and Thomas remained in Richland, where they eventually built up a 500-acre farm. At the same time, they established another large spread in Martin Township in Allegan County that they apparently managed with tenants. Hugh married in 1837. Thomas, unmarried at least as late as 1860, boarded with his neighbor, B. F. Doolittle. Only Hugh was listed as a farm operator on the agricultural censuses. The tenure relation between the brothers, however, was a partnership of equals. Hugh and Thomas jointly owned and were assessed for all of their properties. The active partnership lasted until 1876, when the sixty-two-year-old Hugh, whose first wife had died the year before, remarried. His new wife, Helen Upjohn, twenty-five years his junior and one of the first women to graduate from the medical school at the University of

Michigan, shared a practice with her father and brother, also doctors, in Kalamazoo.[30] The Kirkland brothers put a tenant in charge of their farm in Richland, and Hugh retired from farming and moved to Kalamazoo. Thomas relocated in Petoskey, in northern Michigan, where he again took up farming and was later joined by Hugh's son, Henry.

The impetus for the Kirkland brothers' partnership was their sudden inheritance as young men of their father's property. Hugh was twenty-one when the family came to Richland, and Thomas was probably younger.[31] It made economic sense for Hugh and Thomas to manage their inheritance together. What was unusual was how long they did so. The Kirklands kept their father's property and added to it in common. Even Hugh's remarriage did not really end the partnership because the two continued to divide between them the revenue generated by their farms. The fact that the brothers were Scottish may have had some bearing on the durability of their partnership, although the evidence suggests that inheritance practices of British immigrants in the nineteenth-century Midwest were not dissimilar from those of Yankees.[32] It may also be that Thomas's failure to marry helped to sustain his partnership with Hugh. The childless Thomas had no need to build up an estate for the provision of patrimony. Whatever the explanation for Hugh and Thomas Kirkland's partnership, nothing quite like it existed among the Yankee families of Richland, Climax, and Alamo Townships.

The closest approximation was the partnership of John and William Vandewalker, neighbors of the Kirklands in Richland in the 1850s and 1860s. The beginnings of the Vandewalker family in Richland are obscure. William first appeared on the township tax rolls in 1844, when he was thirty years old. John was first listed in 1847 but only for payment of the militia tax—a levy on all men over twenty-one years of age to raise revenue for the Mexican-American War. He did not begin to pay property assessments until 1855. The brothers' father, also named William, died in Richland in 1854 at the age of seventy-three. In addition, a George Vandewalker paid the militia tax in 1847, and an L. Vandewalker paid property taxes in 1848. John and William first bought land in Richland in 1849 when they jointly acquired eighty acres in section 4 from Lawrence Vandewalker, a land speculator with properties scattered throughout Kalamazoo County who was probably a kinsman. In 1855, John acquired an adjacent eighty acres. Both John and William married. William eventually fathered seven children; nothing is known of John's family.[33] William was listed as operating a quarter section farm on the 1850 and 1860 agricultural censuses, and at least through 1860, he paid taxes on the entirety. John paid only personal property taxes. William died in 1862. In January 1863, John deeded his share of the northern half of the northeast quarter of section 4 to William's heirs. Later that year, he sold the southern half to another settler and left the township.

Several facts stand out in the Vandewalker story. First, although William appears the stronger partner in the enterprise, judging by his visibility in the public record, John actually owned over half of the acreage in the brothers' farmstead—his own 80 acres plus some portion of the other 80 acres that he had purchased with his brother. William's payment of the taxes on the farm may have been a way of balancing investments. William worked rented land for five years before he and John bought eighty acres in 1849. He may have provided a capital stake for the farmstead, and capital may have been his continuing contribution to it. This surmise leads to the second fact: after William's death, John made no attempt to run the farm by himself, either by buying out William's heirs to preserve the integrity of the holding or by working a reduced acreage. Whatever William's contribution to the Vandewalker farmstead, John was not prepared to do without it.

Thus, tenure relations among brothers were temporary associations designed to generate sufficient capital to allow the partners to set up farms for themselves. In other words, they functioned exactly as they did between fathers and sons, and they extended the parental relation by enabling sons to maximize their patrimony. The advantage of cooperative farming to Richland, Climax, and Alamo families is intuitively obvious. Systematic proof is more difficult to uncover, but a case for savings in capital and labor can be made by showing how the tenure of family-owned properties reflected cooperative farming.[34] The point of departure for this case is the likelihood that the closer an individual came to owning a farm, the less complex were his tax assessments. A farm owner ought simply to pay taxes on his own property. And since the purpose of family farming was to promote independent farm ownership and the assessments of family members were exceedingly complex, it follows that the tenure of landholding farmers who did not have family on the rolls should in the aggregate be simpler, more reflective of outright ownership, than that of family members. Accordingly, all landholding farmers were first sorted by family membership. On the basis of a case by case comparison of land owned and land taxed, they were then divided into five categories of tenure: owners, who paid taxes on all of the land they owned; renters, who paid taxes on land but owned none; owners who were also renting land; owners who were renting out land; and owners who paid no real property taxes. The difference between owners who rented land and those who rented out land was between taxpayers assessed for more property than they owned and those who did not pay taxes on all of the property they owned.

But farm ownership was also a function of age. A simple breakdown shows clearly that individuals on the 1860 population census who called themselves farmers were underrepresented among township farm operators and taxpayers until age thirty, overrepresented between the ages of thirty and fifty, and thereafter about evenly represented.[35] An undifferentiated family-membership category containing fathers, sons, and brothers therefore obscured evidence of the effect of age on property ownership; the former would appear at either end of the scale, while the latter would cluster in the middle. Furthermore, brothers' tenure would in the aggregate tend to resemble that of landholding farmers generally because their assets were not a function of familial relations but of capital accrued. One did not rent property because one was a brother, but one might well rent because one was a son.

Thus, when family members were divided into two categories of fathers and sons and brothers and then grouped by age, the former showed a tendency toward rental arrangements, and the latter toward ownership.[36] Of the brothers, 55.7 percent were between the ages of thirty and fifty, while 51.8 percent of the fathers and sons were between twenty and thirty and sixty or over. Of the brothers, 45.1 percent either owned or owned and rented out property, compared to 30.6 percent of the fathers and sons; 57.6 percent of the fathers and sons either rented or owned and rented property, compared to 47.5 percent of the brothers. Tenure arrangements within families did indeed reflect cooperative farming, and changes in them between fathers and sons did indeed signal the distribution of patrimony. Once again, the history of the Barrett family is instructive.

Consider how Hildah Barrett dealt in turn with each of his sons. Merritt was twenty-two when the family arrived in Richland. Economic relations in the 1830s between Hildah and his eldest son suggest that Merritt came to the township equipped with the capital to acquire a farm of his own. If anything, Hildah appears the poor partner in the tenure arrangements linking the farmsteads of father and son. For Marvin, John M., and Wright L., however, all of whom attained their majorities in Richland, the distribution of patrimony began when they first appeared on the tax rolls, assessed for land they worked but their father owned, and ended when they began to pay taxes on their own farmsteads. In all three cases, this last change indicated that they had acquired and begun to work their own farmsteads. Marvin and John M. married and established separate households shortly thereafter. Because Wright L. took possession of his father's farmstead, he remained in Hildah's household, not marrying until after his father's death.

Thus, the appearance of the son of a Richland, Climax, or Alamo settler on the township tax rolls indicated that the son had received from his father the means to acquire a capital stake. He paid taxes because he had begun to work for himself. These first assessments were normally for either real or personal property, unlike those of established settlers who paid on both. When a son was occasionally taxed for both real and personal property, the latter valuation was usually very small—less than $20.[37] Clearly, what mattered patrimonially in these instances was the real property assessment. It is difficult to say whether sons commonly paid more on real or personal property because the same individual might be taxed for either in different years. Such, for example, was the case with the assessments of Marvin, John M., and Wright L. Barrett.

Payment of real property taxes meant that a son had obtained a portion of the family holding to work, as the county histories later put it, "on his own account."[38] He was entitled to the proceeds of his labors, which were intended eventually to enable him to buy land of his own. The parcel for which a son was taxed was small—roughly forty acres. Although the father usually owned the property, a son sometimes paid on land owned by an elder brother. Such an arrangement nevertheless reflected the distribution of patrimony because the tenure of his older brother's and his father's lands was enmeshed. Merritt Barrett owned and periodically paid taxes on part of Hildah's farmstead, while his younger brothers were assessed for other properties of their father.

In contrast, payment of personal property taxes meant that a son labored for cash wages, as Marvin Barrett initially did. He did not work a specific piece of property in his own right. Who such a son's employer was, whether his father or someone else, is virtually impossible to tell. However, the occupations of young men between the ages of fifteen and thirty who were not heads of household and whose fathers also appeared on the 1860 census were suggestive of who employed these sons. (Unlike the 1850 census, the 1860 census consistently listed occupations for all males age fifteen and over.) It is fair to assume that a son who lived in a household other than his father's and who called himself a laborer was working out, while one who did not live at home and called himself a farmer was boarding out. In any event, few sons fell within either of these categories. More to the point is what sons living in their fathers' household called themselves. The vast majority took their fathers' occupations: sons of farmers were farmers; sons of laborers, laborers. Of the latter, nothing more need be said. But in a handful of instances, sons of farmers called themselves laborers.[39] The conclusion is not that farmers' sons who called themselves farmers did not work for wages whereas those who called themselves laborers did, but that the latter worked out and the former did not. What has this innocuous surmise got to do with the distribution of patrimony as revealed by a son's payment of personal property taxes?

Patrimony consisted of a father's provision for his son of a means to acquire capital. Either a son's employment for wages or his access to property to work on his own account satisfied the condition of distribution. Who paid the son who secured his "start in life" by working as a wage laborer was, in a strict sense, irrelevant. In law and custom, a father owned his child's labor and the fruits of that labor until the child turned twenty-one.[40] A father was not obliged to pay his son for his labor on the family holding before the son attained his majority. If the son worked out, the father was entitled to his wages. Thus, when a father paid his son a wage or allowed him to keep what he had earned working for somebody else, he distributed patrimony—the means whereby his son acquired capital.

Here the contrast between the experience of single men and women living in the townships is instructive. Whereas Thomas Dublin has shown that New England farm women between the ages of fifteen and twenty-one who left home for mill work, teaching, or domestic service were allowed, if not encouraged, to keep their own wages, the evidence from Richland, Climax, and Alamo suggests a more restricted experience. On the frontier, the distribution of patrimony to daughters did not include the provision of capital stakes. Although some may have worked for wages and kept them, most were directed toward lives of domesticity. Whereas young women in antebellum New England had open to them opportunities for economic independence through wage work, opportunities that closed after the Civil War, Dublin shows, with the reabsorption of daughters into a family labor system, their contemporaries on the frontier enjoyed no such life chances.[41]

In the first place, 29.9 percent of the young women in the townships in 1860 were married by their twenty-first birthdays, compared to only 2.2 percent of their brothers. Roughly two-thirds of both single men and women lived at home. Of these, more than three-quarters of both single men and single women attended school. However, only 24.8 percent of the women compared to 83.4 percent of the men listed an occupation, strong evidence that between the ages of fifteen and twenty-one, young men were involved in the distribution of patrimony while their sisters labored at home in anticipation of marriage. Even single men who attended school were over twice as likely as single women to list an occupation (25.3 percent and 11.3 percent, respectively). The women's occupations, moreover, indicate meager possibilities for wage earning. Indeed, most women who listed occupations probably engaged in work little different from the work of formally "unemployed" women. Most employed women performed some sort of domestic work; only four were teachers. In contrast, more than nine in ten of the single men living at home were listed as farmers or laborers. They were already in pursuit of independent farm ownership.

The pattern was similar for young men and women living away from home but grimmer, for it reveals the limited opportunities of children from the poorest families in the townships. Far fewer of either sex attended school—less than one in five of the women and less than one in four of the men—and of these, roughly half of both women and men were also employed. The women's occupations were again largely domestic, except for three teachers. More than nine in ten of the men were laborers.

The experience of young women in the townships therefore suggests some continuity with the traditional notion of patrimony that discriminated between the bequests to sons and daughters by awarding sons land and daughters personal property. It also suggests that women, although they seldom owned land themselves, were instrumental in familial alliances involving property. Fathers did not stand to lose daughters in marriage so much as to gain sons-in-law. On the frontier, to which whole families did not always move intact and where rates of population turnover were high, the involvement of sons-in-law, like brothers, in family-farming arrangements was a way of extending the patrimonial relationship between fathers and sons.

For young men, however, a more complete obversion of the traditional landed bequest in situ is hard to imagine. It was not simply that fathers on the Michigan frontier conferred capital as readily as land because land was capital but that they defined negatively their role in securing starts in life for their sons. They conceived of patrimony as a removal of an impediment, filial obligation, to the acquisition of capital. What, then, remained of the economic bond between fathers and sons; or more precisely, when and how did a son achieve economic independence from his father?

## "Buying Time"

We have seen that as the conception of patrimony was transformed from land to capital and as patrimony ceased to confer local status, receipt no longer guaranteed perpetuation of the family in its community from one generation to the next. In Richland, Climax, and Alamo, distribution sometimes began when a son was as young as fifteen, was largely complete by the time he turned twenty-one, and had nothing to do with whether he stayed on the family holding or even in the township. In other words, the earlier patrimony was conferred, the shorter the period of customarily enforced filial obedience. The law, however, enforced filial obedience until a son turned twenty-one by giving to fathers a property right in their sons' labor. The ability of sons to secure capital stakes before the age of majority thus clashed with the legal definition of when a boy became a man. In New England and the Midwest in the two generations before the Civil War, sons roughly between the ages of seventeen and twenty-one entered a peculiar period of semi-independence from their fathers, defined by a notion known as "time."[42] They were obliged to turn their earnings over to their fathers, but the obligation was negotiable. Depending on his relationship with his son, a father might demand the entirety or a portion of the earnings, or he might give his son the "balance of his time," either as a gift or in return for a lump sum.

There is, of course, no way of knowing how often sons "bought their labor from their fathers" or "received their time," as the county histories put it. The important point is that a father's right to his son's labor was enforced in law and custom. Of the 277 Kalamazoo County men born between 1810 and 1840 whose biographies appeared in the 1892 *Portrait and Biographical Record*, for example, 61 percent stated the ages at which they left home, thus providing evidence of the custom.[43] Of these, 58.6 percent left home at the age of twenty-one or older, 25.4 percent in the year they attained their majorities. The right had been fixed in American law since the colonial period and was an article of English common law governing the relations between parents and children. By the first quarter of the nineteenth century, however, the right was something quite different from what it had been before the Revolution. As economic expansion and commercialization transformed the conception of patrimony from land to capital, so it redefined the function of the law of property from protector of individual security and status to guardian of the market. The property right of fathers to their sons' labor ceased to be a legal compensation for patrimonial obligation and became a device for maximizing the capital generated by the parent-child relation.

It is worth reviewing the theories of William Blackstone, whose *Commentaries on the Laws of England* first appeared in 1765, because his formulation was the departure point for the reworking of the American law of parent-child relations following the Revolution. The concern here is not to compare parent-child relations in law and practice in colonial America and contemporary England but to examine changes in the relations from the colonial period to the generation before the Civil War as experienced in

American law. It should also be noted that despite the seeming neutrality of the legal language with regard to gender, Blackstone, like later American commentators, clearly means "father" by "parent," and when he refers to "children," his greater concern is for sons. According to Blackstone, the bond between parent and child had the force of law until the child turned twenty-one. The bond was one of reciprocal obligation. "The duty of parents to provide for the maintenance of their children" is "an obligation . . . laid on them not only by nature herself, but by their own proper act, in bringing them into the world. . . . By begetting [children] . . . [parents] have entered into a voluntary obligation, to endeavour . . . that the life which they have bestowed shall be supported and preserved." It followed, therefore, that the duty of children adhered to a principle of natural justice and retribution: "For those who gave us existence, we naturally owe subjection and obedience during our minority, and honor and reverence ever after."[44]

Parental obligation extended beyond provision of food, drink, clothing, and shelter. The duty by "far the greatest of any" was to give children "an education suitable to their station in life." The parent conferred no benefit on a child by bringing him into the world "if he afterwards entirely neglected his culture and education, and suffered him to grow up like a mere beast, to lead a life useless to others, and shameful to himself."[45] The phrase "education suitable to their station in life" assumes a hierarchical social order in which status was largely fixed by birth and an agrarian economy undergoing commercialization. For the vast majority of the English population of Blackstone's day, education did not mean formal schooling so much as training for a life on the land or an apprenticeship in a trade. In this sense, education was directly linked to patrimony: the instruction of a child to his status and the conferral of that status.

A father's power in law over his children derived from his duty. His authority was partly designed "to enable . . . [him] more effectively to perform his duty, and partly as a recompense for his care and trouble in the faithful discharge of it." To keep the child "in order and obedience," for example, he was allowed to correct him or to empower another to do so "for the benefit of his education." A father's power over his son's estate was that of a trustee or guardian, "for, though he may receive the profits during the child's minority . . . he must account for them when he comes of age." In other words, property that a child acquired independently of his parents was sacrosanct. Blackstone continues, "[A father] may indeed have the benefits of his children's labour while they live with him and are maintained by him: but this is no more than he is entitled to from his apprentices or servants."[46] This last sentence is so couched in conditional language—"may indeed," "but this is no more than"—that its importance needs emphasis. Apprentices or servants were a form of property, and so were children.

The view that children, like indentured servants, apprentices, and, of course, slaves, were regarded as a form of property in colonial America predated Blackstone's formulation of the common law principle. Parents in prerevolutionary Massachusetts could sue for wages if they hired their offspring out and for loss of labor if someone abducted their children or otherwise caused them to abscond. As William Nelson has explained, pleadings, issues, and substantive law were identical in suits involving slaves, indentured servants, apprentices, and children. The "master" of any of these laborers could, during their term of service, forbid them to work for someone else and by court order or reasonable corporal punishment compel them to work for them. Nelson's larger point about the law of property— indeed, the entire legal system—in colonial Massachusetts is that it was designed to guard the foundations of a society and an economy that were becoming unstable. Law functioned to preserve the hierarchical distribution of wealth and status and what Nelson calls the "ethical unity" of Massachusetts society: every man should know his place in his community and in relation to every other man. To that end, the law of property militated against the threat of social dislocation posed by economic competition by consistently favoring customary usages.[47]

In the thirty years following the Revolution, however, the ethical unity of Massachusetts society crumbled under the impact of dramatic economic growth, and the law responded to new social and economic values. In the immediate postrevolutionary years, rules of property were tightened and extended to new forms of wealth created by changes in the economy. Nelson is not completely certain why the expansion of property concepts in law occurred. Although the courts were following colonial precedent, he suggests that the expansion is best explained by the postrevolutionary generation's tendency to associate the protection of property with the preservation of liberty. The new rules for the allocation of property, however, did not increase liberty; they simply specified who owned what, ensuring that those who had rights would continue to have them. By the 1820s, this libertarian attitude toward property had given way to a concern that rights should be assigned to sponsor economic development, that the law should be an engine of economic progress. The Massachusetts courts were disposed to view landed wealth "not as a legally protected source of individual security, but as a commodity whose price in the market depended on its productivity." Whereas formerly the law had protected customary usages in the distribution of resources, it now assigned rights on the basis of utility. The shift was from a monopolistic conception of property rights in a society of fixed wealth and status to a notion of free competition for rights in a society that also competed for wealth and status.[48]

What happened to the right of fathers to their children's labor during this period of fundamental reorientation in social and economic values as reflected by changes in the law of property? Nelson sees the libertarian trend in property law of the late eighteenth century as applying to the regulation of laborers.[49] Although slaves were freed in Massachusetts after the Revolution, the law continued to recognize the right of heads of households to the labor and wages of their servants and children. Seemingly, the courts were testing how far that right extended. The case of *Benson v. Remington* (1806) is illustrative.[50] A father successfully sued for the wages of his daughter that accrued while she lived with her employer between the ages of thirteen and eighteen. The opinion of the community where the daughter, employer, and father lived was that the father had abandoned the girl and was not entitled to compensation. The court determined, however, that since the father had not authorized the employer to pay the child her wages, they were his. In other cases, fathers sued their daughters' employers after the girls became pregnant and recovered on the grounds of loss of services.

Nelson does not extend his consideration of fathers' rights in their children's labor to the 1820s, the period, he argues, in which the value of free competition replaced that of monopoly in the determination of property law. He notes, however, several later cases that indicate a redefinition of the parent-child relation according to the value of free competition. In *Freto v. Brown* (1808), the court determined that a stepfather was not entitled to his stepchild's wages, although he could recover his support for the child. In the cases of *Jenney v. Alden* (1815) and *Whiting v. Howard* (1825), Nelson points out, a father "who had expressly agreed to emancipate his son or whose agreement could be inferred from a son's conduct lost his right to his son's wages."[51] Subsequent precedent cases suggest that by the 1820s courts in New England were as concerned with the father's right to waive his right to his children's labor as they were with his entitlement. The Vermont case of *Chase v. Elkins* (1829) succinctly lays out the issues.[52]

In 1825, Samuel Chase, a bankrupt, gave his son, Joseph, his time for a consideration of $16 a year until the son turned twenty-one. Joseph Chase was about eighteen when he "bought his labor" and went to work "on his own account" as a hired man. He received his own wages, and his father made no attempt to control him or his property. After two years, Joseph paid his father the entirety of his time, or $48. From his wages of the next year, he bought a pair of oxen, which he lent to his father. In March 1828, Curtis

Elkins, a creditor of Samuel Chase and a deputy sheriff, issued a writ to attach the oxen, which were then seized and sold to pay Chase's debt. Joseph Chase, now twenty-one and therefore able to bring suit on his own behalf, demanded damages from Elkins. Both the pleadings and the judgment in the case are worth quoting at length.

Plaintiff's counsel urged:

> The father has a right to sell to his minor son his time, or a right to his future earnings. He may think this to be the best for the son, and for the family. He may have no business in which to employ the son to any advantage; and it may be altogether prudent to encourage his son to be faithful and industrious, by giving him his earnings or a portion of them. If he has not this right, and the creditor can hold this property against the plaintiff, it would virtually render the children bond slaves to their father's creditors; and entail the poverty of the father upon the children, in all its discouraging and depressing circumstances.[53]

The gist of the defense was that the contract between Samuel and Joseph Chase for the sale of the son's labor was void because the "law does not emancipate until twenty one years." All of Joseph's wages, and the oxen purchased with them, belonged to Samuel because "the father is entitled to the earnings of the son while a minor." Therefore, by selling Joseph his time and claiming the oxen as a loan from his son, Samuel had perpetrated a fraud upon his creditors.

On the facts of the case, the court rejected the defense's contention of fraud. It then considered Samuel's right to sell Joseph his time:

> If the father's right to the son's labor can be called property, he has the same right to dispose of it, in good faith, as he has to dispose of other property. He should have this right that he may consult the genius, capacity, and inclination of his son, and direct the whole for the best interest of himself and son. If he deems it best for his son to serve as an apprentice to some trade, or enjoy the patronage of some gentleman of the bar and become a lawyer; or the patronage of some clergyman, and become a preacher, no creditor has a right to interfere with this, and claim the son to labor, that he may attach his earnings.[54]

The point was not whether Joseph's labor was property or whether his father had a right in it, but what that right was. Did Samuel Chase have the same right to dispose of his son's labor "as he [had] to dispose of other property"? Under colonial law, the answer would have been no. A colonial father could sell his child's labor, but he could not divest himself of his right in the child because divestiture would also relieve him of his parental responsibilities. The situation was analogous to the legal regulations governing the treatment of indentured servants and apprentices. Masters could hire servants and apprentices out but remained accountable for their welfare for the contracted period of service.[55] The Vermont court not only declared that Samuel Chase had the right to terminate his responsibility for Joseph but argued that it might be in the "best interest" of father and son that he be allowed to do so. Utility determined the proper disposition of a child's labor. If labor was property like any other, then the market set its value. Giving or selling a son his time was just as much a conferral of patrimony as securing for him an apprenticeship in a trade or the patronage that would allow him to learn a profession.

*Chase v. Elkins* makes clear that the chief legal obstacle to this line of thinking was its potential for fraud. If a father gave his minor son his time, what were his legal responsibilities toward the child and the child's toward him? To what extent should the debts of the father be visited upon the son and vice versa? Beginning in the 1810s, the courts moved steadily toward a severance of legal ties between fathers and minor sons who had received their time. Thus, in 1815, a Massachusetts court upheld the right of a son to his earnings against the creditors of his father, an absconding debtor. In an 1818 Pennsylvania case in which a father permitted his son to improve and settle on a tract of land, the son's title was considered valid even though he began the improvement while a minor. A New York court in 1827 allowed a child to maintain an action in his own name for wages against his employer. The same year in Connecticut, a father was precluded from suing his son's employer for his son's services. Finally, in the Vermont case of *Varney v. Young* (1839), in which a father had, at the request of his son's employer, relinquished all claim to the boy's labor, the court upheld the father's refusal to pay for expenses incurred by the employer during the son's illness.[56]

By 1846, the second edition of the legal commentary of the well-known jurist, Tapping Reeve, first acknowledged the father's right to his child's labor and then declared: "The relation between parent and child is so far relaxed, that the father may, at any time, relinquish his claim for such services, and when he does, the profits of the infant's labors belong to the infant himself . . . and the relinquishment of such right by the father may be proved by parol. . . . The infant after having thus purchased his time, is entitled to his own earnings, as against those of the creditors of his father."[57]

Thus, by the 1840s, the legal right of a father to his son's labor as property existed only insofar as parent and child agreed to its existence. In law, a son achieved economic independence and the status of an adult when he acted

independently. If he acted independently without his father's express consent, the courts were disposed to consider his behavior as consonant with
parental consent. In Michigan, the law of apprentices retained a provision
through the 1880s that nothing in the statutes could be construed to conflict
with the father's right to his children's labor while minors, but the article
had no force.[58] The law remained the same, but it had been stripped of its
original purpose.

This lengthy consideration of Yankee families and their farms on the
Michigan frontier in the generation before the Civil War has revealed that the
function of the family holding was to generate capital and that the economic
bond between fathers and sons was an exchange of labor for access to
capital. The value of both holding and bond to the settlers was the result of a
centuries-long process by which conferral of a landed patrimony in situ
ceased to confer position in the social order and by which the rural community, under the impact of economic expansion and commercialization,
ceased to be the fundamental social reality. This is not to say that the settlers
of Richland, Climax, and Alamo did not live in a nation of farmers. Instead,
the argument is that as commercial opportunity—the possibility of earning a
livelihood away from the land—widened, life on the land became commercial. It was no accident that the court in *Chase v. Elkins* equated a father's
giving his son his time with provision of an apprenticeship in a trade or
patronage in a profession. When ownership of property in a place no longer
determined status, farming became an occupation like any other—a means
of livelihood, a career on which a son might decide to embark.

However, before the Civil War, that son probably chose to become a
farmer, and this choice is directly to the point: Richland, Climax, and Alamo
settlers, firm in their faith in economic growth, invested their holdings and
their relations with their sons with capital value because the world was
composed, as it always had been, of rural communities. They had seemingly
secured a future promising more of the same, only better. Nevertheless, the
cost of their investment was considerable: a reorganization of the farming
family as a mutual self-help association whose members remained active as
long as it suited them. In their efforts to preserve the capital-generating
capacities of their farms, families spoiled a different whole—their unity. The
lasting impression of the story of the Barretts is its nastiness. There was
Marvin, who clearly did not receive as much assistance from Hildah as did
his brothers; Wright L., who stuck it out on his father's farmstead until both
parents died and then left farming and Richland; and John M., who built up
his own estate with the inheritance of his deceased brother's son while the
rest of the family looked on. How many other farming families in the town-

ships encountered such unpleasantness as the Barretts experienced is immaterial. Speculation over whether domestic relations on traditionally run farms were happier is superfluous. What does matter is that the nastiness of the Barrett relations was systematic, and it was perpetrated in the name of capital.

# A Pretty Joining of God and Mammon

RELIGION AND COMMUNITY

In March 1836, the Reverend William Page reported to the American Home Missionary Society (AHMS) on the state of organized religion in western Michigan. He had found Gull Prairie

> inhabited by one hundred or so Presbyterians and Congregationalists, who in the infancy of the settlement were going to have an Eden on a footstool, with nothing but Angels for neighbors—nine deacons and three ministers—But so much salt of the earth piled upon one place, lost its savor . . . sourness and discord has been the result—These Christian townships on prairie land, however well intended, and fascinating in the prospect . . . are a sort of religious selfishness—a holy worldly minded-ness—a pretty joining of God & mammon—a smug way of laying up treasures on earth under the show of benevolence and self denial which will sooner or later turn into a hornet's nest.[1]

Page was clearly enjoying his flight of rhetoric, but he was dead serious. "I write," he explained to the secretary of the society, "not for publication—

but as intellect fancies and conscience approves." And, truly, he did not exaggerate the sourness of life on Gull Prairie, nor was he wrong to single out Christian aspirations as the source of discord. With nine deacons and three ministers on the prairie, Isaac Barnes had good reason to repent that he had ever solicited the pious and respectable to come to the settlement. At the time of Page's visit, the session of the Presbyterian Church of Gull Prairie was in the midst of an inquiry into the "Christian character" of Isaac Barnes.

The accusations against Barnes were part of a larger religious controversy dating almost from the arrival of the Kalamazoo Emigration Society on Gull Prairie six years earlier. It was of "vast importance" that the new settlement "be commenced under Christian principles," all settlers agreed, regardless of whether they had signed the "articles of agreement." Because as Yankees they believed in the expression of moral order through institutions, they also agreed that a church should be organized and a minister "procured and supported." The sticking point was who should take these matters in hand. The moral directive of Gull Prairie was a litmus test of communal leadership.

For over a year after the arrival of the Kalamazoo Emigration Society, Gull Prairie had no church. The settlers met for worship and Bible study in one another's homes and occasionally heard the preaching of the Reverend William Jones, a Presbyterian attached to the AHMS, and the Reverend Luther Humphrey, head of the Saint Joseph Presbytery. The failure to organize a church signaled not a lack but an intensity of interest in the spiritual life of the community. In September 1830, when the settlement probably consisted of no more than fifteen families, Jones reported a strong Presbyterian colony on Gull Prairie.[2] Yet the Kalamazoo Emigration Society, which comprised half of the settlement, had pledged to organize a Congregational church. From the beginning, Gull Prairie drew Presbyterians and Congregationalists in roughly equal numbers. Since the two groups only agreed on the desirability of organizing a single church, each tried to organize before the other.

The Presbyterians managed to strike first, but just barely. In March 1831, William Jones wrote to the AHMS asking for financial assistance that would enable him to accept an invitation to labor on Gull Prairie. A day later, Erie Prince, an agent for the society, reported on his visit to the settlement. He had learned of the Kalamazoo Emigration Society's desire to support as soon as possible a Congregational minister and had written on its behalf to the Reverend John Seward of Aurora, Illinois, urging him to come to Gull Prairie in the spring. For some reason, Seward did not come to the settlement, but Jones was ensconced there by midsummer, at which time he reported a call to form a church, maintaining that the people would support him after one year, and requested aid from the society.[3]

With Jones's appointment, the competition between Presbyterians and Congregationalists flared into open conflict, to which Jones himself greatly contributed. He was a man whom many found easy to dislike, and not only for his denominational affiliation. As Arvilla Smith, wife of George N. Smith, himself later a Congregational minister and laborer for the society, wrote in her diary after Jones offered to board the newly arrived couple in exchange for Smith's work as a hired hand: "[Jones] appeared very fine and smooth. . . . As he was a minister of the gospel [Smith] supposed him to be a good man . . . but I soon had some hints of his character. Neighbors about advised us not to go. We should stay but a short time if we did. . . . Of his character I shall say very little and that will be enough to [say?] of a Minister that he was anything but a Christian."[4] Jones apparently had an eye for both spiritual and economic opportunities. Like many missionaries, he was perpetually short of funds, but he hustled for cash as did few of his brethren. While negotiating his relocation on Gull Prairie, he solicited support from his old churches in Ypsilanti and Detroit. On Gull Prairie, he ran a farm while ministering to that settlement and several others in the eastern Kalamazoo River valley. In 1834, the society rebuked Jones for being "so much engaged in worldly business" and threatened to withdraw his commission.[5]

Far worse than Jones's worldliness for the organization of a church on Gull Prairie was his irascible self-righteousness. By September 1831, Jones was writing to the society in high dudgeon describing his "trials & difficulties." He had been brought to Gull Prairie under false pretenses. He had wrongly supposed that his invitation had come from the settlement as a whole. Now he had discovered that without consulting him some in the community had formed a committee "to write abroad for ministers." One member of this committee was a man "who reports to have come from Rhode Island and to be a deacon of the church," yet he brought "no letter of recommendation." He "pretended to be worth $25,000," yet "it is well known that he is a bankrupt and that he and his family have . . . made a final separation." Without Jones's knowledge, the committee had decided on a date for organizing a church. Gull Prairie was so caught up in "internal neighborhood broils" that Jones had administered a reproof, but it had been so badly taken that some now sought to replace him with another missionary supported by the society. All fault lay with the deacon from Rhode Island and a few others. Jones would go elsewhere if the society thought it best, "but in my view it matters not who is here—the elements of discord are here & in order to [have?] harmony there must be a change in materials."[6]

Despite the competition between Presbyterians and Congregationalists to organize a church, denominational controversy explains only one dimension of the Gull Prairie "broils." Nor is it possible, following Jones, to view the trouble as the work of a few congenitally contentious individuals. Little is known of the deacon from Rhode Island except his name, Philip Gray. What is clear is that the settlers, whether members of the Kalamazoo Emigration Society or not, had expected to live in Christian harmony on the prairie and that they had fallen out over who should orchestrate their unity. High expectations of unity had turned disagreement into discord. As the Congregationalist Isaac Barnes put it in a letter supporting Jones enclosed in the missionary's report: "I arrived . . . at this place . . . with flattering hopes of a pleasant and Christian settlement." But "unhappy measures" and "unchristian feelings" would make the organization of a church now "highly improper."

Improper or not, one month after Jones's angry letter to the AHMS, the settlers of Gull Prairie met to organize a church. Luther Humphrey presided as moderator, and Jones served as clerk. A vote to determine the new church's denomination resulted in a tie that Humphrey broke, and the Presbyterian Church of Gull Prairie was duly constituted. William Jones, supported by society funds, was retained as minister. Divisiveness was now institutionalized. Within a few months, some settlers asked John D. Pierce, a Congregational missionary in neighboring Calhoun County, to spend part of his time with them, and Isaac Barnes wrote again to the society, this time declaring that Jones was not fit to unite the community: "Where he is there is [sic] the seeds of discord."[7]

Both the struggle to organize a church on Gull Prairie and the absorption of Congregational settlers into a Presbyterian church reflected a Yankee conception of community embraced by locality. By the time Yankees came to Michigan, of course, the state churches of the colonial period had given way to competing denominations. The fundamental change in Yankee religious institutions, if measured by their social power within communities, was in their ability to control dissent. Puritan churches that in the seventeenth century forced religious malcontents from the colonies tolerated dissenting sects in the eighteenth century while taxing them for the support of the standing order. Revolution raised the cry for disestablishment, but the abolition of state churches was not complete until well into the nineteenth century. Connecticut severed its ties with the Congregational Consociation in 1817; Massachusetts and the Congregational Association parted company in 1834.[8]

The drive for disestablishment heralded the passing of a conception of churches as the chief upholders of social and moral order. The phenomenal proliferation of Methodist and Baptist churches in the first generation after the Revolution presaged a new evangelical conception of church and ministry. The object of the Methodist ministry was to organize societies of committed Christians. To this end, the Methodist episcopacy sent clergy into the field not to become "settled" pastors but as itinerants who were able to organize rapidly small societies under lay leadership. The Methodist strategy of itinerancy was quickly adopted with equally striking success by the Baptist leadership, and although the Baptist organization always remained looser than that of the Methodists, the operations of the two denominations were similar.

Calvinist churches in turn became Methodized as they viewed with alarm the speed and thoroughness of Baptist and Methodist evangelizing on the frontier. They did not so much abandon the old conception of the church as the foundation of social and moral order as they attempted to graft onto it the techniques of the new conception of the church as a missionizing agency. By adapting the practices of revivals and itinerancy and by cooperating with one another, the Calvinist churches intended to colonize the West. The classic example of denominational cooperation on behalf of community churches was the Plan of Union, compacted between the Presbyterian General Assembly and the Congregational Consociation of Connecticut. The chief instrument for furthering the Plan of Union was the AHMS, founded in 1826, which subsidized the work of clergymen in new settlements too poor to support a minister on their own. It was under the Plan of Union that the Presbyterian Church of Gull Prairie was organized with a congregation half composed of Congregationalists.[9]

In recognition of the denominations' differences in polity and sameness of doctrine, the Plan of Union allowed for the formation of three types of churches: Presbyterian, Congregational, and a mixed church that, depending upon local circumstances, might seek admission either to a presbytery or an association. Presbyterian and Congregational ministers could serve churches of either denomination; committeemen and elders could sit at presbytery or association meetings; and churches could join either a presbytery or an association while retaining an internal polity of their own choosing. Both the Consociation and the General Assembly reserved for ministers authority over doctrine, discipline, ordination, dismission, and the transfer of pastors and candidates. The General Assembly differed from the Consociation in local church order. Whereas in Presbyterian churches elders ruled indefinitely, Congregational churches elected their committeemen to rotating terms of office.[10]

The fact that the denominational tug-of-war on Gull Prairie resulted in the organization of a Presbyterian church was hardly surprising. Presbyterianism's hierarchical organization enabled it to penetrate the frontier far more quickly and thoroughly than Congregationalism, with the result that Presbyterian polity predominated among Plan of Union churches for the first thirty years of the plan's existence. Even in the Western Reserve, Congregational churches were attached to presbyteries, not associations.[11] The Gull Prairie church was seemingly yet another example of the long-standing if unequal relationship between the Consociation of Connecticut and the General Assembly.

By the 1830s, however, the Plan of Union was under attack from Old School Presbyterians for doctrinal looseness and from conservative Congregationalists for discriminating against the denomination's ways. In 1837, the General Assembly split, the northern New School synod leaving the rump organization in the control of the largely southern Old School, which repudiated the Plan of Union. The Congregational challenge to the plan was more direct: increasingly, Congregationalists squabbled with Presbyterians over the polity of frontier churches and sought to establish associations and consociations where presbyteries and synods had once held sway. On the Calvinist frontier in Michigan, Old School Presbyterianism was not a serious issue, but nowhere else was the feuding between Congregationalists and Presbyterians more in evidence. Newly opened to settlement, the territory was regarded as fair game by both camps. Richland Township was not an insignificant locus of the conflict, for the denominational struggle was played out locally: new churches were prizes to be won or lost. The Presbyterian Church of Gull Prairie was one of the earliest of at least fifteen Michigan churches founded in the 1830s whose Congregational constituents bitterly resisted the imposition of Presbyterian polity under the Plan of Union.[12]

Although shaped by the war of Calvinist institutions that raged around it, the struggle of the Gull Prairie church to give voice to the Congregationalists lining its pews while retaining its Presbyterian identity was a community fight. It was not that denominational integrity in itself mattered so much to the congregation; rather, the settlers perceived polity as the outward manifestation of an integral relationship between church and community. Church informed Yankee communal order. This understanding was fully consonant with the intent of the Plan of Union: to fill a vacuum between the organic need of frontier communities for religious organization and the inability of frontier churches to maintain a minister. However, although the Plan of Union reserved for clergymen authority over local churches, it effectively enabled churches to function without them.

The laity drew power from the anomalous position of the clergy who served the frontier churches. Laborers for the AHMS served many masters: the society, their denominations, and the collection of settlements, with or without organized churches, to which they ministered. They depended for their support on yearly commissions from the society and local voluntary contributions. Congregations were under no illusions that they should accept charity with deference. On the contrary, they did not hesitate to rebuke their ministers, to insist on their conformity to local tastes in preaching, and to demand their reassignment when they felt it was necessary. When George N. Smith, for example, had the temerity to address a neighboring church on the evils of prostitution, disgruntled men from his Plainfield (later Plainwell) congregation took swift action. They placed a wooden horse in front of his door with a note declaring, "As for whores we don't care anything about them, [and] we don't care about having our young folks hear about [them]," and threatening to make Smith ride the horse if he ever preached on the subject again.[13] This displacement of ministerial authority explains why the rivalry between Presbyterians and Congregationalists was so bitter, why it was locally prosecuted, and why the denominational dimension of the trouble on Gull Prairie was really beside the point. At issue was the nature of authority itself in the community. Thus, when Isaac Barnes and the deacons fell out over the session's right to question his Christian character, they also fought over Barnes's claim to communal leadership.

The Presbyterian Church of Gull Prairie functioned without internal government for a little over two years. In January 1833, the congregation elected a session consisting of deacons Samuel Brown and Simeon Mills and elders James Porter, John B. Barnes, and Samuel Woodruff. The election indicated a compromise between Congregationalists and Presbyterians, Kalamazoo Emigration Society members and later arrivals, with Barnes and Porter representing the latter. Barnes refused to accept his election, however, and since he was not replaced, Presbyterians acquired the dominant voice in the church.

The session acted quickly to establish the church's authority. The day of their election, the elders ruled that all settlers who had lived in the township for at least a year and had not united with the church were to "be excluded from communion unless they presented a certificate or a satisfactory reason why not." The purpose of this edict was to remove from the congregation anyone who was not a member. The session could not deny a settler's right to attend services, but it could deny the sacrament, without which a profession of faith was meaningless. The certificate was a letter of dismission from a settler's home church recommending admission to the Gull Prairie church.[14] In effect, the session was attempting to force all of the Gull Prairie community within the confines of the Presbyterian church. If church and community were one, to refuse to present a certificate was to place oneself beyond the fellowship of both.

By the time of the session's organization, the Gull Prairie church had for six months been rid of its obligation to support William Jones. The AHMS had allowed Jones's commission to expire without renewal. Presiding over the session's organization was the Reverend Levi White, a Congregationalist from Sandisfield, Massachusetts, who with his family had joined the church. Shortly thereafter, White, an "aged man," received a commission from the society to minister on Gull Prairie. He soon had the assistance of another Congregational minister, the Reverend Mason Knappen from Connecticut, who had received a commission to preach elsewhere in Kalamazoo County. With a minister in residence and the occasional preaching of Knappen, Jones, and Humphrey, the congregation experienced a revival for much of 1833 and therefore exhibited considerable compliance with the January edict. In August, White reported that the church had gained forty-five new members.[15]

Despite this drive for spiritual unity in the community, however, the quarreling continued. Finally, the Western Reserve Synod, which oversaw the organization of Presbyterian churches in southwestern Michigan, intervened. In February 1834, clergymen assembled on Gull Prairie to organize the Saint Joseph Presbytery and place the Richland church under its care. A fifteen-day revival ensued, during which, Luther Humphrey happily reported, differences were reconciled and 70 new converts were brought into the church out of a community of fewer than 300 souls.[16]

Humphrey's optimism was premature. As Arvilla Smith, herself united with the Gull Prairie church during the revival, explained in her diary: "There had been much difficulty among the inhabitants of Gull Prairie for two years past. They had gone to great lengths slandering and injuring each other's characters and at the time of this meeting [of the presbytery] they had divided the church. Two meetings were held with[in] a mile of each other. The difficulty originated from where this [meetinghouse] should be erected. . . . It is now erected but fresh wars are breaking out and what will be the result Lord only knows."[17] Exactly how the Gull Prairie church had divided and where the two sites for a meetinghouse were located is unknown, but it is extremely likely that the split followed both denominational and economic fault lines in the community. The meetinghouse was ultimately built in Gull Corners, next to the home of Deacon Samuel Brown, who owned many of the lots in the village. The competing site was undoubtedly located in Isaac Barnes's Geloster. If the organization of the Saint Joseph Presbytery and the revival had strengthened the partisans of Presbyterian order, they also brought the embattled proprietor, Isaac Barnes, to the fore as the leader of the opposition.

The departure from Richland Township early in 1835 of Elder James Porter, the sole Congregationalist and member of the Kalamazoo Emigration Society on the session, left the Gull Prairie church for all practical purposes in the hands of Samuel Brown, Simeon Mills, and Samuel Woodruff. Congregationalists chafed under this Presbyterian leadership, and none more so than Isaac Barnes. The session members found Barnes equally irritating. On August 31, 1835, they met to discuss his "Christian character." They were undeterred in their deliberations by Levi White, who presided over the meeting. The session devoted itself to examining correspondence with the Congregational church of Medina, Ohio, of which Barnes had once been a pillar. Medina had responded to the session's earlier communication of concern over Barnes with a request for more facts.

The session's authority to make the inquiry was questionable. First, it took into its own hands a matter that required ministerial approval. Whatever Levi White's role in the inquiry, he was not properly called to the church, so the session acted on its own. Second, under the Plan of Union, in the case of mixed churches like the Gull Prairie church, adult male members of the congregation disciplined erring Congregationalists. Isaac Barnes's case never received a congregational hearing. Operating as they did on the margins of legality, the session members proceeded cautiously. They never specified the charges against Barnes, as they did against Andrew Rowell, who sold tickets on the Sabbath, or Czar Giddings, who fought and swore outside Mumford Eldred Jr.'s store.[18] Nor did the members of the session themselves attempt to discipline Barnes, as though he were a Presbyterian. Instead, they prepared a brief for the prosecution and submitted it to the Medina church, hoping for a conviction.

The peculiarities of the session's investigation of Isaac Barnes all stemmed from the colonel's refusal to comply with the edict of 1833 and to present his letter of dismission to the session. Clinging to his role as proprietor, Barnes fused and personalized his religious and economic concerns. He refused to give up the Geloster post office when everyone could see that Gull Corners would be Richland's town. He rejected the Gull Prairie church because it was not Congregational and not located in Geloster and because he was not its principal benefactor. He was perhaps also imbued with the orthodoxy of David Hudson, who in the early 1830s led a successful fight to dissociate his church from a presbytery and to attach it to an association. Whatever the exact mixture of motivations behind Barnes's opposition, he had come to view the Gull Prairie church as a personal challenge to his communal leadership.

Barnes paid a high price for his stubbornness. According to Milton Bradley, who became pastor of the Gull Prairie church in the 1840s and whose statement is corroborated by a comparison of church rolls with land records for 1835, the revivals of 1833 and 1834 raised the proportion of church members in the community to a number "larger than at any subsequent period in our history."[19] Among the communicants were all of the former members of the Kalamazoo Emigration Society, including Barnes's kinsmen, John B. and Orville, and their wives and his son, Carlos. Barnes's brother, Tillotson, and his wife, Ursula, also joined the church. Barnes's wife, Martha, and his sons, George, Lester, and Lucius, stood by him. Isaac Barnes's refusal to join the Gull Prairie church set him at odds with his family, his fellow Christian colonists, and his community—a tenuous position for a would-be proprietor.

As for Brown, Mills, and Woodruff, the seriousness of Barnes's offenses overrode the dubiety of the investigation. What galled the session was that Barnes continued to attend church services while refusing membership. Had he simply registered his disapproval with his absence, the session would have had no grounds for its inquiry. The church's authority did not extend to settlers who did not worship with it. Isaac Barnes dissented by sitting, Sunday after Sunday, in the Gull Corners meetinghouse. Barnes's presence gave the lie to the proposition that church and community were one on Gull Prairie. It negated the 1833 edict, which was intended to bring all those who attended services under the discipline of the church as members. In this sense, the members of the session did not so much deny communion to Barnes as he refused to accept it, and membership in the Gull Prairie church, from them. For Barnes, complete withdrawal from the Gull Prairie church would have been tantamount to an admission of the defeat of his proprietorship and a declaration of victory for supporters of the Presbyterian church and Gull Corners. Dissent by absence would have placed him beyond the pale of the community over which he claimed proprietary authority. Dissent by abstention from the sacrament was an assertion of that authority and could not be ignored. By denying the right of the session to serve communion to him, Barnes questioned the church's legitimacy. In the eyes of Brown, Mills, and Woodruff, his act of denial must have approached blasphemy. Deacon Simeon Mills's description of the inquiry as "an inquiry into the Christian character of Isaac Barnes" was precisely to the point.

Any opportunity to arbitrate Barnes's differences with the Gull Prairie church was lost once the session began its investigation. Nothing in the characters of Barnes, Brown, Mills, or Woodruff offered much hope for compromise. According to Milton Bradley, Barnes seemed "exclusive and bigoted" to the Richland community. The Presbyterian Bradley wrote approvingly of Brown, Mills, and Woodruff, but his assessments make clear that the members of the session were as difficult as Barnes. Samuel Brown, recalled Bradley, was "neither a bigot, nor in any sense loose and unreliable in his character and life." Deacon Brown presided over the session that in 1839 suspended his son, Samuel T., from the church for "not liv[ing] agreeably to his profession and giv[ing] occasion to the enemies against our holy religion." Bradley called Deacon Mills "an open, fearless defender of Christianity." Mills had sold to his brothers, Willard and Sylvester, the land on which they platted the town of Richland. As for Elder Woodruff, he was "decided as a Christian, unbending as the hills when once established in his opinions."[20]

In its reply to the session's inquiry, the Medina church requested that the session have a "friendly conversation" with Barnes. This request followed standard disciplinary procedure for cases in which official concern for an errant member had not yet been translated into a formal charge. It was also a delaying action. The Medina church could not ignore the session's complaints about Barnes, but it was reluctant to discipline him on the members' word alone. At the very least, a friendly conversation between Barnes and the session would establish Barnes's position. At best, Barnes, Brown, Mills, and Woodruff would resolve their differences. The session viewed the conversation, however, not as an opportunity for conciliation but as a way of forcing Barnes to plead guilty. Barnes, predictably, proved equally obdurate. "No confessions were made on the part of Isaac Barnes," Deacon Mills wrote of the actual conversation in the session minutes for January 25, 1836. Determined to get satisfaction, the session reported the conversation to Medina.

Not long after the meeting with Barnes, two changes occurred in the religious life of Richland Township: the session voted to increase its body to eight members, and John D. Pierce, a sometime laborer for the AHMS who had been occasionally preaching on Gull Prairie since 1832, organized a Congregational church.[21] Whether the session's decision to increase its size was designed to forestall the formation of the church or to contain the damage is unknown. Both the increase in the size of the session and the organization of the Congregational church, however, resulted from external pressures placed on the Gull Prairie community. Instructed by the society, which was heavily subsidized by General Assembly funds, to organize only

Presbyterian churches, the militantly Congregational Pierce openly rebelled against what he considered a Presbyterian territorial imperative. He became one of the first Congregational ministers in Michigan to work for the severance of his denomination's ties with the Plan of Union. As Pierce acidly explained to the secretary of the society in reporting the formation of the first Michigan association in March 1837, the "most slanderous stories and reports" circulated to prevent Congregational churches from receiving aid from the society and "to put down Congregationalism." The Saint Joseph Presbytery discouraged the organization and support of Congregational churches.[22]

At least insofar as the Gull Prairie church was concerned, Pierce had a point. In moving to enlarge the session, Brown, Mills, and Woodruff did not act on their own initiative but submitted to the directive of the Michigan Presbyterian hierarchy. The vote followed the session's receipt of letters from Luther Humphrey and John P. Cleveland, one of the most prominent Presbyterian clergymen in the territory. Humphrey and Cleveland were staunch supporters of the Presbyterian version of the Plan of Union, favoring concession to Congregational forms in internal polity but preferring that churches attach themselves to a presbytery.[23] When Pierce complained that such maneuvers were discriminatory, he accurately reflected Congregational opinion on Gull Prairie, where the association was organized with Isaac Barnes and other local discontented Congregationalists in attendance. The preamble of the association's constitution captures some of the insurgent sentiment in its statement that the members felt "as the descendants of the Pilgrims Veneration for the Religious institutions of our fathers."[24]

Denominational drumbeating drove the religious reorganization of Gull Prairie. Despite the competitive intent of the changes, however, and the structural incongruity of the result, communal worship was little affected. The reconstitution of the session returned it to denominational parity. Dauphin Brown, Samuel's son, joined his father, Mills, and Woodruff on the session. Representing the church's Congregationalists were Edwin Mason, John B. and Orville Barnes, and James Porter, son of the first Elder Porter. The new session thus reached out reconciling hands to Presbyterians and Congregationalists, Kalamazoo Emigration Society settlers and later arrivals, Isaac's family and his enemies. Members of the Congregational church, although firm in their separateness, pursued amicable relations with the Presbyterians. Mason Knappen served unofficially as the congregation's spiritual leader and helped it to establish a close, cooperative relationship with the Presbyterian church. The cooperation was partly born of necessity, for the Congregationalists could afford neither a pastor nor a church of their own. They worshipped with the Presbyterians and shared the same ministers. By April 1836, the Presbyterian Church of Gull Prairie had gathered to it three distinct constituencies: Congregationalists who preferred Congregational usage, Congregationalists who accepted the Presbyterian hierarchy in exchange for more broadly based church leadership, and Presbyterians. On any one Sunday, the same minister admitted communicants of either denomination to either church.[25]

Organization of a Congregational church and reorganization of the Presbyterian church ought to have broken the deadlock between Barnes and the session. Had Barnes joined the Presbyterian church, he would have removed the session's objections to his character; had he joined the Congregationalists, he would have removed himself from the session's purview. When the newly constituted session met in April to consider his case, however, Isaac Barnes remained a member of the Congregational church of Medina, Ohio. Had Barnes decided that he could not be a Congregationalist in the presence of Presbyterians? His failure to seek admission to either church must have looked to the session like sheer willfulness. At least one Congregationalist sided with the Presbyterians to continue the inquiry, for the session voted to dispatch a letter to Medina "stating plainly the facts in [the] Barnes case which can be attested to by competent witnesses & if the church feel it to be their duty to prosecute the case we will furnish affidavits without delay."[26]

What the Medina church did when it received this pointed missive is unknown, but the "Barnes case" was not fully resolved for nearly two years after the April meeting. In the meantime, the two congregations continued to worship together, and the Presbyterians began to build a permanent edifice and to seek a minister. With the completion of the new church, into which both congregations moved in November 1837, came a second Gull Prairie revival. Shortly thereafter, the session issued a call to the Reverend Calvin Clark, who was installed on February 7, 1838.

On February 10, Deacons Brown and Mills and Elder Woodruff apologized to Isaac Barnes: "Whereas . . . [we] made a record . . . militating against the character of Isaac Barnes of the Congregational Church of this place, and . . . complaints to the church in Medina Ohio to which he then belonged . . . we acknowledge after more mature reflection & investigation of the case, that it was without just cause & unwarranted, & cheerfully make an injured brother . . . just restitution."[27]

Barnes had probably joined the Congregational church sometime before his participation in the formation of the association in March 1837. Perhaps he had been pressured to yield by the Medina church or had decided to give

up his lonely resistance and to make common cause with other Congregationalists. In any event, the timing of the session's apology, following on the
heels of Clark's installation, cannot have been accidental. If the purpose of
their inquiry was either to coerce Barnes into joining or to force him completely out of the church, why would Brown, Mills, and Woodruff have
made restitution unless pushed by Calvin Clark? Again, Simeon Mills wrote
precisely to the point: the case against Barnes was "unadvised." The session
admitted the illegitimacy of its inquiry. Although Brown, Mills, and Woodruff had once thought Barnes guilty of blasphemy, perhaps they now saw
their own actions as prideful. Only a minister called to the church could
have provoked the concession. Practical and moral authority in the Presbyterian Church of Gull Prairie lay finally and indisputably in the hands of one
man.

In its choice of Calvin Clark, the church was singularly fortunate. Clark
had a rare talent for fence-mending and a genuine commitment to broadly
based lay participation. He was a Presbyterian but did not believe in *jure
divino* denominations.[28] After Clark had been in Richland a little over a year,
an event unprecedented in the history of the Gull Prairie church occurred.
At an afternoon Sabbath meeting, the congregation "expressed their nearly
unanimous wish to have the Session . . . vacate their office." Since the
church's organization, membership had increased over fivefold to 109 communicants who wished to "express . . . feelings in the choice of a new
session."

The congregation's request signaled the shifting of authority from a session occasionally subject to outside ministerial guidance to a "settled" pastor and the congregation as a whole. Although "for some time cherished by
many," the call for a new election was not another flare-up of the discord that
had long troubled the church but a sign that it was at last abating. "Almost
unanimously elected," the new session retained four old members: Samuel
Brown as deacon and Simeon Mills, Orville Barnes, and Dauphin Brown as
elders. Josiah Buel became the fourth elder. Gone were John B. Barnes,
Edwin Mason, and Samuel Woodruff.[29] Thus, the session returned to its
original size, and its composition was remarkable only for its continuity with
the old board. The election had not served to clean house but to recognize
the church's achievement of institutional security. It no longer relied upon
mission charity or the leadership of a few laymen, nor was it threatened by
disharmony among its members.

From this secure base, Calvin Clark worked steadily to bring about a
reconciliation between Presbyterians and Congregationalists. By June 1841,
when the Congregational association met on Gull Prairie, his efforts had

begun to bear fruit. The association devoted itself to a single question: "Is it or is it not the duty of any church belonging to this body to unite & amalgamate itself with a church of any other denomination for the sake of greater gospel privileges? is it, or is it not for the spiritual benefit of such a church?" Here, plainly put, was the conundrum facing the Congregational Church of Gull Prairie. It had formed because its members thought themselves badly used by a rival denomination, but it could not wean itself from the local Presbyterian church. The Congregational church had neither a meetinghouse nor a minister of its own. Since it was unable to sustain itself, was it not then obliged to reunite with the Presbyterian church? The association opened its deliberations to the widest possible communal discussion by inviting Calvin Clark and all members of both churches to participate as corresponding members of the association. The debate lasted much of the day and was followed by a vote "to lay [the matter] on the table sine die & that the churches be advised to act their wisdom on the subject." If the Congregationalists wished to reunite with the Presbyterians, the association would not stand in their way.[30]

A little less than a year later, the Calvinist churches of Gull Prairie met for the last time to consider reunification. The hidebound continued in their resistance—some Congregationalists claiming, with the self-interested backing of some Presbyterians, their right to a church of their own. Nevertheless, the reunification plan gained approval, and the presbytery authorized the merger of the two churches in September. The session then resigned, and a board of six completely new members began three-year rotating terms of office in accordance with Congregational usage. Calvin Clark left the church the following July and was replaced by Milton Bradley, another firm supporter of the Plan of Union.[31] By 1848, Bradley had returned to his fold all except the most extreme denominational partisans, and the frontier years of the Richland Presbyterian Church were over. Bradley remained with the church until his retirement in 1877.

Thus, the long struggle between Presbyterians and Congregationalists on Gull Prairie was finally resolved by the formation of a unified church of compromised polity. The trouble in the settlement had reflected the larger denominational conflict over the Plan of Union, yet it had also taken a distinctly local course. It had been born of highly charged local expectations for an organic relationship between church and community years before the Congregationalist revolt from the Plan of Union. It resolved itself four years before a Congregational convention composed of delegates from throughout the Old Northwest met in Michigan City to abrogate the Plan of Union. By the time of the Gull Prairie church's reunion, the worst of the denominational strife was yet to come. Indeed, Calvin Clark left his ministry on Gull Prairie to accept a position as an itinerant, supported by AHMS funds, to "bishopize" western Michigan and so to resist the Congregational insurgency.[32]

The key to the struggle was local control. As the Reverend Vernon D. Taylor, whose own church was within months of splitting apart, explained in a letter to the society: "The worst feature of eastern Congregationalism is it is so agrarian in its character as to almost entirely an[n]ihilate the pastoral relation & the influence is very much, if not entirely, to destroy a pa[s]tor's influence over his flock. It is largely suf[f]used with distrust & jealousy and nothing is worse than this in a church."[33] Congregationalism was "agrarian" because it emphasized the autonomy of local churches. Congregationalists in Taylor's church resisted their attachment to a presbytery, which Presbyterian supporters of the Plan of Union saw as critical for maintaining order in frontier churches too poor to call ministers of their own and dependent on missionary support. When the Presbyterian version of the Plan of Union attempted to substitute denominational hierarchy and missionizing for locally settled ministers, however, it inadvertently opened the door to lay leadership and therefore to communal discord.

The problem on Gull Prairie was that too many individuals with pretensions to leadership wanted to impose their version of moral order on the community. The fact that the differences among them were chiefly variations on the theme of church and communal unity only personalized the divisiveness. In the end, the issue was not about the acceptability of superintendence by a presbytery but about who would locally direct the religious life of the settlement. Only a "settled" pastor could impose order on so many deacons, elders, and missionaries. Thus, the Plan of Union triumphed on Gull Prairie even as it shattered elsewhere.

But it was a deeply ironic triumph. Reunification of the Presbyterian and Congregational churches resolved long-standing discord within the community, but it did not unite Richland residents within a single church. While Calvinists squabbled, Methodism took root in the township. A Methodist class was organized as early as 1833 under Brother Samuel Boyles, who arrived in Richland in 1831. Boyles eventually became a minister and rode circuit in Kalamazoo and Barry Counties. At least one other Methodist minister settled in Richland. English-born William Daubney came to Richland from Hinesburg, Vermont, in 1835. He, too, divided his time between farming on Gull Prairie and circuit riding.[34] Methodist and Presbyterian churches gradually divided Richland between them, the Presbyterians drawing members from the eastern half of the township, and the Methodists from the west.[35] Thus, whereas the Presbyterian Church of Gull Prairie in its early years embraced most of the township's settlement, by the time Milton Bradley took over as pastor, it would clearly never again draw all of Richland into its fold. Despite the settlers' yearning for the integration of church and community, the Presbyterian church came to serve a locality within a community. Over the older, organic impulse of Yankee settlement lay the new denominationalism.

As for Isaac Barnes, vindication of his Christian character was not enough to compensate for his rebuffing as a town proprietor. The colonel left Richland for Allegan County a year before the reunification. He had tried to make Geloster Richland's town; he had tried to make a Congregational church Richland's church; but he had failed at both because the challenges to his leadership were too many and too great. Across Kalamazoo County, Caleb Eldred succeeded where Barnes failed.

Like Barnes in Richland, Eldred equated Climax Township with possession: his land, his village, and his church. Unlike Barnes, the judge was able to sweep aside the objections of other settlers to his leadership. In the matter of Climax's churches, Francis Hodgman, whose father, Moses, came to the township before 1840, neatly captured Eldred's uncompromising stance: "He was a rigid Baptist. . . . So long as there were no church organizations in the town he worked ardently for the spread of the gospel without asking the denomination of the man who preached it. As soon, however, as the different churches were organized . . . he was square on the Baptist side."[36] Although devoted to Christian principles, Eldred made no pretense of the unity of church and community. He associated communal leadership with moral directive rather differently than did the Gull Prairie Calvinists. Eldred was interested in fostering a moral climate in the township, but he regarded churches as spiritual amenities. If other denominations wished to establish beachheads in Climax, let them try, but he would have a Baptist church, even if it meant elbowing out the competition. Baptist, Methodist, and Presbyterian churches formed in Climax in the late 1830s, but by 1840, only the Baptists remained, a singular testimony to, unlike Barnes again, Eldred's control of township resources and his will.

Caleb Eldred opened his home to Baptist circuit riders as early as 1833 and shortly thereafter to their Methodist brethren. In the winter of 1834–35, the Reverend James T. Robe, head of the Kalamazoo Mission, organized a Methodist class in the township, which by then also had regular Baptist preaching. Two Baptist and two Methodist ministers, who coordinated their circuit riding, fueled a great revival during the winter of 1836–37, during which most of the township's unconverted professed and the covenanted reaffirmed their faith. The evangelical surge, however, fragmented the Climax community into denominations. Presbyterians organized shortly after the revival ended. Yet so pervasive was the Baptist-Methodist influence in Climax that the church soon drew most of its members from adjacent Leroy Township in Calhoun County. Three years later, the Presbyterians relocated permanently in Leroy.

Baptists and Methodists continued to cooperate after the revival, but they had clearly become institutional rivals. The Baptists organized under the leadership of Elder John Harris of Battle Creek, who stayed with the judge when he came to preach. Since neither group could afford a church of its own, Baptists and Methodists shared the District Number 1 schoolhouse in Climax village and alternated Sunday services. Sharing the schoolhouse accelerated the rivalry. The building had been Caleb Eldred's first home on the prairie, and he still considered it his property, although it now belonged to the township. Eldred had built a new house for his family in 1836, moved the old dwelling closer to the center of the village, refurbished it, and sold it to the township to use as a schoolhouse for what some settlers thought was an exorbitant price. But for Eldred, the sale had literally been all in the family: he was serving on the township board when it bought the building, while his son-in-law, Daniel Lawrence, was director of District Number 1.[37]

The Methodists finally gave up trying to negotiate with Eldred and the Baptists and, by 1839, with the township supervisor (Caleb Eldred) and the school inspectors (Daniel and Stephen Eldred). The church moved north to Charleston Township before 1840. The Baptists used the schoolhouse until 1847, when they erected a brick church nearby. Late in the next decade, Caleb Eldred built a parsonage on an adjacent lot that he owned and gave both to the church. Eldred's world was by then nearly complete. The old man delighted in walking from his home, past his church, through his orchard, to his school, where he distributed his apples to the schoolchildren.[38]

The Richland settlers eventually arrived at a position similar to the one embraced by Eldred in Climax Township from the beginning. Christian principles mattered more than their institutional embodiments; churches were more matters of personal preference than expressions of communal moral order. In this, the experience of both townships points to the profound impact of evangelical Protestantism in the antebellum period as both a centrifugal and a centripetal force—splintering community churches yet blurring the doctrinal differences among them. One consequence of the Second Great Awakening, no less important for being local, was that it altered the meaning of moral leadership within small, rural communities like

Richland and Climax. In a world of shared principles, which churches were organized was less important than who organized them, as Isaac Barnes discovered at a cost. Personal eminence and communal prominence, as reflected in issues of faith, no longer went hand in hand.

The colonel did not experience in his old age the proprietary ease enjoyed by the judge. For Barnes, Allegan County was a last frontier.[39] In the early 1840s, the county was not yet fully occupied, for it lacked the plenitude of prime farming land that had attracted settlers to Kalamazoo in the previous decade. Wayland, where Barnes located, was not for him the prospected site of a Christian colony but a place to make money. Barnes's business in Wayland was strictly a family business. In the winter of 1836–37, in the midst of the session's inquiry into his Christian character, Barnes and his son, George, had located a mill site on the Rabbit River in section 2, had a log house built on it, and made extensive purchases of nearby pine forest. Another son, Lucius, had the mill in operation by the following winter and, as long as water power remained adequate, conducted an extensive lumbering business in southwestern Michigan.

The Barnes interest in Wayland was purely extractive. Isaac and his sons never intended to stamp the township permanently with their presence. They made no effort to plat a town but called the entire township "Lumberton"—a place to secure capital. Lumberton as a place name did not survive the Barnes milling operation, but Isaac probably did not expect that it would. He and his sons were not looking for a new Geloster. Isaac Barnes was well into his sixties when he moved to Wayland Township. Perhaps he was tired or embittered by his experience on Gull Prairie, for his actions in Wayland showed little of his old proprietary instincts. Instead, Lumberton was apparently the site of a family retrenchment. The mill was a scheme to provide for Isaac and his wife, Martha, in retirement and to build stakes for George and Lucius.

George Barnes came to Wayland with Isaac and Martha in 1841. He had been living in nearby Martin Township, developing land and serving as state representative and township supervisor. The Barnes family sold its mill when the Rabbit River ran low in the mid-1840s. Lucius left Wayland and lived variously in Allegan County and Ohio before returning to the township in 1854, presumably to take over the family estate. George, who never married, Isaac, and Martha seem to have lived out the rest of their lives in Wayland on the family's accumulated assets. Despite their indifference to Wayland's prospects outside the mill, however, Isaac and George were still Barneses and men of prominence. When the township was organized in

1844, Isaac served as moderator and George as inspector of the township meeting and election. George was elected supervisor, Isaac was made a director of the poor, and both were chosen as school inspectors. Isaac then vanishes from the record. He and Martha died in February 1848; George died in 1853. A Congregational church was not organized in Wayland until 1860.

# All of the Whiggs and Some of the Democrats

POLITICS AND COMMUNITY

As bitter as Isaac Barnes's experience was with the Presbyterian Church of Gull Prairie, religious controversy alone did not force him from Richland Township. On New Year's Day 1845, an angry, aged, and probably ailing Barnes dictated a letter from his Allegan County home to his old political "friend," Senator Lucius Lyon. Barnes had been Lyon's occasional correspondent in the 1830s while Lyon served as territorial delegate to the U.S. Congress, providing information relevant to Lyon's speculations in western Michigan lands and seeking assistance in obtaining political appointments for himself and his son, Carlos. Now Barnes wrote to Lyon about a matter of honor. The old man asked the senator to examine a transcript of a letter from Mumford Eldred Jr. to Congressman Isaac E. Crary dated June 18, 1840, in the files of the federal Post Office Department. The nephew of Judge Caleb Eldred of Climax, Mumford Eldred Jr. was in 1840 Richland's principal merchant and Barnes's most deadly political rival.[1]

To Barnes, the transcript was proof that Eldred had plotted to remove him from his position as postmaster in Richland and thereby to expel him from the township. For his part, Eldred had vigorously denied the charge and declared the transcript a forgery. Besmirched by a controversy that would not die, Barnes sought Lyon's help in clearing his name: "Although some length of time has elapsed since the transaction yet truth is the same now as then or ever, and I have been censured for not proving facts and bringing the truth to light." Eldred's letter was a tissue of lies, Barnes wrote. Would Lyon not go to the post office headquarters and verify the accuracy of the transcript?

Eldred's letter referred to a citizens' petition of February 1839 to the Post Office Department. In the petition, seventy-five settlers requested Barnes's removal as postmaster and Eldred's appointment in his stead. The petition was a fraud, declared Barnes, who evidently had a copy of it; the signatures were of persons living outside his post office district or "those, according to good authority, by direct falsehoods relative to the office and its concerns." In April 1839, Eldred had submitted a second petition with thirteen signatures, and Barnes earnestly requested that Lyon prepare for him a transcript of the petition, claiming that the reputed signatories "declair . . . it was done by forgery." Finally, Barnes asked for a transcript of a letter that could also be found in the post office files, allegedly from the influential county Democrat, H. H. Comstock, "charging me with false facing at the election of 1840." "In a most solemn manner," Comstock had sworn to Barnes that the letter was "a forgery of a very dark character." Closing his appeal to Lyon for aid against Eldred's "anniquity," Barnes resoundingly affirmed his Democratic principles: "Wishing you the enjoyment of happiness in looking forward to the Inauguration of Polk and Dallas, the Reannexation of Texas, and the exclusive occupancy of Orrigon, all justly our own."

The most direct proof that Barnes was right to charge Eldred with fraud and forgery comes from Eldred's letter to Congressman Crary, a copy of which Barnes enclosed in his letter to Lyon. Not only is Eldred's letter of a piece with his known career in Richland, but its rhetoric strongly resembles that of Eldred's own correspondence with Lucius Lyon. An active participant in the county Democratic organization, Eldred began the letter by affirming his partisan credentials with a promise to "spend $100" to get out the vote for Van Buren.[2] Then the letter got down to business: "Isaac Barnes our Post Master has come out for Harrison the whole hog . . . and all Parties here in this town has tried to put him out of office & to put me in his stead and change the office to Richland being the name of our town." Here Eldred compressed a mixture of truth, untruth, and possibility into fact: many Richland settlers did wish to move the post office from Geloster to Gull Corners; Barnes emphatically denied that he was a closet Whig; and some may have thought Eldred, as the principal merchant, a good candidate for postmaster. The petition to remove Barnes had included "all the democratic Partys names and most of the Whiggs," "most of the Prominent men" of the county, and the postmasters "in this region of the county." This attempt to demonstrate widespread anti-Barnes sentiment inadvertently lends support to Barnes's charge that many of the signatories lived outside the post office district.

The case against Barnes established, Eldred laid out his program. First, the peremptory demand: "Now I want you [a characteristic phrase] to go to the [Post Office] Department and see that Petition because he is being against us all." Then, a halfhearted recognition of overreaching: if Crary did not wish to plump for Eldred, his political associate in Richland, Alvan Hood, would make a good postmaster. Next, the assertion of Crary's political self-interest: "I Barnes opposed you in your election and so did his family." And finally, the proposed deal between political friends: "I will not let any one [k]now that your name is in the question—and likways that there is no one Els—here that wants the office in the democratic Party [so much for the candidacy of Alvan Hood!]—I keep Store—at the Town center and am Permently Sattld &c—the ownly store now [in] the Place—of any consequence."

Mumford Eldred Jr. was appointed postmaster of Richland shortly after Barnes's departure from the township in 1841, and the office was moved from Barnes's house in Geloster to Eldred's store in Gull Corners. Eldred's successful attempt to link partisanship to personal economic ambition, although singularly nasty, was hardly unique. Such maneuvers were a feature of local politics in Michigan at the end of the territorial period and during the early years after statehood. As the national party in power, the Democratic organization controlled political appointments, such as post office and district land office posts, which were critical to the establishment of new communities and therefore vital to sponsors of local development schemes. Lucius Lyon's personal papers both as representative and as senator contain hundreds of letters from "friends" pledging loyal support and asking for an appointment.

Typical, except perhaps for its wry candor, was a letter that Lyon received from Isaac Barnes in 1836, when Barnes was already under assault in Richland and considering opportunities elsewhere. The letter provided a wealth of information about land values in western Michigan that was helpful to Lyon in his speculations. It flattered him for his "masterful exposition of the rights of Michigan" to retain a southern boundary disputed by Ohio and to be brought swiftly into the union. Then it made its pitch. Would Lyon promote Barnes's candidacy as registrar of the new land office to be opened north of Grand River? "It is the order of the day, (and as honorable in my view as the old-fashioned Yankee practice) that if a man desires a favor to ask for it."[3]

Mumford Eldred Jr. was obviously much less gracious in his demands. Indeed, his rough rhetoric rested on two key assertions: first, organized opposition to the Democratic Party required the vigilance of the faithful. Eldred did not simply make his case against Barnes by claiming that Gull Corners, not Geloster, was Richland's town. He also charged that Barnes was a traitor to the Democracy and was therefore unfit to hold office. As Ronald Formisano has shown, competition between Whigs and Democrats first appeared in Michigan in 1835. In Kalamazoo County, Whig organization probably began in the summer of 1837, when a convention of "those opposed to the state and national administration" elected delegates to a state convention.[4] Local elections in most communities, Formisano argues, did not become partisan until the mid-1840s, although in Kalamazoo the process was under way in at least some townships as early as 1838.[5]

But the emergence of partisanship in local elections in the mid-1840s does not mean that partisan politics had previously been absent from local affairs. On the contrary, partisanship in the last years of the territorial period was an excellent avenue for self-advancement, as the case of Isaac Barnes demonstrates. Barnes took asking for political favors as a matter of course, such as when he wrote to Lucius Lyon that he was tired of serving as probate judge of Kalamazoo County and would like instead to become an associate judge of the circuit court, an appointment of "much more convenience to myself and to the public."[6] Such political appointments, which both advanced personal fortunes and fostered local development, were by definition competitive, for they favored some individuals and communities over others. Within a new settlement, ambitious men jostled to control local resources, to direct the establishment of township infrastructure, and, not incidentally, to carve out a prominent place for themselves in a nascent social order. Partisan politics thus played a key role in defining local status on the frontier by singling out some men for preferment.

By the time that Mumford Eldred Jr. began to work the lever of patronage, however, the organization of Whig opposition had altered the arena of partisan politics. Eldred's rhetoric reflected the change, as did his political activism. He first served as a delegate to the county Democratic convention in 1838 and ran unsuccessfully for state representative in 1838 and 1842.[7] When this partisanship penetrated the townships sufficiently to affect local affairs, it began to redefine the relationship between local status and local politics. Partisanship emerged in local elections as the rudiments of township infrastructure fell into place, and it divided a new, fractious, and unstable elite into warring camps. Soon the elite competed less over who would take charge of local development than over who should set the moral tone of the community. In township elections, partisan, personal, and communal identities merged. Mumford Eldred Jr. would play a key role in Richland in the transition from developmental to cultural politics.

Eldred's second assertion in his letter to Crary was that political patronage as a reward for party loyalty was a legitimate vehicle of capital accumulation. For Eldred, personal advancement and party loyalty were complementary. A good Democrat should get ahead and help his family, good Democrats all, get ahead, too. Eldred's first appeal to Lucius Lyon, for example, was a request in 1844 that his father be appointed farmer for the Indians at the Baptist and Episcopalian missions in Barry and Allegan Counties. The current farmer, Stephen Fairbanks of Richland, was a "violent Political Abolitionist." Mumford Eldred Sr., however, was perfect for the post—a "strong Democrat for 45 years" who "never has had the first office of Proffit from the Government." Besides, his father was the "best practical farmer in the state."[8] Several months later, Eldred wrote again to Lyon to ask that Uncle Caleb (who made his own request the same day) be appointed postmaster at Climax and that his father now be considered for the post of farmer, or instructor in agriculture, to the Indians at the Old Wing Mission near present-day Holland. This letter achieved a level of personal and partisan invective remarkable even for Eldred. The farmer at Old Wing was also a "violent Abolitionist," a Richland "Boy some 22 years old and nearsighted" who "could not tell a Horn from a Corn 15 rods," appointed only because his wife and the missionary's wife were sisters.[9]

Most telling about Eldred's partisanship, however, is the way it blossomed along the upward curve of his career in Richland as a local officeholder and as an entrepreneur of no mean ability. He had emerged as a figure of consequence in 1835 when he and John D. Batcheldor opened the first general store in the township in Gull Corners. In contrast, the year marked for Isaac Barnes the beginning of a long fall from grace in the Presbyterian Church of Gull Prairie and in the eyes of his fellow settlers. Two years before, Barnes had played a key role in the organization of Richland Township and had been elected to the office of supervisor, the highest local office, as well as commissioner of highways and pound master. The following year, he was reelected supervisor and commissioner of highways. But in 1835, Barnes found himself thrust from the center of politics. Until his departure from Richland, he served in only two other local offices—fence viewer and commissioner of highways in 1837 and 1838, respectively. He was badly defeated as a candidate for commissioner of highways and clerk in 1839 and 1840.[10]

In the same period, Mumford Eldred Jr.'s political fortunes rose as rapidly as Barnes's declined. First elected clerk in 1836, he was thereafter continuously in office, serving as supervisor, fence viewer, treasurer, and assessor. By 1840, Eldred had been elected to local office six times, a feat that placed him among an elite group of seven men who had held five or more township positions between 1833 and 1840. Eldred's extreme youth made his rise all the more remarkable. He was not yet thirty years old in 1840, while all of the other major officeholders were over forty and three were over fifty.[11]

Despite his tender years, Eldred had much in common with his fellow officeholders, and these shared characteristics reveal a good deal about the relationship between local status and local politics in the early years of settlement in Richland. In the first place, Eldred and the others truly dominated the township's public life in the 1830s. Of the fifty-six men elected to office between 1833 and 1840, these seven men (12.5 percent) occupied slightly under 40 percent of 144 positions. They dominated also by the ubiquity of their service. Most often elected as supervisors, highway commissioners, and assessors—particularly important positions in a new community because they were executive as well as administrative—they also occupied lowly offices. Isaac Barnes and Mumford Eldred Jr., for example, served as both fence viewers and supervisors, while Simeon Mills was elected pound master and supervisor.

Richland's major officeholders achieved their preeminence in part simply because they had lived in the township much longer than most other settlers. As a number of scholars have noted, the extreme mobility of nineteenth-century Americans made persistence the first requirement for the formation of a stable elite in new communities.[12] In any one year, roughly one-third of Richland's population had either just arrived or was about to leave. In contrast, all of the major officeholders resided in the township for much of the 1830s.[13]

The social and economic profile of Eldred and his compatriots is also revealing. Although all were landowners, they were neither simple nor simply farmers. As a group, they were well-off. Three of them—Eldred, Simeon Mills, and Samuel Boyles—were among the wealthiest men in Richland in 1838. The mean assessed value of the cohort's property was $2,200, ranging from $5,050 for Eldred to $895 for Isaac Briggs, compared to a little over $1,080 for all taxpayers. Besides their wealth, the major officeholders also shared a commercial orientation and a prominence in local religious affairs that mirrored their leadership in town governance. Eldred was a merchant. Timothy Mills owned a tavern in Gull Corners and with his brother, Simeon, speculated in town sites, as did Samuel Brown. Isaac Barnes, of course, was the putative proprietor of Richland Township. Simeon Mills, Brown, and Briggs were deacons in the Presbyterian church; Barnes was a Congregationalist insurgent; and Samuel Boyles, a Methodist minister, organized a Gull Prairie class. In short, Richland's major officeholders in the 1830s were Christian entrepreneurs who had identified their interests with a vision for the development of the township. The partisan appointments sought by Barnes and Eldred meshed well with the communal denotation of local status.

Whether the major officeholders were selected as township leaders by their fellow settlers or whether they selected themselves comes down to the same thing, as the case of Mumford Eldred Jr. demonstrates. Eldred's political career in Richland Township was the logical outgrowth of an aggressive campaign of capital accumulation begun when, no more than twenty years old, he came to southwestern Michigan from New York State with his uncle Caleb in 1830. Uncle and nephew were the advance guard of a wholesale removal of Eldreds to Michigan. Caleb's family joined him on Climax Prairie, as did his brother Daniel and his family. Mumford Sr. and his family followed Mumford Jr. to Richland. Eldred's earliest efforts to raise capital— a cattle drive to Indiana in 1831, followed by the rapid purchase and resale of several parcels of government land—were probably backed by his family: his uncle Caleb, who had worked in the cattle trade in New York, and his new father-in-law, Hazel Hoag, next to whose tract Eldred also purchased government land.[14]

By late 1834, Eldred's efforts had coalesced into a distinct commercial program in which he maximized short-term gains by rolling over property bought on margin with borrowed capital. Before 1838, when he pulled out of the local land market just before the second financial contraction of the panic of 1837-39, Eldred bought and sold nearly 1,000 acres of government land. His purchases dwarfed those of the forty-nine other Richland settlers who bought government land in the same period. Only three, besides Eldred, acquired more than 300 acres. At the same time, Eldred bought Spring Brook, a tract in section 19 containing a town plat, timberland, and Richland's first sawmill. He was forced to sell Spring Brook when he found himself overextended, but ever nimble, he managed to turn potential disaster into yet another financial triumph. Eldred sold the tract to Hosea B. Huston, a prominent merchant in Kalamazoo and backer of his and Batcheldor's store, then used the renewal of credit through Huston to buy out Batcheldor and to repurchase a quarter interest in the mill property.

By 1839, Eldred had consolidated his profits from land speculation into sole ownership of the only general store in Richland. He then turned to partisan politics, with his first aim to replace Isaac Barnes as postmaster and move the post office to his store in Gull Corners. After this successful maneuver, Eldred continued to prosper for several years in Richland. He remained in township office, serving as justice of the peace in 1843 and 1844. He expanded his merchandising operation by buying out the stock of Stephen Cummings, a bankrupt competitor. And he became the local "champion of the Democrats." In achieving this last feat, he also made himself obnoxious to a good many people in the community.

Thanks in no small part to Eldred, in 1844 partisan politics for the first time determined the annual spring election for township offices. In state and national elections, Richland had returned large Whig majorities since 1840 and was known as a banner Whig township in a strongly anti-Democratic county.[15] Despite this Whig strength, support for the Liberty or Abolitionist Party, as it was called, began to split the local, though not the state or national, Whig vote in 1841. In Kalamazoo, Abolitionist candidates for county or township offices were occasionally popular enough to win, but the usual effect of the three-way competition was to give the Democrats an opportunity to beat the Whigs. In the 1844 election in Richland, however, strong Abolitionist and Whig tickets cast the Democrats not in the role of conquerors of the divided but in the role of spoilers of a Whig victory.[16]

In the morning polling, the Democrats, believing they could not win, refused to vote. But in the afternoon, Mumford Eldred Jr., having decided that delight at Whig embarrassment would outweigh hatred of Abolitionists, marched into the polling place with about twenty followers. Taunting the Whigs—"as we go so goes the election"—he and his men voted Abolitionist. Whigs then began a mad scramble throughout the township to round up voters, and Eldred's ruse failed. Unabashed, he turned his attention to the coming national contest. Throughout the summer, anyone who wished to enter Eldred's store was forced either to pass under a hickory pole or to duck under the railing. Few missed the arrogance of the symbolism. To do business in the store, and everyone had to, customers were obliged to bow or squat to the Democratic Party and Mumford Eldred Jr. Not surprisingly, the presence of the pole "produced a good deal of bitterness" in the community.

While the hickory pole stood outside his store, Eldred calculated another demonstration of his political and commercial prowess that was more than a gesture. In August, he wrote the first of a series of letters to Lucius Lyon. As had been the case with his appeal to Crary, he sought Richland's post office, but this time he wanted to take it with him to Yorkville, in neighboring Ross Township. Eldred had used up his commercial and political opportunities in Richland and was ready to try again elsewhere. If he thereby hurt Richland's chances for further development, he reasoned that only some Whigs would suffer. "You know," he declared to Lyon, "that our place here [Richland] has no water power and cannot be much of a place and you know that [at Yorkville] Gull Mills Power is first rate." He had bought Gull Mills the day before and intended to move his store there. The whole village of Gull Corners would have to follow him: "The shoemaker—blacksmiths sadler & harnessmaker they are all stocked by me." The boast spoke the language of the hickory pole: whether you move to Yorkville or travel to it, you will have to do business with me.

Then Eldred betrayed his awareness of the riskiness of his latest maneuver. He "*confidently*" thought he could get two-thirds of Richland's citizenry to sign a petition in favor of the move, but he did not want to make a fuss. In any event, a petition was unnecessary. All of the Democrats in Richland supported the relocation of the post office; only the Whigs opposed it. As he had done before, Eldred wrapped the truth in a lie. Even if the Democrats favored the move, they were in the minority in Richland. Thus, the matter of the post office had to be settled quietly.[17]

Eldred was right to worry about opposition to his plan. As rumor of his intentions spread, he wrote again to Lyon in December. "All of the Whiggs and some of the Democrats" opposed the relocation of the Richland post office, and "rather than have some trouble about it I will withdraw the application."[18] Eldred had finally overplayed his hand. Despite his commercial and political clout, the community was in an uproar. Eldred, however, would not let the matter drop. At the end of January 1845, he wrote for the last time to Lyon to propose an audacious, even reckless, scheme. One can only wonder what Lyon thought when he opened Eldred's letter less than a month after his receipt of Isaac Barnes's appeal.

Since his last missive, Eldred had opened a store in Yorkville and had begun making flour at the mill and sending it to Grand Rapids for transshipment around the lakes. He had maintained his store in Gull Corners and wrote that if he could not get a post office at Yorkville, he would be glad to continue as postmaster in Gull Corners. This hedging was perhaps an acknowledgment of a movement to replace him as postmaster in Richland, for Eldred then presented a plan to promote Yorkville and to kill Gull Corners as a Whig center of trade. His proposal, Eldred wrote grandly, would solve the compound "problem" of the post office in northeastern Kalamazoo County: Yorkville residents were badly served by the Richland post office, he now lived in Yorkville, and he wished to be postmaster. His solution was so simple and logical that it would upset only a few "Whiggs at the Corners." He enclosed in support of his plan a petition, which has not survived, signed by the "prominent Democrats of Kalamazoo."

Eldred again proposed to move the post office at Gull Corners to Yorkville and then to open a new post office on the west side of Gull Prairie, to be supplied from Yorkville. The plan was designed to cut off Gull Corners from direct mail service, while accommodating Richland's Democratic constituency, which tended to live on the western side of the township.[19] Eldred then argued for a mail route between Yorkville and Augusta. The latter village lay to the south near the Territorial Road and was also on the intended line of the Michigan Central Railroad, which followed the Territorial Road west from Detroit. When the line went through—Eldred thought by the following season but in fact in the spring of 1846—mail could be off-loaded at Augusta, brought to Yorkville, and carried north to the Grand River Road near the Baptist Indian mission just north of Richland Township. From there, it could be transported to Grand Rapids. If Richland would not bow, Eldred would make it squat. Gull Corners would become a satellite of Yorkville.

Lyon apparently temporized in his reply to Eldred, for a note on the envelope containing Eldred's letter reads, "Arrangement can't be carried into effect until cars run as far west as Augusta." Nevertheless, Eldred was sufficiently encouraged to press on with his campaign against Gull Corners. He resolved to acquire the bell of the Presbyterian Church of Gull Prairie to call people to Yorkville. The bell had a peculiar history.[20] Around 1841, the partnership of Stephen Cummings and Simeon Howe rented the mill at Yorkville, intending to grind, barrel, and ship east locally produced wheat. It was the same scheme that Eldred later pursued after his purchase of the same mill. Cummings also proposed to accept subscription pledges of flour for the purchase of a bell for the Presbyterian church steeple. The offer, which was accepted, was clearly intended to enhance Cummings's status in the community. He was not a church member. Mumford Eldred Jr., incidentally, Richland's nemesis in the events that followed, was.

In the spring of 1842, Cummings traveled to Troy, New York, to purchase a bell from a Mr. Meneely. The latter refused the subscription pledges but agreed to accept Cummings's own note if Cummings would take the Richland paper. The deal was struck, and the bell was duly delivered. Unfortunately, the harvest of 1842 was poor, and Richland residents delivered only a portion of their flour, and late at that, to Cummings, now operating without Howe. To make matters worse, high overhead halved Cummings's return. His business failed, and he left Richland for Wisconsin.

What Meneely received in payment for the bell from the bankruptcy settlement of Cummings's business is unknown. In any event, the debt was not satisfied, and Meneely had no legal means of holding the bankrupt Cummings to his obligation. Nor could he collect from the Richland community because he did not own their paper. Two parties, however, derived some satisfaction from Cummings's downfall. The first was the subscribing Richland residents who had got off cheap. The second was Mumford Eldred Jr., who bought out the stock of Cummings's store and thereby acquired an "interest" in the bell. After his move to Yorkville, Eldred wrote to Meneely that Richland would give up its bell and that he, Eldred, would settle Meneely's debt.

Rumor of Eldred's intentions leaked across the Ross Township border to Richland. In May, the disquieted session of the Presbyterian church sent a representative to Eldred to learn the truth. The emissary found Eldred and a party of men ready to ride on Richland. Eldred and his posse discovered a crowd of angry Richland residents waiting for them at the church. When Eldred attempted to force entry into the church, the bell began to ring "as it was never rung before." From throughout the township, men and boys responded to the alarm. Eldred and his men retired in defeat. The Richland residents then hastily settled their debt with Meneely.

As the episode of the bell ended, so ended Eldred's other plans for himself and Yorkville at the expense of Gull Corners. Although he managed to get himself made postmaster at Yorkville, he failed to capture the Richland post office and to reroute the mail service. Yorkville did not replace Gull Corners as the center of trade for northeastern Kalamazoo County. The settlement pattern was set, and the strenuous efforts of one man could not budge communal interest. For Richland Township, the heyday of frontier development schemes had passed. Not long after Eldred's attempt to seize the bell, Chauncey W. Calkins, his clerk and brother-in-law, bought the store in Gull Corners and became Richland's principal merchant. Eldred's career as a political partisan likewise went into eclipse. He wrote no more letters to Lucius Lyon, and he ceased to serve as a delegate to the Democratic county convention. Sometime in the 1850s, Eldred left Yorkville for California, where he invested in gold mining.

Mumford Eldred Jr.'s trajectory highlights several features of local politics in the early years of Richland Township. The first is the conflation of politics with political economy. Personal aggrandizement and local development were mutually reinforcing. Local officeholding reflected the local status accrued from the identification of individual with communal fortunes. Partisan politics functioned in this process both as an enabler and as a spoiler. Patronage appointments, such as the contested Richland post office, were by definition highly competitive. They could both help and hurt individuals and communities. Gull Corners and Eldred gained when Barnes lost the Geloster post office. Gull Corners would have lost if Eldred had succeeded in relocating the post office in Yorkville. As it was, in losing his bid to build himself up by gaining a patronage appointment, Eldred lost local status.

The final point is that once partisan politics came to inform local as opposed to state and national elections, it channeled competition for local status by dividing the pool of potential township officeholders into opposing camps. Here the cases of Isaac Barnes and Mumford Eldred Jr. offer only the beginning of an analysis. Both of these men were Democrats, able for much of their time in Richland to tap nonlocal sources of patronage. Their local status, however, as manifested by their participation in communal development programs and service as officeholders, did not in and of itself depend upon party affiliation. Yet clearly, by the fateful township campaign of 1844, local elections in Richland had come to mean something very different from what they had meant earlier. It now mattered that Eldred was champion of a Democratic minority.

The significance of officeholding as an expression of local status needs further clarification here. Local government was the government that mattered most in the lives of township residents. Antebellum Americans had little experience with or understanding of an intrusive, impersonal state, and the concerns of government that did impinge upon their lives—taxation, internal improvements, and education—were to a great extent mediated at the local level. Michigan localities were governed by a system of town meetings modeled on Massachusetts law. Township residents met annually in early April to set the yearly budget and to elect a board, composed of a supervisor, clerk, and treasurer, four justices of the peace who served rotating terms of office, and at least one assessor, highway commissioner, school inspector, and constable. Supervisors collectively constituted a county board, an intermediate level of government between the township and the state that was borrowed from New York.[21] As these offices indicate, it was primarily in the townships that citizens felt the effect of government in their lives: in the assessment and collection of all taxes, maintenance of law and order, economic regulation through debt litigation in the justice courts, and establishment and oversight of local infrastructure, principally schools and roads.

Small wonder, then, that in the early years of Richland Township the settlers elected to office men who had visibly identified their interests with those of the community.

The appearance of partisanship in local elections both complicated and reinforced that identification. The centrality of politics in antebellum American life is well known. Hard-fought contests; frequent elections for local, state, and national offices; the association of the Whig Party with evangelical Protestantism; and the politicization of reform movements all contributed to voter turnouts unsurpassed before or since. Voting was seen as an ideological act, a defense of the republic from the internal enemies that had threatened it since the Revolution. Mass political participation required dogged, efficient party organization. To whip up voter enthusiasm, party cadres distributed pamphlets; organized parades, barbecues, and rallies; and distributed inebriating treats on election day. Party loyalties were ardent and constant; for many Americans, they were lifelong commitments passed on from father to son. Such attachments were ideological if not necessarily, or even usually, intellectually sophisticated. As many scholars have shown, partisanship involved a complex identification of basic values with projected party image in which ethnocultural affiliations served as both negative and positive reference groups. Evangelical Yankees, for example, voted heavily Whig because they associated the party with social regeneration whereas they viewed the Democratic Party as the home of Catholic foreigners and undisciplined imbibers of liquor.[22]

Party affiliation, in other words, testified publicly to personal identity. As William Gienapp has argued, it affirmed deeply held values in a fluid society lacking such traditional sources of authority as an aristocracy and a state church and riven by ethnic, religious, and cultural conflict. The Whig and Democratic Parties literally represented two opposing worldviews. Whigs championed both economic development and the demand for cultural uniformity of a rising middle class that sought to remake American society in its image. Whig allegiance to bourgeois capitalism later fed the ideology of the Republican Party. Opposed to both economic and cultural consolidation, the Democrats were, in contrast, localists, proponents of laissez-faire economic principles, local sovereignty, and cultural diversity. Their vision was of a prosperous, economically undifferentiated world of farms and villages.[23]

In their synthesis of the recent historiography of the Midwest, Andrew R. L. Cayton and Peter Onuf have persuasively applied this framework for understanding the differences between Whigs and Democrats by arguing for common ground between economic and ethnocultural interpretations of politics in the Old Northwest. To studies of politics in Ohio and Illinois that depict Whigs as commercially inclined Protestant Yankees and Democrats as agrarian southerners, Cayton and Onuf reconcile Ronald Formisano's insistence that in Michigan ethnic and religious, as opposed to socio-economic, differences framed partisan conflict. Cayton and Onuf's main point is that economic and cultural issues are not incompatible explanations of the ideological cleavage between the parties. The key is the slowness of Michigan's development in the 1840s and 1850s compared to that of states to the south. Whether Michigan should progress, rather than how, was an issue on which all partisans could agree. In Michigan, therefore, "cultural differences that underlay much of the political and social life of the Old Northwest came to the fore more easily."[24]

What Cayton and Onuf's synthesis does not address, however, is how to explain partisan conflict in supposedly homogeneous, evangelical Yankee townships like Richland. One might expect that in such Whig bastions party loyalty, as a vehicle for the expression of personal identity, had little to do with local elections and denotations of local status except insofar as it associated the individual with communal culture. Communities predicated on shared ethnicity, religion, and other values would have no need for partisanship in local politics. But homogeneity is a relative concept, and as we will see, Formisano's ethnocultural sieve is too coarse to capture differences among the ostensibly like-minded. Once Whig and Democratic committees organized in Kalamazoo County, it proved impossible to restrict partisanship to nonlocal politics, as the case of Mumford Eldred Jr. amply demonstrates. Although Eldred was clearly an opportunist, there can be no doubt of his party loyalty nor of his merger of that loyalty with his personal fortunes. Partisanship gave names and faces to threadlike fault lines already present in the community, much as the bitter squabble between Presbyterians and Congregationalists had revealed the conflict between two closely allied evangelical Protestant groups over the locus of moral authority. Partisan politics, in contrast, was the arena for a communal debate over what constituted status in a rural township.

A few words about the sources for an examination of partisanship and local status are necessary. In the first place, although Kalamazoo was an intensely anti-Democratic county, it supported continuously only a Democratic paper, the *Kalamazoo Gazette*.[25] Much less is known, therefore, about the composition of the county Whig organization than about leading Democratic operatives. Second, there are no surviving poll books for Richland, Climax, and Alamo, so the analysis concentrates more on candidates for office than on the voters who elected them. Finally, complete township records survive only for Richland, and these include local election returns—

slates of candidates and votes cast—for over half of the period from 1833 to 1860.[26] Why the township clerk reported election returns only ·for 1839 through 1841 and 1846 through 1860 is unknown. Nevertheless, the record is sufficiently full to make it possible to trace the course of partisanship in township politics and to construct a social and economic profile of the candidates for office.

## "Three Cheers for Richland!"

If the returns for 1839 through 1841 are any indication, local elections in Richland before the arrival of partisanship were not so much competitions for office as they were affirmations of those deemed best suited to direct communal affairs. Such electoral intent doubtless enabled the coterie of Christian entrepreneurs to lead the township before 1840. Some candidates ran unopposed, as did Mumford Eldred Jr. for treasurer and Samuel Brown and Josiah Buel for directors of the poor in 1839. Many ballots were essentially victories by acclamation, the losers receiving only one, presumably their own, vote. Nor were the candidates organized by slates, for the number of aspirants for any one office varied from year to year. Five men ran for three positions as justice of the peace in 1839, for example, and five and six individuals jockeyed for one opening in 1840 and 1841, respectively. Even real competition in the sense of voter-generating opposition apparently conformed to the principle that acceptable candidates should take turns in office. In 1840, Samuel Brown beat L. H. Jones and Samuel Boyles for supervisor by a total of 50 votes to 39 and 1, while Mumford Eldred Jr. bested Uriah Upjohn and Samuel Boyles for treasurer by 50 votes to 39 and 1. The following year, Boyles won over Brown for supervisor, 55 votes to 27, and Upjohn ousted Eldred as treasurer, 63 votes to 16.

By 1846, however, the character of township elections had changed dramatically. Partisanship had come to stay, with full slates for every office and consistent margins between winners and losers, indicating straight-ticket voting. If local elections in Richland before the emergence of fusion tickets in 1854 had involved a stable competition between Whig and Democratic partisans, the former would have swept township offices year after year. But as Formisano has shown, Yankee townships in Michigan were more strongly anti-Democratic than they were pro-Whig.[27] Richland was no exception. Between 1846 and 1854, the township experienced three contests in which Whigs, Democrats, and antislavery men (indiscriminately labeled "Abolitionists" in the *Kalamazoo Gazette*) all mounted full slates. The effect was to reduce to a thread the Whig margin of victory. In the polling for supervisor in 1847, for example, the Whig candidate, Augustus Mills, beat the Democrat, Stillman Jackson, by a mere 62 votes to 61. The Abolitionist candidate, Samuel Boyles, received 21 votes that in a two-way race would doubtless have gone to Mills.

Further complicating local elections in Richland in this period were substantial fluctuations in voter turnout. These variations were in part a function of population growth and turnover. The township's adult male population grew from 153 in 1840 to 200 a decade later to 275 in 1854, increases of 30.7 percent in 1850 and 37.5 percent in 1854. As Kenneth Winkle has shown, winning elections in the antebellum period meant managing a pool of voters in constant flux.[28] The ability or determination of Whig and Democratic operatives to mobilize Richland's shifting population varied enormously. Sometimes the Democrats simply gave up the fight, as in 1849, when a drastic drop in voter turnout from 152 to 96 (36.8 percent) enabled the Whigs to take most of the offices and to elect unanimously Uriah Upjohn and Milton Bradley as supervisor and treasurer, respectively. In other years, the Democrats rallied their forces to good effect. Turnout in 1850 returned to 151, and the Democrats elected all of their candidates except those for treasurer and one assessor. This triumph, however, was so remarkable that the *Kalamazoo Gazette*, which was inconsistent in reporting local returns, felt compelled to gloat: "Three cheers for Richland! This stronghold of the Whigs has been gloriously carried by the democracy!!"[29] Except in contests that pitted Democratic candidates solely against antislavery men, the chances of Democratic victory remained tantalizingly close—enough to make the competition heated—but for the most part unrealizable.

Local elections in Richland entered a new phase in 1855 when the fusion ticket consolidated anti-Democratic sentiment and swept the township offices by a margin of about 25 votes. Thereafter, the Republican Party strengthened its hold on Richland. Although the township's voting population increased by 23.7 percent to 339 between 1854 and 1860 and turnover remained constant, the Democrats were unable to dent Republican margins of 40 to 50 votes. Fluctuations in turnout had no effect on the Republican drive to dominance. In 1857, the only year that turnout decreased—from 222 to 158 votes (30.6 percent)—Republican candidates overwhelmed the opposition by a margin of 2 to 1. In 1860, nearly 80 percent of all eligible voters in the township went to the polls, an increase in turnout of 18.4 percent over the previous year, and returned Republican margins of about 40 votes.

But although the Democratic Party's ability to win elections was distinctly limited, particularly after 1854, it was hardly a weak presence in Richland. Even at its weakest, the party still drew 35 percent of the township vote. This healthy plurality begs the question of who was drawn to the Democratic Party in an anti-Democratic stronghold. Formisano's discussion of Vermontville, a staunchly anti-Democratic, mostly Whig township in central Michigan, offers a point of departure. Vermontville in 1850 may have contained the largest percentage of voters born in New England of any township in the state, having been colonized by a Vermont congregation that initially bought land in common. Yet the township was also home to a substantial number of Democratic voters, settled on land outside the colony purchase. "Such cleavage" suggests to Formisano that "many townships may have been similarly conditioned by an outsider-insider axis related to the dominant community ethos."[30]

The Reverend Milton Bradley, pastor of the Presbyterian Church of Gull Prairie and himself a Whig candidate for local office and for delegate to the state constitutional convention in 1850, thought that, like Vermontville, Richland was also politically and geographically divided.[31] After the first partisan election in 1844, Bradley recalled, "the Whigs continued to hold the ascendancy, although the Democrats were constantly gaining from the accession of new voters from the west part of the township, until the spring of 1850, when the Whigs met their 'Waterloo.' From this time, until 1855, the Whigs were in a minority, but by a complete organization and bringing forward their strongest voters they were able to secure most of the offices."[32] It is hardly surprising that new voters came from the western side of the township, for the most valuable and first-alienated prairie land lay to the east. After the land rush of the 1830s, settlers who sought to establish new farms in Richland found wild land for purchase from local and absentee speculators along the township's western border. The geographical separation of new Democratic settlers from established Whigs, moreover, was reinforced by religious affiliation. According to Bradley, Presbyterians tended to live in the eastern half of the township and Methodists in the west. Formisano has shown that although evangelicals—Presbyterians, Congregationalists, and Baptists—voted heavily Whig, Methodists, until the formation of the Republican Party, tended to support the Democracy.[33] What did this fault line—geographical, economic, religious, and political—mean to Richland's settlers? A profile of the men they deemed worthy of conducting local affairs and therefore nominated for township office offers an answer.

Whig, Democrat, or Abolitionist, Richland's candidates for local office comprised a stable cohort within the township's ever-changing population. This stability was reinforced by the fact that a male Richland resident's chances of nomination, let alone election, to local office decreased in the two decades before the Civil War. Population growth expanded the pool of potential voters, increasing voter turnout. Maturation of the township's settlement system limited the number of officeholders needed to direct township affairs; one highway commissioner came to do the work of three, for example, and one school inspector replaced three school commissioners. Between 1846 and 1850, an adult male in Richland had a slightly better than 1-in-5 chance of election to office; in the next decade, his chances declined to 1 in 8.[34]

Even more significant in explaining the candidates' hold over local elections were their persistence and their family ties in the township. The reality of an adult male's opportunity to run for office was even narrower than its numerical possibility. More than 2 in 5 (43.2 percent) of the 182 candidates between 1839 and 1841 and between 1846 and 1860 had lived in Richland for at least five years at the time that they stood for election; just under 1 in 5 (19.4 percent) had been residents for ten years or longer. Over half (56 percent) shared a last name with another candidate; 44 percent had a father, son, or brother who was also a candidate. Clearly, to be considered as a candidate for a local office, a settler had to demonstrate a long-term commitment to Richland. Family ties validated this commitment, as politically active fathers provided bona fides for sons and brothers vouched for one another's partisan credentials. Family participation in local politics signaled the consolidation of Richland's social order, despite the township's rapidly changing population.

Twenty-seven men figured prominently among the candidates for local office between 1839 and 1841 and between 1846 and 1860. Standing for election five or more times, they comprised 24.2 percent of all candidates but amassed 42.5 percent of all nominations.[35] In contrast, 73 men (40.1 percent) served only once as candidates and accounted for only 16.9 percent of all nominations. Richland's most active politicians were primarily either winners or losers; those who won did so repeatedly, while those who lost kept coming back for more. The political careers of these men were not crammed into a few years of extraordinary activity but spanned most of the township's period of settlement. Winners lived an average of 15.9 years in Richland. Losers were even more persistent, remaining in the township a mean of 17.1 years. These figures actually underestimate the politicians' longevity since they are based solely on tax roll appearances. In short, despite Richland's growing, constantly changing population, local politics was dominated by competition between two small groups of long-term residents.

The fortunes of Richland's major politicians reflected the course of partisanship in the township. Eleven of the twelve winners were Whigs. The sole Democrat, Mumford Eldred Jr., left the township just after he had made himself notorious for his role in introducing partisanship to local elections.[36] Eleven of the fifteen losing politicians were Democrats. The party may have drawn its voting strength from new settlers on the western side of the township, but its candidates were just as entrenched in Richland as those put forward by the Whigs. The other four politicians were antislavery men—three Whigs and one Democrat.

The presence of antislavery men among Richland's losing politicians demonstrates the conservatism of the township's anti-Democratic sympathies. The sole known antislavery man who compiled a winning record in township elections was Uriah Upjohn, a Whig who ran as a Free-Soil candidate for state senator in 1848.[37] More typical was the case of Rockwell May. May arrived in the township in 1834 from Sandisfield, Massachusetts, and quickly established himself as a prosperous farmer and entrepreneur, acquiring 340 acres of prairie and oak opening land in Richland and 120 acres of pine land in Allegan and Kent Counties.[38] In the years before partisanship came to Richland, he was elected four times to local office, serving as assessor and highway commissioner between 1837 and 1843. May was always, however, a man of ardent partisan sentiment. In his early years in Richland, he was one of the township's leading Whigs, helping to organize the party in Kalamazoo County and serving on the township vigilance committee.[39] During the national campaign of 1840, he "marshalled a great Whig procession from his part of the county which filled the Richland roads, and rode at its head on a powerful bay horse with a broad ax on his shoulder, cutting down the forest trees and hauling them with ox teams to build the famous log cabin [in Kalamazoo village]."[40] Splendid and fantastically ungrammatical as it was, the image of May as the Whig on horseback did not endure. In 1844, May came out for James G. Birney, the Liberty Party candidate, and remained a staunch political abolitionist until the organization of the Republican Party in 1854. He thereby joined the ranks of a political minority. May was badly defeated as the Abolitionist candidate for county coroner in 1850, receiving a mere 22 votes in his home township.[41] In local elections, he fared no better. He was a perpetual candidate for township office between 1846 and 1853 but was resoundingly defeated in every contest.

May left Richland in 1855 to open a dry goods store in Kalamazoo, but the political trajectory of his fellow Whig-turned-Abolitionist, John S. Porter, suggests that had he remained in the township, he might have been restored to local office. Like May, Porter helped to organize the Whig Party in Kalamazoo County and, like him, was elected to local office before township politics became partisan. Porter served as supervisor in 1838. But between 1846 and 1854, he was nominated seven times for local office but was elected only once, as justice of the peace in 1848. After the formation of the Republican Party, Porter's political fortunes took a turn for the better. He was elected school inspector in 1855 and clerk in 1858 and 1860.

What did it mean to be a Whig, Democratic, or antislavery candidate for office in Richland Township? Ronald Formisano has made a forceful argument against an economic interpretation of partisanship in antebellum Michigan. Both native-born Democratic and anti-Democratic politicians, he found, tended to be well-off and to have invested in development schemes for the promotion of banks and internal improvements. Democrats and their opponents instead divided along religious lines between nonevangelical and evangelical Protestants. They were also divided by ethnicity, although Michigan's southern-born population was negligible and the state drew its settlers predominantly from the Northeast. Ethnic conflict instead occurred between Yankees and New Yorkers of New England descent and New Yorkers who retained a historic antipathy to Yankees.[42]

A profile of Richland's 27 major politicians, grouped here as Democrats and anti-Democrats (Whigs, Republicans, and antislavery men), reveals the limited ability of ethnocultural analysis to explain partisanship in an ostensibly homogeneous community. As a group, the politicians were certainly better off than most settlers in the township. Of the 21 who appeared on the 1860 census, nearly half (47.6 percent) declared property worth $5,000 or more, compared to 19.2 percent (48) of the population as a whole. Only 1 of the politicians (4.8 percent) owned property valued at less than $1,000, compared to 34.9 percent (87) of the population as a whole. Despite this shared prosperity, however, anti-Democrats were wealthier than Democrats, although too much weight should not be placed on this conclusion because the numbers are so small. Six of 9 Democrats appearing on the 1860 census owned property worth less than $5,000, whereas the wealth of 7 of 12 anti-Democrats exceeded that sum. Moreover, the property of 4 of the anti-Democrats was valued at more than $10,000, which made them among the wealthiest men in the township. Only 6.5 percent (17) of all adult males in Richland listed on the 1860 census had estates in excess of $10,000, and they included none of the Democratic politicians.

The religious loyalties of Democrats and anti-Democrats cannot be fully explored because only partial records survive for the Presbyterian and none for the Methodist Episcopal or Wesleyan Methodist churches in the township.[43] Following Formisano's analysis and Milton Bradley's contention that Richland was divided geographically along religious and political lines, one would expect to find Methodists among the Democratic politicians and Wesleyan Methodists, a group that separated in 1841 from the Methodist Episcopal church over the issue of slavery, and Presbyterians mainly in the anti-Democratic camp. But, alas, with the exception of Mumford Eldred Jr., who was a Presbyterian, the church affiliation of the Democratic politicians is unknown. The evangelical propensity of the anti-Democrats, however, is striking. Seven of the 15 were Presbyterians, including a deacon and a minister. One, Rockwell May, was one of the Congregationalist insurgents against the Presbyterian Church of Gull Prairie in the 1830s.[44] Another, Henry Knappen, was the son of the Reverend Mason Knappen, a Congregationalist who labored for the American Home Missionary Society in the early years of settlement. Finally, two of the anti-Democrats, Samuel Boyles and Uriah Upjohn, were Wesleyan Methodists.[45]

Evidence for the ethnicity of Democrats and anti-Democrats confirms the Yankee domination of Richland Township but does not point to an ethnic clash with New Yorkers. Eleven of the 15 anti-Democrats were born in New England, and only 1, the Presbyterian minister, Milton Bradley, had origins in New York. Uriah Upjohn, a Welshman of Quaker descent, and William A. Ward were British, the foreign group that Formisano found most likely to vote Whig.[46] The exception was Samuel Boyles from Pennsylvania. As for the Democrats, although 5 were born in New York, 6 hailed from New England, and 1, from Ohio, was the son of a Democratic politician from Connecticut.

Thus, in a township as homogeneous as Richland, ethnocultural variables offer only a partial explanation for the differences between Democrats and anti-Democrats. What is most striking about the Richland Democrats, again with the exception of Mumford Eldred Jr., is their obscurity in the record compared to their opponents. The anti-Democrats resemble, in contrast, nothing so much as a rural bourgeois elite bent on shaping the township to its sensibilities.

The formation of rural elites is a relatively understudied aspect of the transition to capitalism in the countryside. Most analyses of the emergence of the middle class understandably focus on urban areas.[47] In contrast, the literature on rural capitalism, much of it concerned with New England between the Revolution and the Civil War, has concentrated on measures of market participation and the displacement of rural people from the land and into nonagricultural employment.[48] Other studies of the transition to capitalism examine rates of fertility among rural women and alteration in their work roles for evidence of embourgeoisement. Still others have traced the spread of urban amenities and tastes to the countryside.[49] Much less is known, however, about the effect of these changes on the social structure of rural communities.

The prominence of anti-Democrats in county histories and other antiquarian sources points at the very least to their pretensions to elite status. But it is the kind of activities the anti-Democrats engaged in and took care to report that signals the triumph of bourgeois capitalism in Richland Township and attests to the class dimensions of the cleavage between them and the Democrats. Consider, for example, the contrast between Stillman Jackson, leader of the Richland Democrats after the departure of Mumford Eldred Jr. from the township, and Horace M. Peck, antislavery Whigturned-Republican. Jackson was an "old settler" whose birth in Vermont in 1807 and death in Richland in 1887 were reported by the Kalamazoo branch of the state historical society.[50] He arrived in Richland around 1840, his first appearance in a township record being his nomination for highway commissioner in 1841. Deeds, tax rolls, and censuses show that by 1860 Jackson had consolidated a farm worth $6,000 north of the village in section 14. Between 1846 and 1860, Jackson was nominated ten times for office and elected twice, as supervisor in the great Whig rout of 1850 and as justice of the peace in 1852. It is otherwise known only that he helped to found an academy in Richland, the Prairie Seminary.[51]

Horace M. Peck was Jackson's near contemporary and was just as longlived: he was born in Watertown, Connecticut, in 1814 and died in Kalamazoo in 1894. He bought government land in Ross Township in 1836 and moved to Richland when he acquired Isaac Barnes's holding in 1844. Peck's entry in the *Michigan Pioneer and Historical Collections* describes him as a "farmer and a capitalist."[52] In neither of these occupations were his efforts modest. Peck's farm, on which he raised prize-winning sheep, was valued at $29,320 in 1860, and he was an active member of the county agricultural society.[53] As a capitalist, Peck's first venture was in township real estate, and in the scale of his operations, he rivaled Mumford Eldred Jr. Unlike Eldred, however, he preferred long-term investments to quick capital gains. Between 1840 and 1860, Peck acquired 620 acres in eight sections scattered throughout the township, and he rented out parcels he did not work himself.

Besides building up his estate, Peck devoted considerable energy to local politics, in which he experienced a fate like that of other antislavery men in the township. He was five times beaten for office between 1846 and 1849 but was elected four times, as justice of the peace and director of the poor, between 1851 and 1859. Like Jackson, Peck was instrumental in the founding of the Prairie Seminary. After visiting the World Exposition in Paris in 1867, Peck placed a tenant on his sheep farm and moved to Kalamazoo, where he helped to organize the Kalamazoo Savings Bank. He remained with the bank as vice president until a few years before his death.

Most anti-Democrats did not enjoy an economic success as great as that of Horace M. Peck. Even less is known about most of Richland's other Democratic politicians than has been recorded about Stillman Jackson. Nevertheless, the careers of the two men are instructive. Both began with landholding. With the exceptions of the Reverend Milton Bradley and Mumford Eldred Jr., whose time as a farmer was extremely brief, all of Richland's active politicians acquired land and built farms in the township. In a farming community, land was still the foundation of wealth and status. This was true even of the 5 anti-Democrats and 3 Democrats who had other nonfarming occupations: the Whig doctor Uriah Upjohn, the Whig school-teacher Alfred Nevins, the Democratic doctor Alvan Hood, and the Democratic postmasters Elijah N. Bissell and David Daniels, who was also variously a merchant and a carpenter. Of the antislavery men among the anti-Democrats, Samuel Boyles worked a farm in section 28 when he was not ministering to his flock in the Wesleyan Methodist church; Rockwell May was both a farmer and a merchant; and John S. Porter, an artist, built a farm in section 14.

If the vast majority of Richland's active politicians could, and did on the censuses, pronounce themselves farmers, however, only the anti-Democrats and the ever-exceptional Eldred could claim to be capitalists. To a far greater extent than their opponents, the anti-Democrats were inclined to treat their acquisitions of land as commodities for nonfarming purposes. Besides Peck, Samuel Brown and his son, Charles B., Augustus Mills, Uriah Upjohn, and Rockwell May bought a variety of parcels scattered throughout the township. Far more characteristic of the Democrats were Samuel Langdon and David Blanchard, who owned eighty-acre spreads in sections 29 and 35, respectively. It is surely not a coincidence, moreover, that the two self-consciously progressive farmers, Peck and Gilbert E. Reed, were anti-Democrats.[54]

Both Stillman Jackson and Horace M. Peck were involved in communal affairs besides politics, but Jackson was atypical of the Democrats in this regard. Here the litmus test is involvement in the organization of the Prairie Seminary.[55] Richland settlers had wanted a school of higher learning for the township since Isaac Barnes first dreamed of an "academical institution." They incorporated an academy in 1833, and they pledged $7,000 and a building site in 1849 to bring the state normal school to the township. Both plans came to naught. Then, in 1853, public-spirited citizens subscribed stock for a seminary, which opened two years later. Eight of Richland's leading anti-Democratic politicians were among the seminary's subscribers and trustees. Besides Jackson, the only active Democrat to participate in the organization of the seminary was David Daniels, who was also the contractor for the building.

It is worth asking at this point how different Richland's leading politicians in the decade before the Civil War were from the officeholders of the 1830s, and hence, how the denotation of local status had changed over the period of settlement. The most obvious difference is between a pool of acceptable men voted into office by communal consensus and two groups of candidates, representing distinct constituencies in the township, who competed for office. Partisanship expressed the emergence of economic and cultural pluralism in Richland. Yet despite this conflict, what must be emphasized is the continuity of a generation. Samuel Brown, joined by his son, Charles B., and Samuel Boyles continued to hold office long after the 1830s had closed. Augustus Mills was the brother of Timothy and Simeon. Officeholders during the early years of Richland Township were commercially minded evangelical Protestants who identified their personal fortunes with the development of township infrastructure. Twenty years later, the men elected to office in Richland were still commercially inclined evangelical Protestants, but they were less concerned with basic infrastructure than with the improvement of their farms and community. The issue was less how to enable Richland to function as a farming community and as a center of trade than how to elevate it to a cultural standard set by the bourgeois capitalist faith to which they subscribed. Exemplifying this faith was the Prairie Seminary, whose trustees hired Mary E. Hills, a graduate of Mount Holyoke Seminary, as the first teacher. The triumph of the Republican Party in Richland signaled the widespread acceptance of the faith, if not a restoration of communal consensus.

## "The Friends of Order"

In the way that all small places are different yet alike, local politics in Climax Township was also the arena for the consolidation of a rural elite. But unlike Richland, partisan politics came almost immediately to the township as the expression of an intense personal rivalry. Climax Township's more limited prospects for development, over which the Eldred family early on acquired considerable, though incomplete, control, circumscribed and focused competition for status through local politics. There was no room in the township for the coterie of Christian entrepreneurs who ran Richland in the 1830s. Instead, participation in Climax politics meant alliance with or opposition to the Eldreds. Partisanship surfaced more quickly in Climax than in Richland because loyalty to the Democratic Party was an essential feature of the Eldred family's identity. To be anti-Democratic in Climax Township was also to be anti-Eldred.

Caleb Eldred's only competitor for preeminence in Climax was Willard Lovell, who prospected Climax Prairie in 1833 and located with his family in the township two years later. What is known of Lovell before he came to Climax Township suggests that he was a man of some means and standing.[56] He was born in Rockingham, Vermont, in 1782, the son of Enos Lovell of Massachusetts. Not long after Willard's birth, his father moved his family to Grafton, where, prospering as a farmer, he became known as Squire Lovell and served as town representative to the Vermont legislature in 1795. Willard seems to have remained in Grafton until his removal to Michigan. Since the *Kalamazoo County History* refers to him as Major Lovell and he came to the territory after the Black Hawk scare, he may have cut a figure in the Grafton militia. A son, Enos T., was born in Grafton in 1821; another, Lafayette W., in 1823. Lovell and his wife, Zerviah, had at least one other son, George, and a daughter, Mary, who became the wife of Richland settler John F. Gilkey.

Willard Lovell quickly became a presence to be reckoned with in Climax Township. The acquisition of 480 acres of prairie made him the single largest landholder in the township and a challenge to the Eldreds' economic dominance. Challenge soon turned into confrontation. In 1836, Lovell led the opposition to the township's purchase for a handsome price of Caleb Eldred's house for the District Number 1 schoolhouse. Lovell's wife, perhaps not coincidentally, belonged to the Methodist church, then at loggerheads with Eldred and the Baptists over the use of the schoolhouse for services. Then, at the first township elections in 1838, Lovell, a loyal Whig, ran for supervisor against Eldred, as devout a Democrat as he was a Baptist.

"The strife was close and bitter," wrote Francis Hodgman, whose father, Moses, was a Whig candidate in the election, "each side importing voters and hiring them to work on the farms until after the election, when their services were no longer needed."[57] With such tactics, the Whigs squeaked out a victory, but the election ended in a lawsuit. When the new clerk, William Sawyer, kept the ballot box after the votes were counted, Nathan Jaquish, a defeated Democratic candidate who suspected fraud and who was also the maker and owner of the box, replevined it, setting in motion a fool's errand across the township. The case was brought before a new Whig justice of the peace, David Freer, at his home in the western part of the township, but by the time Democratic witnesses appeared, the venue had been moved to the home of a second new Whig justice. The witnesses traveled four or five miles further to meet before John C. Beach, only to discover the case adjourned to the schoolhouse on the prairie, where they arrived after dark. After further delays, *Jaquish v. Sawyer* came to trial. The plaintiff predictably lost and had to sell his horse to pay court costs and the cost of making the box. The Democrats tried again to challenge the election through a grand jury inquiry into fraudulent voting, but this attempt also came to naught.

Willard Lovell's personal triumph in Climax Township was short-lived: he died the following year at the age of fifty-seven. Whig rule proved equally fragile, as the Democrats struck back at the next township elections. Claiming his scepter as supervisor, Caleb Eldred brought into office with him his son, Daniel B., as clerk; his son-in-law, Daniel Lawrence, as treasurer; his son, Stephen, as assessor and school inspector; and his brother, Daniel, as school inspector. This impressive family victory, however, could not be sustained. Climax's voting population was almost perfectly divided between Whigs and Democrats. For most of the 1840s, the township returned the narrowest of Democratic margins in nonlocal elections, aided after 1841 by Abolitionist tickets that cut into the Whig vote. At the township level, the Whigs controlled the office of supervisor but not the township board.[58] Only once, in 1845, did the Democrats manage to elect Stephen Eldred as supervisor. Yet support for the parties was so closely divided that prominent Democrats such as Eldred, his brothers Thomas B. and Nelson, Henry Potts, and Nathan Jaquish all served on township boards.[59]

In the meantime, the Lovell family regrouped, George, Enos T., and Lafayette W. banding together to preserve their father's holding. Enos T. left the Kalamazoo Institute, a branch of the state university, and Lafayette W. abandoned common school. The brothers worked the farm together until 1844, when Lafayette W., having attained his majority, left Climax to study medicine. He financed his education by selling his share of the family holding to his brothers. After attending Rush Medical College in Chicago and interning at an eye-and-ear infirmary in New York City, he returned to practice medicine in Climax in 1849 and bought back into the family estate.

His return marked the reemergence of members of the Lovell family as major figures in township politics. George had already served as supervisor in 1844 and was elected again in 1849, 1851, and 1852. Lafayette W. then took over, first occupying the post in 1853 and enjoying reelection five more times during the decade. The Lovells' only real rival for supervisor in the 1850s was Stephen Eldred, elected in 1850 and 1859. Indeed, the office became a virtual family possession, for between 1855 and 1879, Lafayette W. and Enos T. together served twenty-two terms as supervisor. Both also held state offices. Lafayette W. was elected state representative on the fusion ticket in 1854, handily defeating Stephen Eldred, whom he beat again in 1856 as a Republican candidate for state senator.[60] Enos T. was elected state representative in 1867 and 1869 and state senator in 1881.

The Lovells were able to attain such preeminence in Climax politics in part because of a marked shift in the township's voting population. In 1849, Climax began to return slight Whig margins in nonlocal elections. Stronger support for fusion tickets and then resounding Republican majorities followed.[61] Symptomatic of the shift was Caleb Eldred's transformation from Democrat to Free-Soiler to Republican. About the same time, the judge also converted to temperance. Michigan's version of the Maine Law, passed in 1853, cut strong lines in local party ranks already being reshaped by national concerns. The law reaffirmed the Eldred family unity, even though the judge's sons remained staunch Democrats. It brought the Lovells and the Eldreds together on a local issue, a rapprochement already partially achieved by the marriage of the judge's daughter, Catherine, to Lafayette W. Lovell in 1848. And it split old Whig allies, such as Isaac Pierce, township supervisor from 1840 to 1842 and in 1849, from the Lovells.

For several years before temperance became state law, Michigan townships voted annually on a local option to license vendors of "spirituous liquors." Only once, in a light turnout, had Climax voters opted "for license," and no license had ever been granted in the township, except in the late 1830s to Daniel B. Eldred, then the sole merchant in Climax Corners. Yet when the township voted on the Maine Law, the returns were nearly split—60 votes for and 56 against.[62] For a substantial number of Climax residents, state-mandated abstinence was clearly not the same as local option. "From that time forward," explained Francis Hodgman, "for at least ten years, the liquor question entered largely into the politics of the town, and had not a little influence in deciding elections. Isaac Pierce, a man of poor education but great natural ability, was the leader of the 'jug party,' while the most fearless advocates for temperance were to be found in Judge Eldred and his family."[63]

Hodgman's characterization of Isaac Pierce in many ways rings true, for Pierce's major assets as a Climax settler were energy and will. He was born in 1803 in Berkshire County, Massachusetts, where his father, Longworthy, had moved from Rhode Island.[64] The family moved to New York in 1811, but the record of its travels is unclear. Longworthy eventually bought a tract of wild land in Livingston County out of which Isaac helped him to grub a farm. In 1830, the family relocated in Niagara County. Isaac married a year later and struck out on his own. With his limited capital, he at first worked land on shares and then bought a mortgaged farm for a small down payment. Pierce appeared destined to continue the hard-scrabble existence he had known as a boy. But in 1835, he sold his farm and moved with his young family to Climax Township. None of his immediate family accompanied him to Michigan, although he may have had other kin in the township. Four other Pierces—Levi, James D., Lawrence S., and John M.—arrived about the same time as Isaac, and he later transacted in land with them all, particularly Levi.

Isaac Pierce came to Climax Township too late to enter a federal claim for a large piece of prairie, but he was able to buy a quarter section from an earlier settler and eighty adjacent acres of government land. Within a few years, he reduced his prairie holding to forty acres and began to make speculative purchases in the southern portion of the township. In 1838, for example, he acquired two forty-acre parcels in sections 21 and 22. As a capital-poor, relatively late arrival in the township, Pierce was always invested as much in the local land business as in the business of farming. The Eldreds also bought land speculatively, but their purchases tended to ring the family's main holdings. Pierce, in contrast, kept one foot planted on his prairie farm and the other dancing over his scattered holdings. Nevertheless, his initial investment in a quarter section of prairie gave him the break his father never had. Just as the Eldreds' discovery of Climax Prairie provided the family with the coherent investment opportunity that had eluded Caleb for most of his life, so Pierce was able to build from his original purchase the means and standing that Eldred and Lovell had brought with them to the township.

Isaac Pierce established a record of political activism in Climax Township as impressive as his economic achievements. He was continuously in office from 1838 to 1853, the year of the passage of the Maine Law, serving repeatedly as a justice of the peace, highway commissioner, assessor, and supervisor. He was also briefly involved in county politics, elected county coroner as a Whig in 1840 and badly defeated as the Abolitionist candidate for sheriff in 1842.[65] Such political affiliations do not square well with Pierce's later leadership of the "jug party"; scholars have long noted the close connections between temperance and antislavery advocates.[66] It is possible that Pierce was a freethinker since there is no record of his association with a church. If so, he may have lacked the evangelical zeal that drove many advocates of temperance to view it as state-mandated abstinence. Certainly, Pierce's behavior during the jug war suggests that he was highly intolerant of legal coercion.

Resistance to Caleb Eldred's campaign to enforce the temperance law in Climax built up for several years before Isaac Pierce's opposition became the stuff of public drama.[67] The real commotion began around 1857 when Pierce rented an old building to a man named Lent who opened a saloon in it. The judge began proceedings against Lent and placed him under a heavy bond to prevent his sale of liquor while the suit was pending. But Pierce and another Climax resident and Democrat, Roswell Clark, stood bond for Lent, and he continued to sell his illicit merchandise.[68] Eldred then prosecuted Pierce and Clark, forcing them to pay the forfeited bond. Outraged, Pierce called an antitemperance law meeting that was greatly enlivened by the appearance of "whiskey men," armed with drums, banners, and a keg "for all openly to partake in," from the neighboring village of Galesburg. Again Eldred brought charges and forced the malfeasors to pay the penalty of the law. Thereafter, Climax was the scene of a running war between the judge and the jug party. Prosecuting whenever an opportunity presented itself, Eldred endured public abuse, death threats, and various acts of vandalism.

"Stirred to its very depths," the community took sides. Finally, the friends of order and Caleb Eldred took public action. In September 1857, the *Kalamazoo Gazette* printed a letter from Climax Township citizens reporting the passage of resolutions at a large temperance meeting in August.[69] The letter reviewed Eldred's prosecution of violators of the temperance law and the "injury already inflicted [upon him] by some dastardly hand." Eldred, it declared, had upheld the "majesty of the law" and "fulfilled the part of good citizen." The "friends of order" wished to thank him publicly and pledged their "vigorous cooperation and support for the future." They vowed to "mutually protect" themselves and Eldred "by all lawful means . . . against the hand of lawless violence, or secret meetings." Presiding over the meeting were Lafayette W. Lovell, chairman, and Stephen Eldred, secretary. The jug war would continue in Climax Township for several more years, but the preeminent citizenry, regardless of personal and partisan differences, had closed ranks.

In Climax as in Richland, then, a not insignificant measure of the passage of the generation of settlement was the emergence of a stable local elite. This rural bourgeoisie had established itself in part through sheer persistence. Families like the Lovells and the Eldreds had simply identified their interests with those of the township longer than anyone else. In emerging as the local elites, however, they had also come to identify themselves with something larger than the places where they lived. Their affiliation with the Republican

Party and the moral tone that they strove to impose upon their communities spoke to a transcendent class interest. As the elites came to link their success in the townships to the triumph of a bourgeois moral order, so they saw their experience as settlers as exemplifying the transformation of frontier into civilization. In the process, they produced their own history of the Yankee West.

# Conclusion. The Foundations of an Empire

On August 14, 1879, the Pioneer Society of Kalamazoo County met in Dyckman's Grove in Schoolcraft for its ninth annual reunion. The society enjoyed pride of place among old settlers' associations in Michigan as the oldest in the state. Members of the society, according to the state association, founded in 1874, were required to be at least forty years of age and to have lived in Michigan for at least twenty-five years. The reunion at Dyckman's Grove, however, attracted many participants who probably did not meet even these fairly elastic criteria for membership, for the society arranged for a special train to run from Kalamazoo to Schoolcraft. The gathering was something more than an occasion for the venerable to talk over old times.[1]

Before the luncheon, the president of the society, the Honorable Stephen F. Brown, greeted the crowd with a speech that set the tone for the afternoon program of oratory, music, and poetry. He began with a tribute to Schoolcraft, the county's "cradle of civilization," where "first began that struggle to overcome the manifold difficulties and dangers in reclaiming land from the dominion of wild beasts and the savage and transforming it into fruitful fields and the abode of civilized man." The society met to celebrate this remarkable transformation, to bear witness to the distance, in more than years, of the past from the present. Such an achievement could only be measured, and therefore appreciated, against the "facts" of the early days, which "may seem trivial and unimportant to some, but which are nevertheless of priceless value to the pioneer and his descendants." "The most important period" in the "history of a country," Brown asserted, "is the one when its history began," and he reminded his listeners of the timeless fascination of the story of Romulus and Remus, who "laid the foundations of an empire" that "became the wonder and admiration of the world."

And so, according to Brown, the arrival of white settlers marked the beginning of meaningful time in Kalamazoo County. "Wild beasts" and the "savage" had no history. Nor did the settlers bring a history with them. Brown saluted the old pioneers not only for their conquest of the wilderness but also for their sacrifice in "forsaking . . . the old and cherished land of their birth." The past for Brown was a mere fifty years ago. The settlers' acceleration of the long march of civilization to a full gallop was part of their special triumph. Even Rome had taken considerably longer to build.

After Brown's address, the old pioneers shared a "sumptuous repast" in the shady grove and then settled themselves for the afternoon program. One after the other, speakers elaborated the themes set forth by the society's president in his opening remarks. All agreed that even though fifty years was a wink of an eye, the contrast between the past and the present was nothing short of staggering. Many speakers attempted to gauge the magnitude of the change and in so doing risked denigrating the very achievements they had come to celebrate. Judge Hezekiah G. Wells flatly refused to make invidious comparisons between the past and the present. "Let us all agree to this rule: to praise the past, be satisfied with the present, and hope for the future." Dr. J. A. B. Stone began his remarks in much the same vein but then lost sight of his point in his enthusiasm for the present: "Can any man or woman who has spent forty-five years in this county remember a single evil they passed through? . . . But perhaps the past looks pleasant because the present is so good. . . . Everything is better than formerly. . . . You raise better wheat . . . better grass, bigger potatoes, and more in the hill, better cattle, better horses . . . better sheep, better chickens and bigger eggs; everything to eat is better, better, better." Men and women were better in "mind" and "heart," too, and their children and grandchildren would improve on them. Kalamazoo County had "prove[d] the truth of Darwinism, that mankind is developing upward."

Thus, although no one intended to disparage the old pioneers, many of the speeches served to cut them down to size. There were no lessons to be learned from the past; the rising generation did not stand on the shoulders of giants. Following Brown, no other speaker raised the issue of the settlers' origins, except for one, who did so only to draw attention to his and their role in the Union victory. General Dwight May, son of Richland settler Rockwell May, contrasted the "cool headed and large hearted" descendants of the "Plymouth colony of pilgrims," who peopled Michigan, with "the descendants of the Jamestown colony, hot and rash." Otherwise, the old pioneers were consistently portrayed as quaint relics of bygone days. Judge Wells thought "there was more of individual character among the people than now." E. Lakin Brown remembered that among the early Schoolcraft settlers "there was scarcely more than a dozen who had more than the mere rudiments of education" and that "there were not more than that number who brought to the prairie any considerable money." A. D. P. Van Buren devoted his speech to a sketch of George Gale, the founder of Galesburg. Gale had "ability and energy," but "his imagination was very apt to take him . . . into the realms of Eldorado magnificence." After platting a town for 40,000 inhabitants, Gale went bankrupt in the panic of 1837–39. He was later known for his stirring oratory, fueled by an excess of hard cider, at Whig gatherings.

As the afternoon wore on, few speakers gave much thought to the future. The old pioneers had not gathered to rededicate themselves to the goals of the founding generation, nor did they advocate a departure from those goals. Even Dr. Stone backed away from his zeal for evolution and declared "the men present and on the platform" "nearly perfect." Only W. G. Dewing, lauding the schools, colleges, and universities founded by the settlers, argued that the old pioneers should continue the good work of institution building. He wanted a county poorhouse and a hospital. Only Captain R. F. Stone foresaw a role for the children of the settlers as pioneers in their own right on the frontier of "intellectual development," "in connection with the facts and demonstrations of science."

In essence, then, the old pioneers at Dyckman's Grove celebrated not the founding generation but the realization of what the settlers had so fervently sought: more of the same, only better. Their trophies of civilization were all around them: material prosperity through the market—the train, it was noted, made the evening run back to Kalamazoo in a mere thirty minutes—and institutions of moral order. They had little nostalgia for the past. For those among them who were genuinely old pioneers, life had triumphantly come full circle. Their children saw the present as the culmination of the achievements of the past extending indefinitely into the future.

Amid the welter of self-congratulation, however, there were a few slight indications that despite all of the gains of the past fifty years, something, for better or worse, had been lost. As Judge Wells explained, referring to the county in the old days, "everybody knew everybody." "We were all neighbors," he continued, "all friends, and it might be that this bond of union, this seeming disposition to stand by each other and be one big family," made "men, not quite so good in the country they came from, quite a little better here." His sentiments were echoed by Judge Briggs at the reunion the following year: "Although times were hard . . . they were good . . . happy times; all were equal, all were friends, and shared each other's joy."[2] Neither magistrate paused to reflect on those excluded from their metaphors of friends, neighbors, and family. The old pioneers who had established themselves in their communities through family ties were the minority among the settlers, and their neighborliness ultimately worked to the disadvantage of those who lacked such ties and therefore did not establish themselves. From this group of persistent, well-connected settlers had emerged the rural bourgeoisie, many of whom were proud members of the Pioneer Society.

Wells and Briggs spoke the language of social and economic class formation. By implication, everybody no longer knew everybody, and all were no longer equal. Could everyone, therefore, "share each other's joy"? Could everyone rejoice, as President Brown urged the old pioneers at the tenth reunion, that in the place of the "rude tamarack cabin of Titus Bronson," there now stood a "mart of trade, surrounded by palatial homes, by halls of learning and temples of Christianity"? At neither reunion was this question ever posed. If the history of Kalamazoo County was the triumph of the capitalist order, it was also the story of the transformation of a Yankee culture of hegemonic aspirations into a bourgeois culture of similar ambitions.

It was clear from the speakers' remarks that the long-standing dialectic between market and morality had been subtly but profoundly altered. Key Yankee institutions—local government, church, and school—that made possible the seemingly endless replication of rural communities had been reconfigured and, in the process, had lost their localism. The speakers passed over local government in their salute to the settlers' achievement and gave only a passing nod to churches. Under the new terms of the dialectic, neither institution required much attention. Local government had come to be identified with national party affiliation, and partisanship, in turn, with class interests. In Kalamazoo County, the triumph of the Republican Party had coincided with the rural bourgeoisie's consolidation of its control over local government. In tipping his hat to Kalamazoo's "temples of Christianity," President Brown presumed a plurality of Protestant denominations whose spiritual wares were offered to town residents as part of the amenities of civilization. The organic relationship between church and community that the settlers had sought, and for which they had fought one another, had long since been replaced by an assortment of religious institutions catering to a fairly narrow range of evangelical tastes.

Speaker after speaker focused on schools, but their emphasis was hardly on the local institution. Instead, they pointed out that the common schools founded by the settlers now fit into a statewide system of education capable of preparing students for lives of individual achievement. "Since our state organization," Judge Wells declared at the tenth reunion, "we have set up that ladder on the bottom round of which we see the five year old, with his finger at the alphabet, and on the top round of the same ladder the pupil coming from normal school, the agricultural college and the university, qualified to commence the battle of life full well as though he had lived within the shadow of the great universities of England and Germany." The judge did not linger, in his enumeration of Michigan's educational advantages, to explain why they were so necessary to successful combat in the "battle of life." Had he done so, he might have pointed to yet another measure of the distance between past and present. The aspirations of the sons of the settlement generation, even the eldest who were eligible for membership in the Pioneer Society, were rather different from those of their fathers.

A sense of this difference can be obtained by dividing the men from Kalamazoo County whose biographies appeared in the 1892 *Portrait and Biographical Record* into two cohorts, those born before and after 1840, and then comparing when and why they first left home as young men.[3] The first point is that the age of majority, which before the Civil War had controlled so decisively when sons achieved economic independence and left home, exercised far less effect on men born after 1840. Whereas fewer than two-fifths of the older cohort who reported to the editors of the *Record* their ages at leaving home departed before attaining their majorities, over half of the younger men did so. Far fewer of the younger cohort (48 percent), moreover, recorded their ages at leaving home than did the older men (61 percent).

Why the men left home explains the significance of these figures. Most of the men born before 1840 who left home before their majority found work as laborers (32.8 percent), as clerks or schoolteachers (18.8 percent), or in a trade, usually an apprenticeship (21.9 percent). Most of those who waited until they reached twenty-one either obtained their own land (26.7 percent), went west to acquire it (20 percent), or were impelled out the door by family circumstances—their marriage or the death of their parents (15.2 percent). Little can be said of the men who left home at an unknown age because more than half did so for unknown reasons. Nearly 16 percent, however, departed to acquire formal schooling, compared to 3 percent of the rest of the cohort. Such career paths reflected the distribution of patrimony in the land-based but rapidly commercializing economy of the pre–Civil War period. Whether a man left home before his majority or waited until he had turned twenty-one usually depended upon his access to capital by working his father's land.

By contrast, the single most important factor in the decision of the men born after 1840 to leave home early was the Civil War; one-third of those who departed before their twenty-first birthdays went to serve in the Union army. Others found work as laborers, clerks, or in a trade. Most of those who remained until their majority did so for reasons similar to those of the older cohort; 47.6 percent obtained their own land, and 19 percent were affected by family events. The striking change was in the men who left home at an unknown age: they were far more inclined than was the older cohort to explain why they did so (42.3 percent of the younger men gave no explanation compared to 57.4 percent of the older men), and of these, 44.2 percent sought formal schooling. In this, they were like many men in their cohort, regardless of when they left home; 28 percent of the younger men departed for an education, compared to 7.9 percent of the older cohort.

For the generation born after 1840, therefore, a life on the land was no longer the obvious course that it had been for their fathers. A son's preparation for adulthood was becoming professionalized.[4] It increasingly required a formal education, not an apprenticeship in a trade or training in agriculture on the family farm. The age of majority had ceased to be a milestone for sons in their relations with their fathers. The once-powerful economic bond between them, directed toward the attainment of independent farm ownership, had been vitiated as it came to fit economic reality less than perfectly. As the national economy's expansion, integration, and commercialization had pulled farming communities into its orbit, farming was being pushed from its central place in American life. At the same time, farming itself, at least for the rural bourgeoisie, had become a profession, requiring participation in an agricultural society and possibly attendance at an agricultural college. Small wonder that prosperous sons of the settlement generation whose biographies appeared in the *Portrait and Biographical Record* disdained the term "farmer" and identified themselves as "successful agriculturalists and stockbreeders."

Where, then, did places like Richland, Climax, and Alamo, whose old pioneers gathered annually in shady groves to celebrate what they had wrought, fit in the new social and economic order? By all appearances, the townships in 1880 were what the settlers had intended them to be—stable rural communities with market connections. Each contained a railroad depot: the Kalamazoo and South Haven stopped at Alamo Center, the Peninsular Railway at Climax Corners, and the Mansfield, Coldwater, and Lake Michigan at Richland Village, formerly Gull Corners. The township villages had all responded to the rail connections with increases in population and in goods and services offered, although their growth had proceeded very much along lines established during the early years of settlement. Richland, the largest village, was incorporated and boasted carriage and cider and vinegar factories as well as various mechanics' shops. Alamo Center and Climax Corners remained unincorporated. As the shipping point for township produce and the location of township churches, the former was still primarily important as the geographical center of Alamo. The coming of the railroad had brought a thriving shipping business and new population to Climax Corners, where the American Express Company had opened an office and the Methodist Church had found it financially feasible to return from the exile in Charleston Township imposed on it by Caleb Eldred's stubbornness.[5]

Richland, Climax, and Alamo in 1880 attested to the fulfillment of the settlers' ambitions for the townships. This achievement, however, came at a price. Once lands of opportunity, the townships were on their way to becoming rural backwaters, a transformation prefigured in the commercial goals that the settlers had pursued through the medium of traditional communal life. Because the world had always been composed of small, similar places, the settlers had believed, as an article of faith, that new economic circumstances would enable a fuller realization of that life. They could not then see that the fruition of their aspirations would forever alter what they took for granted.

The changes were already under way in 1880, and they were subtle. Richland, Climax, and Alamo were small, similar places amid a landscape of many others like them. Such places, however, were ceasing to be the organizing principle of American society. When speakers at the old pioneer reunions identified formerly Yankee institutions with class interests, they revealed a great deal about how they construed the relationship between status and community as locality. Belief in communal institutions had enabled the settlers to see status as at once territorially bounded and portable. A culture of self-replication through institutions created small, similar places. Yankees assumed both that institutions were identified with local interests and that those interests did not vary greatly from community to community. But as the old pioneer oratory made clear, once institutions came to be identified with class instead of local interests, they transcended their localism. So, too, did status. Indeed, an individual's purely local identification could be a limiting condition of status. In this regard, what happened to the patrimony of John F. Gilkey, Richland's largest landholder, serves as a fitting conclusion. Upon the history of families like the Gilkeys rested the rhetoric that transformed locally minded Yankees into bourgeois midwesterners.

Gilkey lived forty-six of his seventy-five years and buried two wives in Richland. He arrived in the township with his parents and two brothers from Chester, Vermont, around 1831. A few years later, his father died, and his brothers, William Y. and Charles, relocated in Barry County. On his own in Richland, Gilkey proved indefatigable in his pursuit of the profits of commercial farming. In addition to amassing over 1,000 acres of prairie and other prime land, he owned at various times extensive tracts elsewhere in Kalamazoo County. Gilkey entered at least 7,000 acres in federal land claims in the 1830s. He also built the sawmill at Gull Lake in 1833, later bought Tillotson Barnes's gristmill, organized cattle drives as far south as Missouri, and became known throughout western Michigan for the high quality of his blooded stock. Before his death in 1878, he was instrumental in bringing the railroad to Richland.[6]

Gilkey's various enterprises were intended for the benefit of his Richland farm. Unlike Isaac Barnes, the township's would-be proprietor, he did not invest in communal infrastructure for its own sake. Indeed, as deeply as Gilkey sank his roots in Gull Prairie, his public role in Richland was modest. "Behind none" in contributing barrels of flour to the poor, he was known for his benevolence, but he belonged to no church. He held relatively few township offices. Antiquarian sources assert his interest in politics but disagree on his party affiliation. Yet because the scale of Gilkey's operations dwarfed those of most Richland residents, he was a ubiquitous, dominant presence in the economic life of the township.

As physically imposing as their father, Edgar, Patrick, George, and Julian Gilkey seem to have enjoyed their family's larger-than-life reputation in Richland. As boys, they were reputed to ride their fine horses at breakneck speed through the village, knocking bystanders out of the way.[7] In the 1870s, the senior Gilkey divided his Richland holding among his sons. George and Julian lived out their lives on their father's patrimony. Julian never married. Neither son published an account of himself in the 1892 *Portrait and Biographical Record*. For a while, Edgar operated a grain business in the village, but by the time his biography appeared in the *Record*, he had returned to farming his father's land.[8] In a sense, then, three of John F.'s sons remained the Gilkey boys. They were what their father had given them. They were living demonstrations of that aspect of the old pioneer rhetoric that saw the present as a consolidation of the achievements of the past.

But in the present, it was not such men as Edgar, Julian, and George Gilkey, inheritors of the old, local order, to whom speakers at the old pioneer picnic of 1879 directed their applause. They were not the men whom Dr. J. A. B. Stone called "practically perfect." Had John F. Gilkey's son Patrick been in the audience that hot August day, however, he might have felt a call to destiny. Patrick's life took a different course from that of his brothers. In striving to transcend local concerns, his career exemplified the emergence of a midwestern bourgeoisie that during Patrick's lifetime wrote its history as the history of a region and saw that region as true America. In memorializing himself in the *Portrait and Biographical Record*, Patrick in his own "small" way contributed to that history by linking his identity to his class.

A graduate of the Richland Prairie Seminary and of a business course in Poughkeepsie, New York, Patrick was the only Gilkey son to obtain more than a common school education. He used his commercial training to go into merchandising in Gull Corners, first in partnership with his in-laws, the Parkers, another family of early settlers, and later by himself. By 1892, he was touted as one of Richland's most successful businessmen, who also ran a 345-acre farm specializing in trotters. "Mr. Gilkey," declared the *Portrait and Biographical Record*, "by close application to the duties which lay before him has become one of the wealthy men of the County, and, as a citizen, his integrity, enterprise, and intelligence are highly respected in Richland."[9] Patrick, in other words, had become something more than a Gilkey boy, but he was one of Richland's own. Although the wealth he had acquired by building up his patrimony through trade commanded recognition outside the township, he derived local esteem from his achievement.

In his entry in the *Record*, however, Patrick seemed less interested in resting on his Richland laurels than in flaunting his wealth. Much of his entry was devoted to a detailed description of his new store in the village that could hardly have enlightened the Richland residents who shopped there. Patrick wanted to make sure that his accomplishments received recognition beyond the township. For him, the emergence of a new personal identity paralleled the transformation of Yankee institutions that he had known as a child. If Pioneer Society rhetoric celebrated the association of formerly Yankee institutions with class, and therefore regional, interests, biographical sketches in the *Record* proclaimed the shift from local to bourgeois identity on the part of the descendants of the pioneers.

Patrick's entry in the *Record* expressed in a particularly graphic way his need to attest to his class standing. Seeing himself as more than a successful merchant and good citizen, he invoked a quantitative measure of status designed to transcend the community he and his store served. In his entry, Patrick specified what his store had cost, who built it, what it was made of, and how big it was—how long, how wide, and how high. Of course, Richland had never before seen anything like it; the store was big enough, expensive enough, and therefore pretentious enough for downtown anywhere.

# Appendix

Table A.1 Suitability of Township Soils for General Farming

| Class | Richland Acres | % | Climax Acres | % | Alamo Acres | % |
|-------|-----------|-------|------------|-------|-------------|-------|
| I | 4,433.92 | 21.0 | 3,565.44 | 16.1 | 91.52 | .4 |
| II | 9,983.36 | 47.3 | 8,091.52 | 36.6 | 2,468.48 | 11.3 |
| III | 6,080.00 | 28.8 | 10,376.32 | 46.9 | 17,874.56 | 81.6 |
| IV | 594.56 | 2.8 | 91.52 | .4 | 1,463.04 | 6.7 |
| Total | 21,091.84 | 100.0 | 22,124.80 | 100.0 | 21,897.60 | 100.0 |

*Sources:* Calculated by planimeter from the Kalamazoo County soil map in U.S. Department of Agriculture, Bureau of Soils, *Field Operations of the Bureau of Soils,* Report No. 24 (1922), 2 vols. (Washington, D.C.: Government Printing Office, 1928). Volume 1 contains county survey reports, including S. O. Perkins and James Tyson, "Soil Survey of Kalamazoo County," ibid., 627–62; volume 2 contains loose-leaf soil maps of counties surveyed in 1922. Perkins and Tyson's soil types have been fitted in the above table into a more general soil classification scheme taken from J. O. Veatch, *Soils and Land in Michigan* (East Lansing: Michigan State College Press, 1953).

*Note:* Class I: Supermarginal soils of highest fertility and greatest yields.
Class II: Supermarginal soils of lesser yields.
Class III: Soils better suited to specialized farming or with severe usage problems.
Class IV: Submarginal soils, in some cases untillable.

## Table A.2 Township Farm Production, 1837–1860

| | 1837 | 1850 | | | 1860 | | |
|---|---|---|---|---|---|---|---|
| | All Townships | Rich-land | Climax | Alamo | Rich-land | Climax | Alamo |
| **Grain (% township production)** | | | | | | | |
| Wheat | 46.8 | 46.5 | 62.3 | 61.9 | 67.6 | 68.9 | 61.6 |
| Indian corn | 12.2 | 37.6 | 22.7 | 28.8 | 19.0 | 19.1 | 32.5 |
| Oats | 38.6 | 15.9 | 11.9 | 6.6 | 12.9 | 11.5 | 4.2 |
| Other grain | 2.4 | — | 3.0 | 2.7 | .4 | .5 | 1.8 |
| **Livestock (1837: average per household; 1850–1860: average per farm)** | | | | | | | |
| Horses | .9 | 2.5 | 3.6 | 2.3 | 3.3 | 3.6 | 2.6 |
| Meat stock | 6.0 | 13.9 | 10.9 | 10.3 | 10.1 | 11.7 | 9.1 |
| Milk cows | — | 3.2 | 3.2 | 2.6 | 2.9 | 3.2 | 2.5 |
| Oxen | — | 2.6 | 2.1 | 2.7 | 2.3 | 2.4 | 2.2 |
| Other cattle | — | 8.1 | 5.6 | 5.0 | 4.9 | 6.1 | 4.4 |
| Swine | 6.0 | 11.4 | 7.4 | 6.9 | 6.2 | 7.5 | 6.3 |
| Sheep | .9 | 110.1 | 129.9 | 19.5 | 98.9 | 117.3 | 24.5 |

*Sources:* Kalamazoo County, State Census, 1837, and Richland, Climax, and Alamo Townships, Agricultural Census, 1850 and 1860, all in Regional Historical Archives, Waldo Library, Western Michigan University, Kalamazoo, Mich.

## Table A.3 Township Farm Sizes and Values, 1850–1860

| | | Richland | | Climax | | Alamo | |
|---|---|---|---|---|---|---|---|
| | | 1850 | 1860 | 1850 | 1860 | 1850 | 1860 |
| N of farms | | 86 | 148 | 40 | 105 | 37 | 161 |
| Average improved acreage | | 79.7 | 102.8 | 99.8 | 88.6 | 49.3 | 44.3 |
| % improved acreage in grain | | 64.2 | 60.1 | 46.1 | 61.1 | 41.8 | 53.0 |
| % improved acreage in wheat | | 46.5 | 67.6 | 62.3 | 68.9 | 61.9 | 61.6 |
| Farm size | | | | | | | |
| ≤80 acres | N | 34 | 60 | 14 | 38 | 12 | 101 |
| | % | 39.5 | 40.5 | 35.0 | 36.2 | 32.4 | 62.7 |
| 81–160 acres | N | 26 | 52 | 10 | 39 | 18 | 50 |
| | % | 30.2 | 35.1 | 25.0 | 37.1 | 48.6 | 31.1 |
| 160+ acres | N | 26 | 36 | 16 | 28 | 7 | 10 |
| | % | 30.2 | 24.3 | 40.0 | 26.7 | 18.9 | 6.2 |
| Average | | 147.6 | 195.1 | 199.4 | 181.2 | 128.4 | 97.9 |
| Median | | 120 | 100 | 150 | 120 | 120 | 80 |
| Average implement value ($) | | 151.0 | 148.0 | 135.6 | 145.2 | 99.1 | 136.5 |
| Average livestock value ($) | | 306.4 | 514.3 | 339.8 | 565.5 | 157.4 | 341.6 |
| Average farm value ($) | | 2,344.3 | 6,022.9 | 2,665.0 | 4,173.4 | 1,124.3 | 2,152.2 |

*Sources:* Richland, Climax, and Alamo Townships, Agricultural Census, 1850 and 1860, Regional Historical Archives, Waldo Library, Western Michigan University, Kalamazoo, Mich.

## Table A.4 Distribution of Township Livestock by Size of Farm, 1850–1860

| | Richland | | | | | | Climax | | |
|---|---|---|---|---|---|---|---|---|---|
| | 1850 | | | 1860 | | | 1850 | | |
| Farm size in acres | ≤80 | 81–160 | 160+ | ≤80 | 81–160 | 160+ | ≤80 | 81–160 | 160+ |
| Cattle | | | | | | | | | |
| % of farms | 73.5 | 84.6 | 88.5 | 73.3 | 82.7 | 88.9 | 85.7 | 80.0 | 81.2 |
| Average per farm | 3.3 | 10.5 | 11.0 | 2.9 | 4.4 | 8.6 | 2.7 | 4.9 | 8.8 |
| Dairy cows | | | | | | | | | |
| % of farms | 100.0 | 100.0 | 100.0 | 98.3 | 96.2 | 100.0 | 85.6 | 80.0 | 93.8 |
| Average per farm | 2.0 | 3.1 | 4.5 | 2.1 | 3.1 | 3.8 | 1.7 | 3.0 | 4.6 |
| Swine | | | | | | | | | |
| % of farms | 91.2 | 100.0 | 100.0 | 90.0 | 90.4 | 94.4 | 92.9 | 100.0 | 100.0 |
| Average per farm | 7.5 | 12.5 | 19.9 | 4.1 | 6.3 | 9.5 | 7.5 | 7.0 | 7.9 |
| Sheep | | | | | | | | | |
| % of farms | 55.9 | 84.6 | 96.2 | 38.3 | 82.7 | 83.3 | 85.7 | 80.0 | 87.5 |
| Average per farm | 61.6 | 111.4 | 220.2[a] | 21.6 | 55.1 | 205.3 | 21.5 | 29.4 | 273.6[b] |

*Sources:* Richland, Climax, and Alamo Townships, Agricultural Census, 1850 and 1860, Regional Historical Archives, Waldo Library, Western Michigan University, Kalamazoo, Mich.

[a]148.1 without John F. Gilkey's flock.
[b]195 without George Lovell's flock.

## Table A.5 Distribution of Township Home Manufactures, Orchard and Market Garden Produce, and Maple Sugar by Size of Farm, 1860

| | Richland | | | Climax | | | Alamo | | |
|---|---|---|---|---|---|---|---|---|---|
| Farm size in acres | ≤80 | 81–160 | 160+ | ≤80 | 81–160 | 160+ | ≤80 | 81–160 | 160+ |
| % of farms with | | | | | | | | | |
| Home manufactures | 3.3 | 3.8 | 38.9 | 2.6 | 15.4 | 14.3 | 9.9 | 8.0 | — |
| Orchard produce | 36.7 | 50.0 | 66.7 | 34.2 | 51.3 | 85.7 | 31.7 | 44.0 | 60.0 |
| Garden produce | 76.7 | 73.1 | 80.6 | 44.7 | 59.0 | 57.1 | 2.0 | — | — |
| Maple sugar | — | — | — | 36.8 | 38.5 | 25.0 | 5.9 | 1.9 | 2.0 |

*Sources:* Richland, Climax, and Alamo Townships, Agricultural Census, 1850 and 1860, Regional Historical Archives, Waldo Library, Western Michigan University, Kalamazoo, Mich.

| Climax | | | Alamo | | | | | |
| 1860 | | | 1850 | | | 1860 | | |
| ≤80 | 81–160 | 160+ | ≤80 | 81–160 | 160+ | ≤80 | 81–160 | 160+ |
| 65.8 | 79.5 | 96.4 | 66.7 | 94.4 | 85.7 | 44.6 | 82.0 | 70.0 |
| 3.8 | 5.6 | 9.7 | 4.8 | 4.9 | 5.5 | 2.5 | 4.3 | 9.1 |
| 92.1 | 100.0 | 100.0 | 100.0 | 100.0 | 100.0 | 89.1 | 96.0 | 90.0 |
| 2.4 | 3.5 | 5.4 | 1.6 | 3.2 | 2.4 | 1.8 | 3.0 | 4.0 |
| 94.7 | 94.9 | 96.4 | 100.0 | 88.9 | 100.0 | 82.2 | 94.0 | 80.0 |
| 6.4 | 7.4 | 9.7 | 5.4 | 5.7 | 10.3 | 4.7 | 8.1 | 11.3 |
| 31.6 | 56.4 | 78.6 | 50.0 | 66.7 | 57.1 | 23.8 | 50.0 | 40.0 |
| 25.3 | 46.7 | 244.4 | 14.0 | 18.8 | 33.8 | 12.9 | 29.4 | 37.5 |

Table A.6 Average Assessed Real Property Values for Litigants and All Taxpayers, 1837–1839, 1844–1845

| Assessed Values ($) | 1837–1839 | | | | | | 1844–1845 | | | | | |
| | Repeated Litigants N=13 | % | All Litigants N=42 | % | All Taxpayers N=312 | % | Repeated Litigants N=15 | % | All Litigants N=52 | % | All Taxpayers N=252 | % |
|---|---|---|---|---|---|---|---|---|---|---|---|---|
| 0 | 3 | 23.1 | 6 | 14.3 | 62 | 19.9 | 0 | 0 | 7 | 13.5 | 57 | 22.6 |
| 1–100 | 1 | 7.7 | 5 | 11.9 | 16 | 5.1 | 0 | 0 | 2 | 3.8 | 13 | 5.2 |
| 101–250 | 3 | 23.1 | 8 | 19 | 41 | 13.1 | 8 | 53.3 | 16 | 30.8 | 63 | 25 |
| 251–500 | 2 | 15.4 | 9 | 21.4 | 60 | 19.2 | 4 | 26.6 | 13 | 25 | 60 | 23.8 |
| 501–750 | 1 | 7.7 | 5 | 11.9 | 30 | 9.6 | 2 | 13.3 | 9 | 17.3 | 30 | 11.9 |
| 751–1,000 | 1 | 7.7 | 2 | 4.8 | 30 | 9.6 | 0 | 0 | 3 | 5.8 | 20 | 7.9 |
| 1,001–1,500 | 1 | 7.7 | 3 | 7.1 | 36 | 11.5 | 1 | 6.7 | 1 | 1.9 | 4 | 1.6 |
| 1,501–2,000 | 1 | 7.7 | 2 | 4.8 | 20 | 6.4 | 0 | 0 | 0 | 0 | 3 | 1.2 |
| 2,000+ | 0 | 0 | 2 | 4.8 | 17 | 5.4 | 0 | 0 | 1 | 1.9 | 2 | .8 |

Source: Richland Township Tax Rolls, 1837–39, 1844–45, Regional Historical Archives, Waldo Library, Western Michigan University, Kalamazoo, Mich.

Table A.7 Average Assessed Personal Property Values for Litigants and All Taxpayers, 1837–1839, 1844–1845

| Assessed Values ($) | 1837–1839 | | | | | | 1844–1845 | | | | | |
| | Repeated Litigants N=13 | % | All Litigants N=42 | % | All Taxpayers N=312 | % | Repeated Litigants N=15 | % | All Litigants N=52 | % | All Taxpayers N=252 | % |
|---|---|---|---|---|---|---|---|---|---|---|---|---|
| 0 | 0 | 0 | 2 | 4.8 | 37 | 11.9 | 3 | 20 | 6 | 11.5 | 50 | 19.8 |
| 1–50 | 3 | 23.1 | 5 | 11.9 | 45 | 14.4 | 5 | 33.3 | 20 | 38.5 | 87 | 34.5 |
| 51–100 | 1 | 7.7 | 8 | 19 | 34 | 10.9 | 4 | 26.7 | 17 | 32.7 | 61 | 24.2 |
| 101–200 | 4 | 30.8 | 13 | 31 | 77 | 24.7 | 1 | 6.7 | 6 | 11.5 | 33 | 13.1 |
| 201–300 | 1 | 7.7 | 6 | 14.3 | 37 | 11.9 | 2 | 13.3 | 3 | 5.8 | 9 | 3.6 |
| 301–400 | 2 | 15.4 | 3 | 7.1 | 38 | 12.2 | 0 | 0 | 0 | 0 | 5 | 2 |
| 401–500 | 0 | 0 | 1 | 2.4 | 11 | 3.5 | 0 | 0 | 0 | 0 | 3 | 1.2 |
| 501–750 | 1 | 7.7 | 1 | 2.4 | 19 | 6.1 | 0 | 0 | 0 | 0 | 1 | .4 |
| 750+ | 1 | 7.7 | 3 | 7.1 | 14 | 4.5 | 0 | 0 | 0 | 0 | 3 | 1.2 |

*Source:* Richland Township Tax Rolls, 1837–39, 1844–45, Regional Historical Archives, Waldo Library, Western Michigan University, Kalamazoo, Mich.

## Table A.8 Families among Township Landholding Farmers, 1850–1860

| | | 1850 | 1860 |
|---|---|---|---|
| N on tax roll | | 343 | 591 |
| N landholding farmers[a] | | 280 | 500 |
| % taxpayers | | 81.6 | 84.6 |
| N families[b] | | 48 | 80 |
| N individuals in families | | 119 | 205 |
| % taxpayers | | 34.7 | 34.7 |
| N family members | | 108 | 186 |
| % taxpayers | | 38.6 | 37.2 |
| Family Types | | | |
| Father (mother)–son | N | 19 | 30 |
| | % | 39.6 | 37.5 |
| Brothers (sisters) | N | 20 | 31 |
| | % | 41.7 | 38.8 |
| Unknown but holdings abut | N | 9 | 19 |
| | % | 18.6 | 23.8 |

*Sources:* Richland, Climax, and Alamo Township Tax Rolls, 1850 and 1860, and Richland, Climax, and Alamo Townships, Population Census, 1850 and 1860, all in Regional Historical Archives, Waldo Library, Western Michigan University, Kalamazoo, Mich.

[a]Landholding farmers were defined as those individuals who paid taxes on ten or more acres and who did not declare a nonfarming occupation on the population census.

[b]Family linkages were established through census and biographical sources. Individuals with the same surname whose properties abutted were also considered related.

## Table A.9 Tenure of Township Landholding Farmers Compared to Family Members, 1850–1860

| | 1850 | | 1860 | |
|---|---|---|---|---|
| | N | % | N | % |
| **Landholding Farmers** | | | | |
| Owning | 80 | 28.6 | 72 | 34.4 |
| Renting | 122 | 43.6 | 184 | 36.8 |
| Owning and renting[a] | 39 | 13.9 | 64 | 12.8 |
| Owning and renting out | 38 | 13.6 | 71 | 14.2 |
| Owners paying no real property taxes | 1 | .4 | 9 | 1.8 |
| Total | 280 | 100 | 500 | 100 |
| **Family Members** | | | | |
| Owning | 23 | 21.3 | 55 | 29.6 |
| Renting | 45 | 41.7 | 63 | 33.9 |
| Owning and renting | 19 | 17.6 | 28 | 15.1 |
| Owning and renting out | 21 | 19.4 | 38 | 20.4 |
| Owners paying no real property taxes | 0 | 0 | 2 | 1.1 |
| Total | 108 | 100 | 186 | 100 |

*Sources:* Richland, Climax, and Alamo Township Tax Rolls, 1850 and 1860, and Richland, Climax, and Alamo Townships, Population Census, 1850 and 1860, all in Regional Historical Archives, Waldo Library, Western Michigan University, Kalamazoo, Mich. Property ownership determined from abstracts of deeds at Title Bond & Mortgage Company, Kalamazoo, Mich.

[a]Cases in which a taxpayer was both renting and renting out property were classified by the net effect of the tenure.

## Table A.10 Ages of Township Farmers Operating Farms and Paying Real Property Taxes, 1860

|  |  | Farmers | Operating Farms | Paying Taxes |
|---|---|---|---|---|
| 15–19 years | N | 63 | 3 | 1 |
|  | % | 10.0 | .8 | .2 |
| 20–29 years | N | 148 | 48 | 74 |
|  | % | 23.4 | 13.2 | 17.1 |
| 30–39 years | N | 150 | 112 | 126 |
|  | % | 23.7 | 30.9 | 29.0 |
| 40–49 years | N | 135 | 109 | 126 |
|  | % | 21.4 | 30.0 | 29.0 |
| 50–59 years | N | 74 | 54 | 58 |
|  | % | 11.7 | 14.9 | 13.4 |
| 60+ years | N | 62 | 37 | 49 |
|  | % | 9.8 | 10.2 | 11.3 |
| Total |  | 632 | 363 | 434 |

| | |
|---|---|
| N farm operators on agricultural census | 411 |
| N not on population census or not listed as farmers | 48 |
| N taxpayers | 591 |
| N not on population census, not listed as farmers, or not paying taxes on real property | 157 |

*Sources:* Richland, Climax, and Alamo Township Tax Rolls, 1860, and Richland, Climax, and Alamo Townships, Agricultural and Population Census, 1860, Regional Historical Archives, Waldo Library, Western Michigan University, Kalamazoo, Mich.

Table A.11 Tenure of Township Families Sorted by Age and Family Relation, 1860

| | 15–19 Years | | 20–29 Years | | 30–39 Years | | 40–49 Years | | 50–59 Years | | 60+ Years | | Unknown | | Total | |
|---|---|---|---|---|---|---|---|---|---|---|---|---|---|---|---|---|
| | N | % | N | % | N | % | N | % | N | % | N | % | N | % | N | % |
| **Parent-Child Relation** | | | | | | | | | | | | | | | | |
| Owning | 1 | 100 | 7 | 31.8 | 3 | 20.0 | 2 | 16.7 | 3 | 33.3 | 0 | 0 | 0 | 0 | 16 | 18.8 |
| Renting | 0 | 0 | 7 | 31.8 | 4 | 26.7 | 3 | 25.0 | 2 | 22.2 | 9 | 40.9 | 1 | 25.0 | 26 | 30.6 |
| Owning and renting | 0 | 0 | 4 | 18.2 | 5 | 33.3 | 4 | 33.3 | 4 | 44.4 | 4 | 18.2 | 2 | 50.0 | 23 | 27.1 |
| Owning and renting out | 0 | 0 | 1 | 4.5 | 3 | 20.0 | 2 | 16.7 | 0 | 0 | 4 | 18.2 | 0 | 0 | 10 | 11.8 |
| Owners paying no real property taxes | 0 | 0 | 3 | 13.6 | 0 | 0 | 1 | 8.3 | 0 | 0 | 5 | 22.7 | 1 | 25.0 | 10 | 11.8 |
| Total | 1 | 100 | 22 | 100 | 15 | 100 | 12 | 100 | 9 | 100 | 22 | 100 | 4 | 100 | 85 | 100 |
| **Brother Relation** | | | | | | | | | | | | | | | | |
| Owning | 0 | 0 | 4 | 17.4 | 12 | 34.3 | 10 | 30.3 | 2 | 33.3 | 4 | 44.4 | 8 | 50.0 | 40 | 32.8 |
| Renting | 0 | 0 | 11 | 47.8 | 13 | 37.1 | 8 | 24.2 | 2 | 33.3 | 0 | 0 | 4 | 25.0 | 38 | 31.1 |
| Owning and renting | 0 | 0 | 3 | 13.0 | 4 | 11.4 | 8 | 24.2 | 2 | 33.3 | 2 | 22.2 | 1 | 6.3 | 20 | 16.4 |
| Owning and renting out | 0 | 0 | 2 | 8.7 | 4 | 11.4 | 6 | 18.2 | 0 | 0 | 2 | 22.2 | 1 | 6.3 | 15 | 12.3 |
| Owners paying no real property taxes | 0 | 0 | 3 | 13.0 | 2 | 5.7 | 1 | 3.0 | 0 | 0 | 1 | 11.1 | 2 | 12.5 | 9 | 7.4 |
| Total | 0 | 0 | 23 | 100 | 35 | 100 | 33 | 100 | 6 | 100 | 9 | 100 | 16 | 100 | 122 | 100 |

*Sources:* Richland, Climax, and Alamo Township Tax Rolls, 1860, and Richland, Climax, and Alamo Townships, Population Census, 1860, all in Regional Historical Archives, Waldo Library, Western Michigan University, Kalamazoo, Mich. Property ownership determined from abstracts of deeds at Title Bond & Mortgage Company, Kalamazoo, Mich.

## Table A.12 Age and Residence of Township Farmers and Laborers, 1860

| | | Farmers | | | | Laborers | | | |
|---|---|---|---|---|---|---|---|---|---|
| | | Head of House-hold | In Parents' House-hold | In Other House-hold | Total | Head of House-hold | In Parents' House-hold | In Other House-hold | Total |
| 15–19 years | N | 3 | 62 | 2 | 67 | — | 54 | 43 | 97 |
| | % | 4.4 | 92.5 | 3.0 | 10.6 | — | 55.7 | 44.3 | 30.9 |
| 20–29 years | N | 86 | 46 | 17 | 149 | 29 | 43 | 77 | 149 |
| | % | 57.7 | 40.4 | 42.3 | 23.6 | 19.5 | 28.9 | 51.7 | 47.5 |
| 30–39 years | N | 143 | 5 | 3 | 151 | 15 | 5 | 16 | 36 |
| | % | 94.7 | 3.3 | 2.0 | 23.9 | 41.7 | 13.9 | 44.4 | 11.5 |
| 40–49 years | N | 131 | 1 | — | 135 | 17 | 1 | 5 | 23 |
| | % | 26.7 | .7 | — | 21.4 | 73.9 | 4.3 | 21.7 | 7.3 |
| 50+ years | N | 127 | — | 2 | 129 | 8 | — | 1 | 9 |
| | % | 98.4 | — | 1.6 | 20.4 | 88.9 | — | 11.1 | 2.9 |
| Total | N | 490 | 114 | 27 | 631 | 69 | 103 | 142 | 314 |
| | % | 77.7 | 18.7 | 4.3 | 100 | 22.0 | 32.9 | 45.4 | 100 |

*Sources:* Richland, Climax, and Alamo Township Population Census, 1860, Regional Historical Archives, Waldo Library, Western Michigan University, Kalamazoo, Mich.

*Note:* Six farmers living in a child's household are omitted. There were no such cases among laborers.

## Table A.13 Occupations of Single Township Men and Women, Ages 15 to 21 Years, 1860

| | | Single Women | | Married Women | | Single Men | | Married Men | |
|---|---|---|---|---|---|---|---|---|---|
| | | N | % | N | % | N | % | N | % |
| | | 202 | 75.1 | 67 | 29.9 | 273 | 97.8 | 6 | 2.2 |
| | | At Home | Living Away | | | At Home | Living Away | | |
| School | N | 83 | 6 | | | 27 | 7 | | |
| | % | 62.4 | 8.7 | | | 14.5 | 8.0 | | |
| Occupation | N | 15 | 38 | | | 47 | 64 | | |
| | % | 11.3 | 55.1 | | | 25.3 | 73.6 | | |
| School and occupation | N | 18 | 7 | | | 109 | 14 | | |
| | % | 13.5 | 10.1 | | | 58.6 | 16.1 | | |
| Neither school nor occupation | N | 17 | 18 | | | 3 | 2 | | |
| | % | 12.8 | 26.1 | | | 1.6 | 2.3 | | |
| Total | N | 133 | 69 | | | 186 | 87 | | |
| | % | 100 | 100 | | | 100 | 100 | | |
| **Occupational Breakdown** | | | | | | | | | |
| Farmer | N | — | — | | | 75 | 4 | | |
| | % | — | — | | | 48.1 | 5.2 | | |
| Laborer | N | 13 | — | | | 75 | 72 | | |
| | % | 39.4 | — | | | 48.1 | 93.5 | | |
| Servant/domestic | N | 16 | 40 | | | 3 | — | | |
| | % | 48.5 | 88.9 | | | 1.9 | — | | |
| Trade worker | N | — | 2 | | | 3 | 1 | | |
| | % | — | 4.4 | | | 1.9 | 1.3 | | |
| Teacher | N | 4 | 3 | | | — | — | | |
| | % | 12.1 | 6.7 | | | — | — | | |
| Total | N | 33 | 45 | | | 156 | 77 | | |
| | % | 100 | 100 | | | 100 | 100 | | |

*Sources:* Richland, Climax, and Alamo Townships, Population Census, 1860, Regional Historical Archives, Waldo Library, Western Michigan University, Kalamazoo, Mich.

Table A.14 Reasons for Leaving Home: Kalamazoo County Men Born 1810–1839 and 1840–1869

| | Born 1810–1839 | | | | | | | | Born 1840–1869 | | | | | | | |
| | Left before Majority | | Stayed until Majority | | Left at Unknown Age | | Total | | Left before Majority | | Stayed until Majority | | Left at Unknown Age | | Total | |
| | N | % | N | % | N | % | N | % | N | % | N | % | N | % | N | % |
|---|---|---|---|---|---|---|---|---|---|---|---|---|---|---|---|---|
| Got own land | 2 | 3.1 | 28 | 26.7 | 13 | 12 | 43 | 15.5 | 0 | 0 | 10 | 47.6 | 0 | 0 | 10 | 10 |
| Worked out | 21 | 32.8 | 11 | 10.5 | 4 | 3.7 | 36 | 13 | 3 | 11.1 | 1 | 4.8 | 1 | 1.9 | 5 | 5 |
| Agricultural | 14 | — | 6 | — | 2 | — | 22 | — | 2 | — | 0 | — | 1 | — | 3 | — |
| Nonagricultural | 7 | — | 5 | — | 2 | — | 14 | — | 1 | — | 1 | — | 0 | — | 3 | — |
| Other employment | 12 | 18.8 | 5 | 4.8 | 6 | 5.6 | 23 | 8.3 | 7 | 25.9 | 0 | 0 | 2 | 3.8 | 9 | 9 |
| Commercial | 6 | — | 5 | — | 5 | — | 16 | — | 5 | — | 0 | — | 2 | — | 7 | — |
| Taught school | 6 | — | 0 | — | 1 | — | 7 | — | 2 | — | 0 | — | 0 | — | 2 | — |
| Formal schooling | 3 | 4.7 | 2 | 1.9 | 17 | 15.7 | 22 | 7.9 | 4 | 14.8 | 1 | 4.8 | 23 | 44.2 | 28 | 28 |
| Learned skills | 14 | 21.9 | 0 | 0 | 3 | 2.8 | 17 | 6.1 | 3 | 11.1 | 0 | 0 | 3 | 5.8 | 6 | 6 |
| Apprenticeship | 8 | — | 0 | — | 0 | — | 8 | — | 2 | — | 0 | — | 0 | — | 2 | — |
| Nonapprenticeship | 6 | — | 0 | — | 3 | — | 9 | — | 1 | — | 0 | — | 3 | — | 4 | — |
| Family events | 4 | 6.3 | 16 | 15.2 | 0 | 0 | 20 | 7.2 | 0 | 0 | 4 | 19 | 0 | 0 | 4 | 4 |
| Death of parents | 4 | — | 13 | — | 0 | — | 17 | — | 0 | — | 3 | — | 0 | — | 3 | — |
| Marriage | 0 | — | 3 | — | 0 | — | 3 | — | 0 | — | 1 | — | 0 | — | 1 | — |
| National event | 1 | 1.6 | 9 | 8.6 | 0 | 0 | 10 | 3.6 | 9 | 33.3 | 2 | 9.5 | 0 | 0 | 11 | 11 |
| Went west | 6 | 9.4 | 21 | 20 | 3 | 2.8 | 30 | 10.8 | 1 | 3.7 | 1 | 4.8 | 1 | 1.9 | 3 | 3 |
| Unknown | 1 | 1.6 | 13 | 12.4 | 62 | 57.4 | 76 | 27.4 | 0 | 0 | 2 | 9.5 | 22 | 42.3 | 24 | 24 |
| Total | 64 | 100 | 105 | 100 | 108 | 100 | 277 | 100 | 27 | 100 | 21 | 100 | 52 | 100 | 100 | 100 |

*Source: Portrait and Biographical Record of Kalamazoo, Allegan, and Van Buren Counties, Michigan (Chicago: Chapman Brothers, 1892).*

# Notes

## Introduction

1. On longitudinal migration in the nineteenth century, see John C. Hudson, "Yankeeland in the Middle West," *Journal of Geography* 85 (September–October 1986): 195–200, and "North American Origins of Middlewestern Frontier Populations," *Annals of the Association of American Geographers* 78 (1988): 395–413; Richard H. Steckel, "The Economic Foundations of East-West Migration during the Nineteenth Century," *Explorations in Economic History* 20 (January 1983): 14–36; and Lois K. Mathews, *The Expansion of New England* (Boston: Houghton Mifflin, 1909).

2. See, in this regard, Lawrence Buell's discussion of the invention of a Puritan past in antebellum New England in *New England Literary Culture from Revolution through Renaissance* (Cambridge: Cambridge University Press, 1986), 214–38.

3. James R. Shortridge, *The Middle West: Its Meaning in American Culture* (Lawrence: University of Kansas Press, 1989); Frederick J. Hoffman, *The 20s: American Writing in the Postwar Decade* (New York: Free Press, 1965), 369–71.

4. Frederik Barth, "Introduction," in *Ethnic Groups and Boundaries: The Social Organization of Cultural Difference*, edited by Frederik Barth (Oslo: Universitetsforlaget, 1969), 9–38; Werner Sollors, *Beyond Ethnicity: Consent and Descent in American Culture* (New York: Oxford University Press, 1986), 20–39.

5. On Michigan's Yankee population, see Gregory S. Rose, "South Central Michigan Yankees," *Michigan History* 70, no. 2 (March 1986): 32–39.

6. Richard Lyle Power, *Planting Corn Belt Culture: The Impress of the Upland Southerner and Yankee in the Old Northwest*, vol. 2 (Indianapolis: Indiana Historical Society Publica-

tions, 1953); Constance Rourke, *American Humor: A Study of the National Character* (Tallahassee: Florida State University Press, 1986); William R. Taylor, *Cavalier and Yankee: The Old South and American National Character* (Cambridge: Harvard University Press, 1979). For *Kalamazoo Gazette* articles, see, for example, "Michigan," July 2, 1838, 2, and "Michigan: Her Condition—Prospects," January 13, 1854, 1.

7. James H. Lanman, *History of Michigan, Civil and Topographical, in a Compendious Form; with a View of the Surrounding Lakes* (New York: E. French, 1839), 294, 297-98.

8. Henry Nash Smith, *Virgin Land: The American West as Symbol and Myth* (Cambridge: Harvard University Press, 1970), 142-43; Andrew R. L. Cayton and Peter Onuf, *The Midwest and the Nation: Rethinking the History of an American Region* (Bloomington: Indiana University Press, 1990); Robert F. Berkhofer Jr., "Space, Time, Culture, and the New Frontier," *Agricultural History* 38 (January 1964): 21-30.

9. Lanman, *History of Michigan*, 298-99.

10. E. P. Powell, "New England in Michigan," *New England Magazine* 13 (September 1895–February 1896): 419-28.

11. George N. Fuller, *Economic and Social Beginnings of Michigan: A Study of the Settlement of the Lower Peninsula during the Territorial Period, 1805-1837* (Lansing: Wynkoop Hallenbeck Crawford, 1916). See also W. V. Smith, "The Puritan Blood of Michigan," *Michigan Pioneer and Historical Collections* 38 (1912): 355-61. The full title of the *Michigan Pioneer and Historical Collections* (used here throughout) varies slightly over time. Volumes 1–9 (1874-86) are entitled *Pioneer Society of the State of Michigan: Pioneer Collections*; volumes 10-38 (1887-1912) are entitled *Pioneer and Historical Society of the State of Michigan: Historical Collections*.

12. Lewis D. Stilwell, *Migration from Vermont* (Montpelier: Vermont Historical Society, 1937); Stewart H. Holbrook, *The Yankee Exodus: An Account of Migration from New England* (New York: Macmillan, 1950).

13. Frederick Jackson Turner, "Geographical Influences in American Political History" (1914) and "The Significance of the Section in American History" (1925), in *The Significance of Sections in American History* (New York: Peter Smith, 1950), 195, 38, 48-49.

14. Frederick Jackson Turner, "The Significance of the Frontier in American History" (1893), "Dominant Forces in Western Life" (1897), and "The West and American Ideals" (1914), in *The Frontier in American History* (Tucson: University of Arizona Press, 1986), 27, 239, 302.

15. Frederick Jackson Turner, "The Problem of the West" (1896), "The Middle West" (1901), "The Old West" (1908), and "The First Official Frontier of the Massachusetts Bay" (1914), in *The Frontier in American History*, 205-21, 67-125, 39-66.

16. Frederick Jackson Turner, "Problem of the West," 215-16.

17. Frederick Jackson Turner, "Dominant Forces in Western Life," 228-29.

18. Roy H. Akagi, *The Town Proprietors of the New England Colonies: A Study of Their Development, Organization, Activities, and Controversies, 1620-1770* (Philadelphia: University of Pennsylvania Press, 1924); Frederick Jackson Turner, "The West and American Ideals," 295.

19. Frederick Jackson Turner, "The Children of the Pioneers" (1926), in *The Significance of Sections in American History*, 257, 262, 270. Compare the despairing tone of this essay with the matter-of-factness of Turner's earlier account of the effect of the Yankee exodus on

New England in "Greater New England in the Middle of the Nineteenth Century," *American Antiquarian Society*, n.s., 29 (October 1919): 222–41.

20. Frederick Jackson Turner, "Children of the Pioneers," 286.

21. Brian Q. Cannon, "Immigrants in American Agriculture," *Agricultural History* 65 (Winter 1991): 17–35; Kathleen Neils Conzen, "Immigrants in Nineteenth-Century Agricultural History," in *Agriculture and National Development: Views on the Nineteenth Century*, edited by Lou Ferleger (Ames: Iowa State University Press, 1990), 303–42.

22. Morris C. Taber, "New England Influence in South Central Michigan," *Michigan History* 45, no. 4 (December 1961): 305–36.

23. My thinking about the Yankee landscape in the Midwest has been influenced by the following: Thomas J. Schlereth, "The New England Presence on the Midwest Landscape," *Old Northwest* 9 (Summer 1983): 125–42; D. W. Meinig, "Symbolic Landscapes," in *The Interpretation of Ordinary Landscapes*, edited by D. W. Meinig (New York: Oxford University Press, 1979), 164–92; and Joseph S. Wood, "Village and Community in Early Colonial New England," *Journal of Historical Geography* 8, no. 4 (1982): 333–46, "Elaboration of a Settlement System: The New England Village in the Federal Period," *Journal of Historical Geography* 10, no. 4 (1984): 331–56, and "The New England Village as an American Vernacular Form," in *Perspectives in Vernacular Architecture* (Kansas City: University of Missouri Press, 1986), 2:54–63.

24. On potomac settlement systems, see James E. Vance, *The Merchant's World: The Geography of Wholesaling* (Englewood Cliffs, N.J.: Prentice-Hall, 1970) and *Capturing the Horizon: The Historical Geography of Transportation since the Transportation Revolution of the Sixteenth Century* (New York: Harper & Row, 1986). On grid systems and landscape formation, see William Wykoff, *The Developer's Frontier: The Making of the Western New York Landscape* (New Haven: Yale University Press, 1988); William D. Patterson, *Beginnings of the American Rectangular Land Survey System, 1784–1800*, Department of Geography Research Paper No. 50 (Chicago: University of Chicago, 1957); Hildegard Binder Johnson, *Order upon the Land: The U.S. Rectangular Survey and the Upper Mississippi Country* (New York: Oxford University Press, 1976); and Peter S. Onuf, *Statehood and Union: A History of the Northwest Ordinance* (Bloomington: Indiana University Press, 1987).

25. Edward W. Barber, "The Vermontville Colony: Its Genesis and History, with Personal Sketches of the Colonists," *Michigan Pioneer and Historical Collections* 28 (1900): 197–265; Douglas K. Meyer, "Union Colony, 1836–1870: Pattern and Process of Growth," *Vermont History* 41, no. 3 (Summer 1973): 147–57; Taber, "New England Influence in South Central Michigan."

26. Kathleen Neils Conzen, *Making Their Own America: Assimilation Theory and the German Peasant Pioneer*, German Historical Institute, Washington, D.C., Annual Lecture Series No. 3 (New York: Berg, 1990), 33.

27. Tom Henderson Wells, "Moving a Plantation to Louisiana," *Louisiana Studies* 6 (1967): 280–89; Joan E. Cashin, *A Family Venture: Men and Women on the Southern Frontier* (New York: Oxford University Press, 1991), 32–77; John Solomon Otto, "The Migration of Southern Plain Folk: An Interdisciplinary Synthesis," *Journal of Southern History* 51 (1985): 183–200; Ellen Eslinger, "Migration and Kinship on the Trans-Appalachian Frontier: Strode's Station, Kentucky," *Filson Club Historical Quarterly* 66 (1988): 52–66.

28. Clarence Danhof, "Farm-Making Costs and the 'Safety-Valve,' 1850–1860," *Journal*

*of Political Economy* 49, no. 3 (June 1941): 317–59; Jeremy Atack, "Farm and Farm-Making Costs Revisited," *Agricultural History* 56, no. 3 (October 1982): 663–76.

29. John Mack Faragher, *Sugar Creek: Life on the Illinois Frontier* (New Haven: Yale University Press, 1986), chaps. 9–12.

30. Conzen, *Making Their Own America*, 27–28; Robert Ostergren, *A Community Transplanted: The Transatlantic Experience of a Swedish Immigrant Settlement in the Upper Middle West, 1835–1915* (Madison: University of Wisconsin Press, 1988), 210–13, 356; Jon Gjerde, *From Peasants to Farmers: The Migration from Balestrand, Norway, to the Upper Middle West* (Cambridge: Cambridge University Press, 1985), 161–66, 229–31.

31. Kathleen Neils Conzen, "Peasant Pioneers: Generational Succession among German Farmers in Frontier Minnesota," in *The Countryside in the Age of Capitalist Transformation: Essays in the Social History of Rural America*, edited by Steven Hahn and Jonathan Prude (Chapel Hill: University of North Carolina Press, 1985), 259–92; Sonya Salamon, *Prairie Patrimony: Family, Farming, and Community in the Midwest* (Chapel Hill: University of North Carolina Press, 1992), 13–118; Cashin, *A Family Venture*, 9–52; Allan Kulikoff, *The Agrarian Origins of American Capitalism* (Charlottesville: University of Virginia Press, 1992), 215–16.

32. Susan E. Gray, "Local Speculator as Confidence Man: Mumford Eldred Jr. and the Michigan Land Rush," *Journal of the Early Republic* 10, no. 3 (Fall 1990): 383–406; Joseph F. Kett, "Growing Up in Rural New England, 1800–1840," in *Anonymous Americans: Explorations in Nineteenth-Century Social History*, edited by Tamara K. Hareven (Englewood Cliffs, N.J.: Prentice-Hall, 1971), 1–15; David E. Schob, *Hired Hands and Plowboys: Farm Labor in the Midwest, 1815–1860* (Urbana: University of Illinois Press, 1975), 174–76.

33. James Henretta, "Families and Farms: *Mentalité* in Pre-Industrial America," *William and Mary Quarterly*, 3d ser., 35, no. 1 (January 1978): 3–32.

## Chapter One

1. *Northwestern Journal*, March 10, 1830, 2.

2. Samuel W. Durant, *The Kalamazoo County History* (Philadelphia: Everts & Abbott, 1880), 458.

3. See table A.1, "Suitability of Township Soils for General Farming."

4. Durant, *Kalamazoo County History*, 457.

5. See, for example, the descriptions of these "oak openings" as parks in James H. Lanman, *History of Michigan, Civil and Topographical, in a Compendious Form; with a View of the Surrounding Lakes* (New York: E. French, 1839), 252, and James Fenimore Cooper, *The Oak Openings, or the Beehunter* (New York: G. P. Putnam's Sons, 1890), 290–91.

6. Jesse Turner, "Reminiscences of Kalamazoo," *Michigan Pioneer and Historical Collections*, 2d ed., 18 (1911): 571–74.

7. Lewis D. Stilwell, *Migration from Vermont* (Montpelier: Vermont Historical Society, 1937), 189–91.

8. Edward W. Barber, "The Vermontville Colony: Its Genesis and History, with Personal Sketches of the Colonists," *Michigan Pioneer and Historical Collections* 28 (1900): 197–265; Douglas K. Meyer, "Union Colony, 1836–1870: Pattern and Process of Growth," *Vermont History* 41, no. 3 (Summer 1973): 147–57.

9. *Northwestern Journal*, March 31, 1830, 2. The characterization of Metcalf is from Samuel A. Lane, *Fifty Years and Over of Akron and Summit County* (Akron, Ohio: Beacon Job Department, 1892), 83. On frontier barbarism, see James Axtell, *The Invasion Within: The Contest of Cultures in Colonial North America* (New York: Oxford University Press, 1985), 302–27.

10. Sources on the Barnes family include Rodney Wynkoop, "The Barnes Family of East-hampton, L.I.," *New York Genealogical and Biographical Record* 37 (1906): 140–45, 213–18, 261–65; 38 (1907): 34–37, which carries Isaac's line to Litchfield, Connecticut, by the second quarter of the eighteenth century; Alan C. White, comp., *The History of the Town of Litchfield* (Litchfield, Conn.: Inquirer Printer, 1920), 282, and Payne Kenyon Kilbourne, *Sketches and Chronicles of the Town of Litchfield* (Hartford, Conn.: Case Lockwood, 1859), 227, 229, which give some indication of the activities of the Barneses in Litchfield; Pomroy Jones, *Annals and Recollections of Oneida County* (Rome, N.Y., 1851), 131–35, 288; and Daniel Wager, ed., *Our County and Its People: A Descriptive Work on Oneida County, New York* (Boston: History Company, 1896), 491–92. The sources on Isaac Barnes in Ohio are N. B. Northrup, *Pioneer History of Medina County* (Medina, Ohio: George Redway, 1861), 185–86, and *History of Medina County and Ohio* (Chicago: Baskin & Bartley, 1881), 376–90.

11. *History of Medina County and Ohio*, 392–93.

12. Isaac Barnes's date of birth is unknown, but his four sons were of school age when the family moved to Medina in 1818, which means that the eldest was probably no older than fifteen and the youngest at least five. It is reasonable to conclude that Barnes was well into his thirties when he migrated to Ohio and approaching fifty in 1830.

13. Sources on David Hudson and Hudson Township include Lane, *Fifty Years and Over*, 811–33, and William Henry Perrain, ed., *History of Summit County, with an Outline Sketch of Ohio* (Chicago: Baskin & Bartley, 1881), 411–20.

14. Roy H. Akagi, *The Town Proprietors of the New England Colonies: A Study of Their Development, Organization, Activities, and Controversies, 1620–1770* (Philadelphia: University of Pennsylvania Press, 1924); William Cronon, *Changes in the Land: Indians, Colonists, and the Ecology of New England* (New York: Hill and Wang, 1983), 54–81. On the dispersion of population within towns, see Sumner Chilton Powell, *Puritan Village: The Formation of a New England Town* (New York: Anchor Books, 1965), 92–124.

15. John Frederick Martin, *Profits in the Wilderness: Entrepreneurship and the Founding of New England Towns in the Seventeenth Century* (Chapel Hill: University of North Carolina Press, 1991).

16. Ibid., 247.

17. Ibid., 273.

18. The best works on the eighteenth-century system of land distribution are Akagi, *Town Proprietors of the New England Colonies*, and Shaw Livermore, *Early American Land Companies: Their Influence on Corporate Development* (New York: Oxford University Press, 1939).

19. Joseph S. Wood, "Village and Community in Early Colonial New England," *Journal of Historical Geography* 8, no. 4 (1982): 333–46, "Elaboration of a Settlement System: The New England Village in the Federal Period," *Journal of Historical Geography* 10, no. 4 (1984): 331–56, "The New England Village as an American Vernacular Form," in *Perspectives in Vernacular Architecture* (Kansas City: University of Missouri Press, 1986), 2:54–63,

and " 'Build, Therefore, Your Own World': The New England Village as Settlement Ideal," *Annals of the Association of American Geographers* 81, no. 1 (1991): 32–50.

20. William Wykoff, *The Developer's Frontier: The Making of the Western New York Landscape* (New Haven: Yale University Press, 1988); Harlan Hatcher, *The Western Reserve: The Story of New Connecticut in Ohio*, rev. ed. (Cleveland: World Publishing, 1966); Neil McNall, *An Agricultural History of the Genesee Valley, 1790–1860* (Philadelphia: University of Pennsylvania Press, 1952); Alan Taylor, *Liberty Men and Great Proprietors: The Revolutionary Settlement on the Maine Frontier, 1760–1820* (Chapel Hill: University of North Carolina Press, 1990).

21. Durant, *Kalamazoo County History*, 459; *Northwestern Journal*, June 30, 1830, 2.

22. It is not fully known who the Kalamazoo Emigration Society members were and how they were connected to one another. Family names indicate some associations: Northrups and Nortons, for example, figured in the settlement of Hudson and Medina, respectively. Isaac Barnes's connection to the brothers John B. and Orville Barnes (Durant, *Kalamazoo County History*, 461) is not entirely clear. Isaac, Giles, and John Barnes all arrived in Medina at the same time and affiliated with the Congregational church. John left Medina for Hudson and moved from there to Richland (Northrup, *Pioneer History of Medina County*, 185–86). It is reasonable to assume that the western Connecticut Barneses had maintained ties with the Barneses in Camden, New York. Some of Benjamin Barnes's brothers and more distant Long Island kin eventually joined him in Oneida County (Wager, *Our County and Its People*, 80, 126–27, 232).

23. Durant, *Kalamazoo County History*, 458–59; A. D. P. Van Buren, "Pioneer Annals: Containing the History of the Early Settlement of Battle Creek City and Township, with Vivid Sketches of Pioneer Life and Pen Portraits of the Early Settlers," *Michigan Pioneer and Historical Collections* 5 (1884): 237–59. John F. Gilkey was the son-in-law of Willard Lovell of Grafton, Vermont, who settled his family in Climax Township between 1833 and 1835 (*Portrait and Biographical Record of Kalamazoo, Allegan, and Van Buren Counties, Michigan* [Chicago: Chapman Brothers, 1892], 728–30).

24. "Report of Commissioners and Proclamations Relative to Seats of Justice," *Acts of the Territory of Michigan* (Pontiac, Mich.: Thomas Simpson, 1831), 71–73. On Titus Bronson, see *Kalamazoo Gazette*, September 11, 1983, E-1, and Bernard C. Peters, "Early Town-Site Speculation in Kalamazoo County," *Michigan History* 56 (1972): 204–8.

25. Durant, *Kalamazoo County History*, 459, 462.

26. All references to land sales in Richland, Climax, and Alamo are based on abstracts of township deeds between 1830 and 1860 at the Title Bond & Mortgage Company, Kalamazoo, Michigan. Unless otherwise noted, references to property assessments are drawn from the tax rolls of the three townships in the Regional Historical Archives, Waldo Library, Western Michigan University, Kalamazoo, Michigan.

27. Besides Barnes and his sons George W. and Carlos, at least seventeen other Richland residents bought land in ten Allegan townships before 1840, including the ubiquitous John F. Gilkey, his brother William Y., and two members of the Kalamazoo Emigration Society, one of whom, David Dillie, bought land with Barnes. Lists of entries, or purchases of federal land, by date and section within townships are included in *The History of Allegan and Barry Counties, Michigan, with Illustrations and Biographical Sketches of Their Prominent Men and Pioneers* (Philadelphia: D. W. Ensign & Company, 1880), 147–352.

28. "An act defining the mode of laying out and establishing territorial roads," April 22, 1827, *Laws of the Territory of Michigan* (Lansing: W. S. George & Company, 1874), 2:593.

29. "An act to regulate highways," April 12, 1827, ibid., 495.

30. "An act to provide for laying out a territorial road running from the mouth of Battle Creek to the mouth of the Kalamazoo River," June 18, 1832, ibid., 3:923-24.

31. Durant, *Kalamazoo County History*, 461.

32. Ibid., 464. Richland is not, however, a particularly Yankee place name, for it appears in none of the New England states. Township 1 south, 10 west, got its name, according to Durant, *Kalamazoo County History*, from the suggestion of Simeon Mills, who may have been inspired by the example of the town of Richland in Oswego County, New York. Richland did prove an extremely popular place name in the Old Northwest. Today, thirty-two states contain at least one Richland, but the five states of the Old Northwest (Ohio, Indiana, Illinois, Michigan, and Wisconsin) account for 35.9 percent of the Richlands in the United States. See *Omni Gazetteer of the United States*, CD-ROM, Version 3.11 (Detroit: Omnigraphics, 1992).

33. "An act to organize the township of Richland, in the county of Kalamazoo," June 29, 1832, *Laws of the Territory of Michigan*, 3:972.

34. Durant, *Kalamazoo County History*, 468.

35. Ibid., 461, 468.

36. Ibid., 469; "An act to provide for laying out and establishing certain territorial roads," March 27, 1833, *Laws of the Territory of Michigan*, 3:1001-2.

37. Peters, "Early Town-Site Speculation," 211.

38. Richland Township Records, 1833-61, April 1, 1833, 1-2, Regional Historical Archives, Waldo Library, Western Michigan University, Kalamazoo, Mich.; Durant, *Kalamazoo County History*, 459.

39. Sources on the Eldred family include Durant, *Kalamazoo County History*, 345-48; *History of Allegan and Barry Counties*, 270-71; and Duane Hamilton Hurd, *History of Otsego County, New York, with Illustrations and Biographical Sketches of Some of Its Prominent Men and Pioneers* (Philadelphia: Evert & Fariss, 1880), 26, 161-71, 220.

40. Durant, *Kalamazoo County History*, 324-34. See also table A.1, "Suitability of Township Soils for General Farming." On mid-nineteenth-century drainage technology, see David E. Schob, *Hired Hands and Plowboys: Farm Labor in the Midwest, 1815-1860* (Urbana: University of Illinois Press, 1975), 111-21, and Allan G. Bogue, *From Prairie to Cornbelt: Farming on the Illinois and Iowa Prairies in the Nineteenth Century* (Chicago: University of Chicago Press, 1963), 83-85.

41. Durant, *Kalamazoo County History*, 346.

42. Peters, "Early Town-Site Speculation," 210.

43. Durant, *Kalamazoo County History*, 327, 338, 347.

44. Ibid., 329-30.

45. Ibid., 327, 329.

46. Ibid., 292. See also table A.1, "Suitability of Township Soils for General Farming."

47. George Torry, "Kalamazoo County," *Michigan Pioneer and Historical Collections*, 2d ed., 1 (1900): 209.

48. Alamo Township Records, May 5, 1838, Regional Historical Archives, Waldo Library, Western Michigan University, Kalamazoo, Mich.; John T. Blois, *Gazetteer of the State of*

*Michigan* (Detroit, 1839), 268. On the dispersion of rural services on the frontier, see Juliet E. K. Walker, "Occupational Distribution of Frontier Towns in Pike County: An 1850 Census Survey," *Western Illinois Regional Studies* 5 (Fall 1992): 146–71.

49. Durant, *Kalamazoo County History*, 294; Alamo Township Tax Rolls, 1838, 1845–53, and Alamo Township Records, 1838–43, Regional Historical Archives, Waldo Library, Western Michigan University, Kalamazoo, Mich.

50. Durant, *Kalamazoo County History*, 292.

51. A full discussion of frontier land speculation appears in Chapter 2. On preemptive speculation, see E. Lakin Brown, "Autobiographical Notes," ed. A. Ada Brown, *Michigan Pioneer and Historical Collections* 30 (1906): 449. On absentee speculation, see John Denis Haeger, *The Investment Frontier: New York Businessmen and the Economic Development of the Old Northwest* (Albany: State University of New York Press, 1981), 74–127, and Douglas H. Gordon and George S. May, eds., "The Michigan Land Rush in 1836," *Michigan History* 43, no. 1 (March 1959): 1–42; 43, no. 2 (June 1959): 129–49; 43, no. 3 (September 1959): 257–93; 43, no. 4 (December 1959): 433–78.

52. Quoted in Blois, *Gazetteer of the State of Michigan*, 268.

53. Reprinted in Durant, *Kalamazoo County History*, 297.

54. In 1838, 54.7 percent of absentee taxpayers and 53.1 percent of resident taxpayers owned land in Alamo.

55. Durant, *Kalamazoo County History*, 294–95.

56. Alamo Township Records, November 2–3, 1840, Regional Historical Archives, Waldo Library, Western Michigan University, Kalamazoo, Mich.

57. John R. Stilgoe, *The Common Landscape of America, 1580–1845* (New Haven: Yale University Press, 1982); Wayne E. Fuller, "School District 37: Prairie Community," *Western Historical Quarterly* 12 (1961): 419–32.

58. Durant, *Kalamazoo County History*, 299.

59. Malcolm J. Rohrbough, *The Land Office Business: The Settlement and Administration of American Public Lands, 1789–1837* (New York: Oxford University Press, 1968), 248.

## Chapter Two

1. *Michigan Statesman*, July 2, 1836, 2. An excellent account of the land boom in Michigan that focuses on the Bronson land office is Malcolm J. Rohrbough, *The Land Office Business: The Settlement and Administration of American Public Lands, 1789–1837* (New York: Oxford University Press, 1968), 241–49. See also Willis F. Dunbar, *Michigan: A History of the Wolverine State*, rev. ed. (Grand Rapids: William B. Eerdmans Publishing Company, 1980), 261–85.

2. On the specie circular, see Richard Timberlake, "The Specie Circular and the Distribution of the Surplus," *Journal of Political Economy* 68 (April 1960): 109–17, and "The Specie Circular and Sales of Public Lands: A Comment," *Journal of Economic History* 35 (September 1965): 414–16.

3. *Kalamazoo Gazette*, January 24, 1837, 3 (emphasis in original).

4. *Kalamazoo Gazette*, January 24, 1838, 2; *Report of the Commissioner of the General Land Office, in Answer to the Resolution of the Senate of 22 January 1847*, 30th Cong., 1st sess., 1848, S. Ex. Doc. 41, 156–65, 251–53.

5. Douglas H. Gordon and George S. May, eds., "The Michigan Land Rush in 1836,"

*Michigan History* 43, no. 3 (September 1959): 449. On Bronson and Butler, see John Denis Haeger, *The Investment Frontier: New York Businessmen and the Economic Development of the Old Northwest* (Albany: State University of New York Press, 1981).

6. On the politics of Michigan's free banking system, see William G. Shade, "The Background of the Michigan Free Banking Law," *Michigan History* 52, no. 3 (Fall 1968): 229–44, and "Banks and Politics in Michigan, 1835–1845: A Reconsideration," *Michigan History* 57, no. 1 (Spring 1973): 28–52. The traditional economic assessment of free banking is Bray Hammond, *Banks and Politics in America from the Revolution to the Civil War* (Princeton: Princeton University Press, 1957), 572–604. For a more recent econometric analysis, see Hugh Rockoff, "The Free Banking Era: A Reconsideration," *Journal of Money, Credit, and Banking* 6 (May 1972): 141–67. Alpheus Felch, one of Michigan's banking commissioners, produced a valuable contemporary account, "Early Banks and Banking in Michigan," *Michigan Pioneer and Historical Collections*, 2d ed., 2 (1901): 111–24. See also H. M. Utley, "The Wild Cat Banking System in Michigan," *Michigan Pioneer and Historical Collections* 5 (1884): 209–22.

7. On the internal improvements scheme, see Dunbar, *Michigan*, 267–73, and William L. Jenks, "Michigan's Five Million Dollar Loan," *Michigan History Magazine* 15, no. 3 (Autumn 1931): 575–633.

8. On the completion of the Michigan Central and Southern Railroads under private ownership, see John Lauritz Larson, *Bonds of Enterprise: John Murray Forbes and Western Development in America's Railway Age* (Cambridge: Harvard University Press, 1984), 31–52.

9. Ronald P. Formisano, *The Birth of Mass Political Parties: Michigan, 1827–1861* (Princeton: Princeton University Press, 1971), 16–20.

10. Dunbar, *Michigan*, 314.

11. E. Lakin Brown, "Autobiographical Notes," ed. A. Ada Brown, *Michigan Pioneer and Historical Collections* 30 (1906): 459.

12. John T. Blois, *Gazetteer of the State of Michigan* (Detroit, 1839), 55, 84–86, 294, 306, 367; George N. Fuller, *Economic and Social Beginnings of Michigan: A Study of the Settlement of the Lower Peninsula during the Territorial Period, 1805–1837* (Lansing: Wynkoop Hallenbeck Crawford, 1916), 29, 322; James H. Lanman, *History of Michigan, Civil and Topographical, in a Compendious Form; with a View of the Surrounding Lakes* (New York: E. French, 1839), 366–83.

13. Dunbar, *Michigan*, 313; Donald C. Henderson, "Notes on Saugatuck," *Michigan Pioneer and Historical Collections*, reprint ed., 3 (1903): 305; Mumford Eldred Jr. to Lucius Lyon, January 31, 1845, Lucius Lyon Papers, William L. Clements Library, University of Michigan, Ann Arbor, Mich.

14. Blois, *Gazetteer of the State of Michigan*, 55, 333; James L. Barton, *Lake Commerce: Letter to the Hon. Robert McClelland, Chairman of the Committee on Commerce, in the U.S. House of Representatives in Relation to the Value and Importance of the Great Western Lakes*, 2d ed. (Buffalo: Jewett, Thomas & Company, 1846), 10, Historical Collections, Baker Library, Harvard University, Graduate School of Business Administration, Boston, Mass.

15. John G. Clark, *The Grain Trade in the Old Northwest* (Urbana: University of Illinois Press, 1966), 81–83; James L. Barton, *Commerce of the Lakes: A Brief Sketch of the Commerce of the Great Northern and Western Lakes for a Series of Years, to Which Is Added an Account of the Business Done through Buffalo on the Erie Canal for the Years 1845 and 1846; Also Remarks as to the True Canal Policy of the State of New York* (Buffalo: Jewett, Thomas &

Company, 1847), 31–32, Historical Collections, Baker Library, Harvard University, Graduate School of Business Administration, Boston, Mass.

16. Brown, "Autobiographical Notes," 458–59.

17. Ibid., 476.

18. Alamo Township Records, March 28, 1843, Regional Historical Archives, Waldo Library, Western Michigan University, Kalamazoo, Mich.

19. William Jones to AHMS, January 15, 1833, Papers of the American Home Missionary Society, 1825–46, American Home Missionary Society Archives, The Amistad Research Center, Tulane University, New Orleans, La.

20. Silas Woodbury to AHMS, May 5, 1836, ibid.; *Kalamazoo Gazette*, June 2, 1837, 2.

21. *Kalamazoo Gazette*, July 22, 1837, 2.

22. George N. Smith to AHMS, November 15, 1837, Papers of the American Home Missionary Society, 1825–46, American Home Missionary Society Archives, The Amistad Research Center, Tulane University, New Orleans, La.

23. "A Farmer," *Kalamazoo Gazette*, September 8, 1838, 2.

24. Douglass C. North, *The Economic Growth of the United States, 1790–1860* (New York: W. W. Norton, 1966), 263; U.S. Congress, House of Representatives, *Report of the Secretary of the Treasury on the State of Finances for the Year Ending June 30, 1863*, 38th Cong., 1st sess., 1864, S. Ex. Doc. 3, 284–382.

25. *Michigan Statesman*, March 26, 1836, 3; *Kalamazoo Gazette*, October 28, 1837, 2; October 6, 1843, 2.

26. David E. Schob, *Hired Hands and Plowboys: Farm Labor in the Midwest, 1815–1860* (Urbana: University of Illinois Press, 1975), 37–38, 40; George N. Fuller, *Economic and Social Beginnings of Michigan*, 43; Lanman, *History of Michigan*, 254; Blois, *Gazetteer of the State of Michigan*, 25.

27. Schob, *Hired Hands and Plowboys*, 68, 71; Jeremy Atack and Fred Bateman, *To Their Own Soil: Agriculture in the Antebellum North* (Ames: Iowa State University Press, 1987), 196–97.

28. Lanman, *History of Michigan*, 251; Atack and Bateman, *To Their Own Soil*, 162–64, 172, 174–80. Three of Atack and Bateman's ten sample counties lie north of the line stretching from present-day Saginaw to Muskegon that marks the climatic limits of viable grain-based agriculture. Their estimate, therefore, may be low compared to yields from Michigan's more productive counties, and their correlation of soil type with yield shows considerable variations masked by the state aggregate.

29. Samuel W. Durant, *The Kalamazoo County History* (Philadelphia: Everts & Abbott, 1880), 462.

30. L. M. S. Smith to AHMS, September 8, 1843, Papers of the American Home Missionary Society, 1825–46, American Home Missionary Society Archives, The Amistad Research Center, Tulane University, New Orleans, La. (emphasis in original).

31. John Dudley to AHMS, May 25, 1838, ibid. (emphasis in original); Jeanne Boydston, *Home and Work: Housework, Wages, and the Ideology of Labor in the Early Republic* (New York: Oxford University Press, 1990), 130–36.

32. Sylvester Cochrane to AHMS, March 3, 1840, Papers of the American Home Missionary Society, 1825–46, American Home Missionary Society Archives, The Amistad Research Center, Tulane University, New Orleans, La.

33. Hiram Smith to AHMS, July 1, 1840, and Justin Marsh to AHMS, June 1, 1840, both in ibid.

34. "A Farmer," *Kalamazoo Gazette*, August 17, 1839, 2 (emphasis in original); *Kalamazoo Gazette*, August 10, 1839, 2.

35. State Census of 1837, Regional Historical Archives, Waldo Library, Western Michigan University, Kalamazoo, Mich.

36. These percentages are derived by summing township production and dividing by yields per acre for Michigan, following the formula used in Atack and Bateman, *To Their Own Soil*, 172. Firsthand accounts make clear the ubiquity of potatoes. While working his way west on the Territorial Road from Detroit, John Montgomery Gordon, for example, dined night after night on little else except potatoes and was told that a first crop would yield some 300 to 400 bushels per acre (Gordon and May, "Michigan Land Rush in 1836," 262, 266, 276).

37. On the place of pork in antebellum westerners' diets, see *The Economic History of the United States*, vol. 3, Paul Wallace Gates, *The Farmer's Age: Agriculture, 1815–1850* (New York: Harper Torchback, 1968), 214–18. On the low quality of cattle before the introduction of blooded stock, see ibid., 200–202.

38. John G. Clark, *Grain Trade*, 57–58, 70–71, 75–78, 81; *Kalamazoo Gazette*, October 9, 1849, 2.

39. See table A.2, "Township Farm Production, 1837–1860."

40. See table A.3, "Township Farm Sizes and Values, 1850–1860." For an analysis of the likelihood that individual northern farmers would purchase reaper-mowers, the major innovation in farm mechanization between 1840 and 1860, see Atack and Bateman, *To Their Own Soil*, 194–200.

41. Gates, *The Farmer's Age*, 227–28.

42. John G. Clark, *Grain Trade*, 75, 77–78.

43. Allan G. Bogue, *From Prairie to Cornbelt: Farming on the Illinois and Iowa Prairies in the Nineteenth Century* (Chicago: University of Chicago Press, 1963), 241–43.

44. See table A.4, "Distribution of Township Livestock by Size of Farm, 1850–1860."

45. Gates, *The Farmer's Age*, 221–27.

46. *Kalamazoo Gazette*, November 8, 1850, 2.

47. *Kalamazoo Gazette*, October 17, 1851, 1; Bogue, *From Prairie to Cornbelt*, 116.

48. Hal S. Barron, *Those Who Stayed Behind: Rural Society in Nineteenth-Century New England* (Cambridge: Cambridge University Press, 1987), 64–65.

49. In contrast, nearly seven out of ten Alamo farmers did not raise sheep, and of those who did, only 4.5 percent maintained flocks of more than fifty sheep.

50. The analysis that follows is modeled on Atack and Bateman, *To Their Own Soil*, 157–60.

51. Lee A. Craig, *To Sow One Acre More: Childbearing and Farm Productivity in the Antebellum North* (Baltimore: Johns Hopkins University Press, 1993), 83–86; Nancy Grey Osterud, *Bonds of Community: The Lives of Farm Women in Nineteenth-Century New York* (Ithaca: Cornell University Press, 1991), 139–201. On the association of women with dairying, see Joan M. Jensen, *Loosening the Bonds: Mid-Atlantic Farm Women, 1750–1850* (New Haven: Yale University Press, 1986), 79–91.

52. *Kalamazoo Gazette*, October 10, 1851, 2.

53. Atack and Bateman, *To Their Own Soil*, 206.

54. See table A.5, "Distribution of Township Home Manufactures, Orchard and Market Garden Produce, and Maple Sugar by Size of Farm, 1860."

## Chapter Three

1. Michigan *Session Laws*, Act No. 54, 18–19 (1841); *People of the State of Michigan v. Paris Fletcher*, November 4, 1843, Richland Township Justice of the Peace Dockets, 1841–59, Regional Historical Archives, Waldo Library, Western Michigan University, Kalamazoo, Mich. Unless otherwise noted, all references to litigation in this chapter are drawn from the Richland dockets.

2. Michigan *Revised Statutes*, sec. 1 (1837/38). Most of the additional powers subsequently acquired by the justices before 1860 simply elaborated their purview over petty debt actions. They were empowered in 1837 to enter judgments by confession of up to $200, a sum raised to $250 in 1846 and to $300 in 1855. See Michigan *Revised Statutes*, sec. 2, 389–90 (1837/38); Michigan *Revised Statutes*, sec. 3, 387 (Green 1846); and Michigan *Session Laws*, Act No. 173, sec. 1, 427 (1855). An act of 1838 allowed corporations to sue and be sued as individuals in justice court. See Michigan *Session Laws*, Act No. 109, 238 (1837/38). In 1841, justices were empowered to hear actions of covenant of payment in bonds not exceeding $100. Actions of debt on such bonds were allowed in 1846, and in 1855, the monetary limit of all actions on bonds was raised to $150. See Michigan *Session Laws*, Act No. 49, sec. 5, 82 (1841); Michigan *Revised Statutes*, sec. 7, 388 (Green 1846); and Michigan *Session Laws*, Act No. 173, sec. 7, 427–28 (1855). Finally, justices in 1851 were given "current jurisdiction in all civil actions founded on contract" if the debt or damages were less than $300. See Michigan *Session Laws*, Act No. 149, 204 (1851).

3. Michigan *Session Laws*, Act No. 54, sec. 1, 65–66 (1840); Michigan *Revised Statutes*, sec. 1, 417 (Green 1846).

4. Michigan *Revised Statutes*, sec. 8, 58 (1837/38); Michigan *Session Laws*, Act No. 49, sec. 3, 81 (1841).

5. The residence of a little over 75 percent of the 144 litigants in the Richland justice courts between 1841 and 1845 was determined from the Kalamazoo County tax rolls, the federal census of 1840, and the county history. Of the 110 individuals thus identified, 93 (84.5 percent) lived in Richland and 17 (15.5 percent) came from Alamo, Ross, and Cooper—all townships in the northern tier of the county. A very conservative calculation, made by assigning half of the other 34 litigants to the class of Richland residents and half to the nonresident class, puts the ratio of resident to nonresident litigants at a little over three to one. See Assessment Rolls for Kalamazoo County, 1837–45, Regional Historical Archives, Waldo Library, Western Michigan University, Kalamazoo, Mich., and Samuel W. Durant, *The Kalamazoo County History* (Philadelphia: Everts & Abbott, 1880).

6. Charles A. Weissert, "The Indians of Barry County and the Work of Leonard Slater, the Missionary," *Michigan History Magazine* 16, no. 3 (Summer 1932): 321–33. See also the account of a disbursement of government funds to the Ottawa band at the Old Wing Colony, near present-day Holland, in George N. Smith Memoranda Book, September 30, 1843, Michigan Historical Collections, Bentley Historical Library, University of Michigan, Ann Arbor, Mich.

7. On the early years of the temperance movement in Michigan, see John Fitzgibbon, "King Alcohol: His Rise, Reign, and Fall in Michigan," *Michigan History Magazine* 2, no. 3 (October 1918): 737–46, and Willis F. Dunbar, *Michigan: A History of the Wolverine State*, rev. ed. (Grand Rapids: William B. Eerdmans Publishing Company, 1980), 352–53. On the Ottawa affiliation with the temperance movement, see George N. Smith Memoranda Book, April 27, August 31, December 24, 1844, May 13, 1845, Michigan Historical Collections, Bentley Historical Library, University of Michigan, Ann Arbor, Mich.

8. Durant, *Kalamazoo County History*, 469.

9. Ibid., 468; interview with A. H. Scott, in A. D. P. Van Buren, collector and contributor, "Indian Reminiscences of Calhoun and Kalamazoo Counties," *Michigan Pioneer and Historical Collections*, 2d ed., 10 (1908): 166.

10. Helen Hornbeck Tanner, *Atlas of Great Lakes Indian History* (Norman: University of Oklahoma Press, 1987), 63; Isaac McCoy, *History of the Baptist Indian Missions* (New York: Johnson Reprint Corporation, 1970), 206.

11. Durant, *Kalamazoo County History*, 325; Van Buren, "Indian Reminiscences," 156.

12. *Northwestern Journal*, June 30, 1830, 2; Tanner, *Atlas*, 134; Durant, *Kalamazoo County History*, 457, 468 (emphasis in original); Dwight Goss, "The Indians of the Grand River Valley," *Michigan Pioneer and Historical Collections* 30 (1906): 186.

13. On Potawatomi and Ottawa land cessions in western Michigan, see Alpheus Felch, "The Indians of Michigan and the Cession of Their Lands to the United States by Treaties," *Michigan Pioneer and Historical Collections* 26 (1896): 274–97, and Charles J. Kappler, ed., *Indian Treaties, 1778–1883* (New York: Interland Publishing Company, 1972), 198–201, 283–84, 372–75, 410–15, 450–56, 725–31.

14. Van Buren, "Indian Reminiscences," 156.

15. See, for example, *Czar Giddings v. Hilda Barrett*, April 20, 1842, and *Roswell K. Goodwin v. James S. Waldron*, July 17, 1848, Richland Township Justice of the Peace Dockets, Regional Historical Archives, Waldo Library, Western Michigan University, Kalamazoo, Mich.

16. The effects of the policy of removal in the Old Northwest have received far less attention than has the removal of southern native peoples. Works relevant to Michigan Indians are Ronald N. Satz, *American Indian Policy in the Jacksonian Era* (Lincoln: University of Nebraska Press, 1975), and "Indian Policy in the Jacksonian Era: The Old Northwest as a Test Case," *Michigan History* 60, no. 1 (Spring 1976): 71–93; James M. McClurken, "We Wish to Be Civilized: Ottawa-American Political Contests on the Michigan Frontier" (Ph.D. dissertation, Michigan State University, 1987); and Elizabeth A. Neumeyer, "Indian Removal in Michigan, 1833–1855" (M.A. thesis, Central Michigan University, 1968), and "Michigan Indians Battle against Removal," *Michigan History* 55, no. 4 (Winter 1971): 275–88.

17. Neumeyer, "Indian Removal in Michigan," 22–30; Tanner, *Atlas*, 135–38; James A. Clifton, *The Pokagons, 1683–1983: Catholic Potawatomi of the St. Joseph River Valley* (Lanham, Md.: University Press of America, 1984), 53–76; George M. Blackburn, "Foredoomed to Failure: The Manistee Indian Station," *Michigan History* 53, no. 1 (Spring 1969): 37–50.

18. On the Ottawa's evasion of removal, see James M. McClurken, "Ottawa Adaptive Strategies to Indian Removal," *Michigan Historical Review* 12 (Spring 1986): 29–55, and Neumeyer, "Michigan Indians Battle against Removal."

19. On the Protestant missions, see McCoy, *History of the Baptist Indian Missions*, 494–

97; Mrs. Etta Smith Wilson, "Life and Work of the Late Rev. George N. Smith, a Pioneer Missionary," *Michigan Pioneer and Historical Collections* 30 (1906): 190–212; and Weissert, "Indians of Barry County." The best primary accounts are the journal (1842–45) and memoranda books (1840–48) of George N. Smith, a missionary at the Old Wing Colony, in the Michigan Historical Collections, Bentley Historical Library, University of Michigan, Ann Arbor, Michigan. The Bentley Historical Library also contains miscellaneous papers of James Selkirk, a missionary at the Griswold Mission.

20. Weissert, "Indians of Barry County," 329–31; George N. Smith Memoranda Book, January 10, 1841, Michigan Historical Collections, Bentley Historical Library, University of Michigan, Ann Arbor, Mich. On Indian indoctrination into white civilization, see Robert F. Berkhofer Jr., *Salvation and the Savage: An Analysis of Protestant Missions and American Indian Response, 1787–1862* (Louisville: University of Kentucky Press, 1965), and Virgil J. Vogel, "The Missionary as Acculturation Agent: Peter Dougherty and the Indians of Grand Traverse," *Michigan History* 51, no. 3 (September 1967): 185–210.

21. Tanner, *Atlas*, 133; Richard White, *The Middle Ground: Indians, Empires, and Republics in the Great Lakes Region, 1650–1815* (New York: Cambridge University Press, 1991), 128–41.

22. See, for example, George N. Smith Memoranda Book, April 12, June 14, 1840, March 1, June 11, September 20, 1841, Michigan Historical Collections, Bentley Historical Library, University of Michigan, Ann Arbor, Mich.

23. Ida A. Johnson, *The Michigan Fur Trade* (Lansing: Michigan Historical Commission, 1919), 127–53; John E. McDowell, "Madame La Framboise," *Michigan History* 56, no. 4 (Winter 1972): 271–86; George H. White, "Sketch of the Life of Hon. Rix Robinson: A Pioneer of Western Michigan," *Michigan Pioneer and Historical Collections*, 2d ed., 11 (1908): 186–200; Douglas Dunham, "Rix Robinson and the Indian Land Cession of 1836," *Michigan History* 36, no. 4 (December 1952): 374–88. A good firsthand account of the Grand Rapids outfit is Gurdon Saltonstall Hubbard, *The Autobiography of Gurdon Saltonstall Hubbard* (Chicago: Lakeside Press, 1911), 81–124.

24. Goss, "Indians of the Grand River Valley," 185–86.

25. Jesse Turner, "Reminiscences of Kalamazoo," *Michigan Pioneer and Historical Collections*, 2d ed., 18 (1911): 576, 580.

26. On the rapacity of Indian traders, see Robert A. Trennert Jr., *Indian Traders on the Middle Border: The House of Ewing, 1827–54* (Lincoln: University of Nebraska Press, 1981). For a firsthand account of the operation of Indian traders at the first disbursement of government annuities at Grand Rapids following the Treaty of Washington, see Douglas H. Gordon and George S. May, eds., "The Michigan Land Rush in 1836," *Michigan History* 43, no. 4 (December 1959): 455–75.

27. See also the account of Smith and the Ottawa band's efforts to drive unscrupulous traders from Old Wing in George N. Smith Memoranda Book, November 27–28, December 5, 8, 1841, January 18, 1842, Michigan Historical Collections, Bentley Historical Library, University of Michigan, Ann Arbor, Mich.

28. Interview with A. H. Scott, in Van Buren, "Indian Reminiscences," 165–66; E. Lakin Brown, "Autobiographical Notes," ed. A. Ada Brown, *Michigan Pioneer and Historical Collections* 30 (1906): 459–60.

29. Van Buren, "Indian Reminiscences," 164–65.

30. Goss, "Indians of the Grand River Valley," 186.

31. Christopher Clark, *The Roots of Rural Capitalism: Western Massachusetts, 1780–1860* (Ithaca: Cornell University Press, 1990), 28–36, 156–75.

32. Interview with Mrs. L. W. Lovell, in Van Buren, "Indian Reminiscences," 157 (emphasis in original). For Mrs. Lovell's relationship to Stephen Eldred, see *Portrait and Biographical Record of Kalamazoo, Allegan, and Van Buren Counties, Michigan* (Chicago: Chapman Brothers, 1892), 728.

33. Richard White, *Middle Ground*, 94–119.

34. *Kalamazoo Gazette*, January 3, 1851, 2.

35. Of the claims, 23.3 percent were for less than $10; 73.8 percent for less than $30; and 88.8 percent for less than $50. See Richland Township Justice of the Peace Dockets, 1841–59, Regional Historical Archives, Waldo Library, Western Michigan University, Kalamazoo, Mich.

36. Clarence Danhof, "Farm-Making Costs and the 'Safety-Valve,' 1850–1860," *Journal of Political Economy* 49, no. 3 (June 1941): 317–59. Barns and other outbuildings were among the last improvements made on a frontier farm. Some Richland settlers rented storage space in their neighbors' barns. In 1844, for example, Solomon Birch sued Nelson P. Bowen for the cost of stabling Bowen's horse. See *Solomon Birch v. Nelson P. Bowen*, February 17, 1844, Richland Township Justice of the Peace Dockets, 1841–59, Regional Historical Archives, Waldo Library, Western Michigan University, Kalamazoo, Mich.

37. Promissory notes figured in 100 of 160 debt cases. A seasonal pattern of justice court litigation has been noted elsewhere, where it has been attributed to parties not having enough time to bring suit during the heavy work months of the spring and early summer. See John B. Wunder, *Inferior Courts, Superior Justice: A History of Justices of the Peace in the Northwest, 1853–1889*, Contributions in Legal Studies No. 7 (Westport, Conn.: Greenwood Press, 1979), 159.

38. Cases in 1841–45 involving promissory notes in which both issue and hearing dates are known comprise 73 percent of all promissory note cases and 46.3 percent of all debt cases in the 1841–59 dockets. There are a total of 126 cases involving promissory notes in 1841–45, and these make up nearly 80 percent of all debt cases in the 1841–59 dockets. Of the cases involving promissory notes in the 1841–59 dockets in which dates of issue and hearing are known (83.2 percent of all note cases), 63.2 percent of the notes were issued between April and September and 68.4 percent were litigated between October and March. See Richland Township Justice of the Peace Dockets, 1841–59, Regional Historical Archives, Waldo Library, Western Michigan University, Kalamazoo, Mich.

39. Ibid. Thirty-six of fifty-six.

40. Clarence Danhof, *Change in Agriculture: The Northern United States, 1820–1870* (Cambridge: Harvard University Press, 1969), 84–85. On the variability of marketing dates, see Winifred Rothenberg, "The Market and Massachusetts Farmers, 1750–1855," *Journal of Economic History* 41 (1981): 298.

41. Regulations governing stays of execution, which delayed enforcement of judgment on the basis of the convicted party's acquisition of security for his debit, changed several times between 1841 and 1859. In 1841, regulations permitted stays of three months for judgments less than $50, nine months for larger judgments less than $75, a year for larger judgments less than $100, and fifteen months for larger sums. The scale was simplified in 1846 to permit stays of three months for judgments less than $50 and six months for larger sums and was changed again in 1855 to allow stays of three months for judgments less than $25, six months

for larger judgments less than $50, and ten months for larger sums. See Michigan *Session Laws*, Act No. 49, sec. 77, 102–3 (1841); Michigan *Revised Statutes*, sec. 114, 402 (Green 1846); and Michigan *Session Laws*, Act No. 155, sec. 150, 456 (1855).

42. Michigan *Revised Statutes*, secs. 3, 8, 160 (1837/38); Michigan *Revised Statutes*, secs. 2, 6, 160 (Green 1846).

43. Michigan *Revised Statutes*, sec. 1, 156 (Green 1846).

44. On the history of written instruments in the colonial period and the early nineteenth century, see Frederick K. Beutel, "Colonial Sources of the Negotiable Instruments Law of the United States," *Illinois Law Review* 34 (1939): 137–50, and "The Development of Statutes on Negotiable Paper prior to the Negotiable Instruments Law," *Columbia Law Review* 40 (1940): 836–65; and Morton J. Horwitz, *The Transformation of American Law, 1780–1860* (Cambridge: Harvard University Press, 1977), 211–26.

45. See Michael Merrill, "Cash Is Good to Eat: Self-Sufficiency and Exchange in the Rural Economy of the United States," *Radical History* 5 (1977): 55–56.

46. Michigan *Revised Statutes*, sec. 7, 156 (Green 1846).

47. Twenty-nine of 173 litigants appeared in 65 of 160 debt cases.

48. Calculated for 20 of 29 litigants from assessed property values in the 1844 and 1845 tax rolls.

49. In 1844 and 1845, Bowen's real property was assessed as $250 and $245 and his personal property as $53 and $350, respectively. Mills's real property was worth $200 and $190 and his personal property $39 and $78, respectively, in those years. Holden did not appear on any Richland tax rolls in the 1840s but had real property assessed at $360 in 1838 and personal property valued at $220 in 1838 and $224 in 1839.

50. In 1844 and 1845, Hooker was assessed for $202 in real property and $20 in personal property, and Wells for $210 in real property and $60 in personal property.

51. For a detailed analysis of federal land buying in Richland Township, see Susan E. Gray, "Local Speculator as Confidence Man: Mumford Eldred Jr. and the Michigan Land Rush," *Journal of the Early Republic* 10, no. 3 (Fall 1990): 383–406.

52. Evidence of recovery is drawn from seventy-four cases with documented executions in the dockets. See Richland Township Justice of the Peace Dockets, 1841–59, Regional Historical Archives, Waldo Library, Western Michigan University, Kalamazoo, Mich.

53. Summary figures are as follows:

N litigants, 1841–59 = 178
N litigants, 1841–45 = 144 (80.9%)
N Richland litigants = 93 (64.6%)
N litigants elsewhere resident = 17 (11.8%)
N litigants residence unknown = 34 (23.6%)
N Richland litigants appearing on at least one tax roll, 1837–39, 1844–45 = 71 (76.3%)
N paying taxes, 1837–39 = 43 (60.6%)
N paying taxes, 1844–45 = 53 (74.6%)
N paying taxes in both 1837–39 and 1844–45 = 21 (29.6%)
Persistent Richland litigants, 1841–45 = 21 (22.6%)

54. See table A.6, "Average Assessed Real Property Values for Litigants and All Taxpayers, 1837–1839, 1844–1845," and table A.7, "Average Assessed Personal Property Values for Litigants and All Taxpayers, 1837–1839, 1844–1845."

55. David Thomas Konig, *Law and Society in Puritan Massachusetts: Essex County, 1629–1692* (Chapel Hill: University of North Carolina Press, 1979); Bruce H. Mann, "Rationality, Legal Change, and Community in Connecticut, 1690–1760," *Law and Society Review* 14 (1980): 187–221, and *Neighbors and Strangers: Law and Community in Early Connecticut* (Chapel Hill: University of North Carolina Press, 1981).

56. Christopher Clark, *Roots of Rural Capitalism*, 124–26, 224–27.

57. One hundred and thirty-five cases (70.3 percent) occurred between 1841 and 1844, 35 between 1845 and 1848 (18.2 percent), 5 between 1849 and 1855 (2.6 percent), and 17 between 1856 and 1859 (8.9 percent).

58. *Kalamazoo Gazette*, January 3, 1851, 2.

59. *Kalamazoo Gazette*, January 17, 1851, 2; Weissert, "Indians of Barry County," 331.

## Chapter Four

1. The following account of the Barrett family is based largely on Richland Township tax rolls, land abstracts, federal censuses, and cemetery records for Richland Village. Additional sources are noted as necessary.

2. See the biography of Benjamin Cummings in Samuel W. Durant, *The Kalamazoo County History* (Philadelphia: Everts & Abbott, 1880), 461.

3. Marvin may have paid taxes earlier, but the rolls for 1840–43 are lost.

4. No record of the patent exists, but Hildah eventually deeded the property to another son, Wright L.

5. Michigan *Revised Statutes*, sec. 1, 267 (1837/38); Michigan *Revised Statutes*, secs. 5, 7, 341 (Green 1846).

6. James Kent, *Commentaries on the American Law* (reprint, New York: Da Capo Press, 1971), vol. 2, *Of the Law Concerning the Rights of Persons*, 181–82, vol. 4, *Of the Law Concerning Real Property*, 35–36, 59–70; Michigan *Compiled Laws*, vol. 2, secs. 1, 12, 851–52 (1857).

7. Michigan *Compiled Laws*, vol. 2, sec. 12, 852 (1857).

8. Michigan *Session Laws*, Act No. 66, 77–78 (1844).

9. F. W. Beers, comp., *Atlas of Kalamazoo County, Michigan* (New York: F. W. Beers & Company, 1873), 19.

10. Ibid. In the 1870s, John M.'s farmstead was among the ten largest in Richland Township.

11. *Portrait and Biographical Record of Kalamazoo, Allegan, and Van Buren Counties, Michigan* (Chicago: Chapman Brothers, 1892), 522.

12. See the discussion of "spoiling the whole" in Christopher M. Jedrey, *The World of John Cleaveland: Family and Community in Eighteenth-Century New England* (New York: W. W. Norton, 1979), 75.

13. Michigan *Revised Statutes*, sec. 10, 301 (Green 1846).

14. On inheritance practices in seventeenth-century England, see Cicely Howell, *Land, Family, and Inheritance in Transition: Kibworth Harcourt, 1280–1700* (New York: Cambridge University Press, 1983), 237–70, and "Peasant Inheritance Customs in the Midlands, 1280–1700," in *Family and Inheritance: Rural Society in Western Europe, 1200–1800*, edited by Jack Goody et al. (New York: Cambridge University Press, 1976), 112–55; Margaret Spufford, *Contrasting Communities: English Villagers in the Sixteenth and Seventeenth Centuries* (London: Cambridge University Press, 1974), 7, 104–10, 159–60, and "Peasant

Inheritance Customs and Land Distribution in Cambridgeshire from the Sixteenth to the Eighteenth Centuries," in Goody, *Family and Inheritance*, 156–77; and Keith Wrightson and David Levine, *Poverty and Piety in an English Village: Terling, 1525–1700* (New York: Academic Press, 1979), 73–109.

15. Joan Thirsk, "The European Debate on Customs of Inheritance, 1500–1700," in Goody, *Family and Inheritance*, 177–92.

16. Alexis de Tocqueville, *Democracy in America*, edited by J. P. Mayer (Garden City, N.Y.: Vintage, 1969), 51–55.

17. On the colonial New England law of inheritance, see George L. Haskins, "The Beginnings of Partible Inheritance in the American Colonies," *Yale Law Journal* 51 (1942): 1280–1315, and *Law and Authority in Early Massachusetts* (New York: MacMillan, 1960), 163–221; and William E. Nelson, *The Americanization of the Common Law: The Impact of Legal Change on Massachusetts Society, 1760–1830* (Cambridge: Harvard University Press, 1975), esp. 48.

18. On New England inheritance practices during the first generation of settlement, see John Demos, "Notes on Life in Plymouth Colony," in *Colonial America: Essays in Political and Social Development*, 3d ed., edited by Stanley N. Katz and John Murrin (New York: Alfred D. Knopf, 1983), 121–41, and Philip J. Greven Jr., *Four Generations: Population, Land, and Family in Colonial Andover, Massachusetts* (Ithaca: Cornell University Press, 1970), 72–102.

19. Darrett B. Rutman, *Husbandmen of Plymouth: Farms and Villages in the Old Colony, 1620–1692* (Boston: Beacon Press for Plimouth Plantation, 1967), 52–62.

20. W. G. Hoskins, *The Midland Peasant: The Economy and Society of a Leicestershire Village* (London: Macmillan, 1957), 190–204.

21. Kenneth Lockridge, "Land, Population, and the Evolution of New England Society, 1630–1790," *Past and Present* 39 (April 1968): 62–80; Paul Boyer and Stephen Nissenbaum, *Salem Possessed: The Social Origins of Witchcraft* (Cambridge: Harvard University Press, 1974), 30–50; Robert A. Gross, *The Minutemen and Their World* (New York: Hill and Wang, 1976), 68–108.

22. Jedrey, *World of John Cleaveland*, 58–94; Greven, *Four Generations*, 222–60; Douglas Lamar Jones, *Village and Seaport: Migration and Society in Eighteenth-Century Massachusetts* (Hanover, N.H.: University Press of New England, 1981), 86–102.

23. See, for example, Jedrey, *World of John Cleaveland*, 81–84.

24. Toby Ditz, *Property and Kinship: Inheritance in Early Connecticut, 1750–1820* (Princeton: Princeton University Press, 1986), 61–81.

25. Kent, *Of the Law Concerning Real Property*, 369–81.

26. Persistence rates were calculated from the 1850 and 1860 tax rolls for Richland, Climax, and Alamo Townships. Family relationships were primarily determined from the 1850 and 1860 population censuses for Richland, Climax, and Alamo and antiquarian sources. A full discussion of these relationships and how they were determined follows.

27. Glenda Riley, *The Female Frontier: A Comparative View of Women on the Prairie and the Plains* (Lawrence: University of Kansas Press, 1988), 118, 133–38.

28. See table A.8, "Families among Township Landholding Farmers, 1850–1860."

29. Kirkland family sources include *Portrait and Biographical Record*, 970, 973, and Henry Bishop, "Memorial Report—Kalamazoo County," *Michigan Pioneer and Historical Collections* 29 (1901): 447.

30. *Portrait and Biographical Record,* 841–42.

31. The surmise is based on Hugh's greater visibility in the public record.

32. British immigrants and Yankees shared a tendency toward inter vivos transmissions and intestacy. See Mark Friedberger, "The Farm Family and the Inheritance Process: Evidence from the Corn Belt, 1870–1950," *Agricultural History* 57 (January 1983): 1–13.

33. John Vandewalker's marriage is certain only because his wife's name appears on the deed. He is not listed in either the 1850 or the 1860 population census.

34. See table A.9, "Tenure of Township Landholding Farmers Compared to Family Members, 1850–1860."

35. See table A.10, "Ages of Township Farmers Operating Farms and Paying Real Property Taxes, 1860."

36. See table A.11, "Tenure of Township Families Sorted by Age and Family Relation, 1860."

37. The health of the local economy, degree of township development, and willingness of taxpayers to pay on the full worth of their properties influenced the ratio of real to personal property valuations. In Richland Township, for example, the ratio climbed from 2.7 in 1837 to 5.3 in 1847 and then fell to 2.9 the following year, where it remained for the rest of the decade. At issue here is the difference between the assessments of established settlers, who, regardless of fluctuations in the ratio, paid on substantial amounts of both real and personal property, and those of young men whose property was concentrated in either personalty or realty. Thus, in Richland in 1837, 27.1 percent (26) of all taxpayers did not pay on real property, whereas 10.4 percent (10) did not pay on personal property. The percentages of taxpayers not assessed for real or personal property were 10.7 (13) and 33 (27), respectively, in 1847 (excluding 17 individuals who appeared on the roll only because they paid the militia tax for the Mexican-American War) and 15.4 (24) and 12.8 (20), respectively, in 1848.

38. References to this expression are legion in the county mugbooks of the 1880s and 1890s and are phrased either as "began work on his own account" or "began life on his own account." A son became an adult when he kept the fruits of his labor.

39. See table A.12, "Age and Residence of Township Farmers and Laborers, 1860."

40. Kent, *Of the Law Concerning the Rights of Persons,* 163.

41. Thomas Dublin, *Women at Work: The Transformation of Work and Community in Lowell, Massachusetts, 1826–1860* (New York: Columbia University Press, 1979), 23–57. Dublin's recent work, *Transforming Women's Work: New England Lives in the Industrial Revolution* (Ithaca, N.Y.: Cornell University Press, 1994), situates the experience of the mill girls in the context of both native- and foreign-born women's participation in wage work in nineteenth-century New England. See also table A.13, "Occupations of Single Township Men and Women, Ages 15 to 21 Years, 1860."

42. David E. Schob, *Hired Hands and Plowboys: Farm Labor in the Midwest, 1815–1860* (Urbana: University of Illinois Press, 1975), 174–76; Joseph F. Kett, "Growing Up in Rural New England, 1800–1840," in *Anonymous Americans: Explorations in Nineteenth-Century Social History,* edited by Tamara K. Hareven (Englewood Cliffs, N.J.: Prentice-Hall, 1971), 9–10, 15.

43. See table A.14, "Reasons for Leaving Home: Kalamazoo County Men Born 1810–1839 and 1840–1869."

44. William Blackstone, *Commentaries on the Law of England: A Facsimile of the First*

*Edition of 1765–1769*, edited by Stanley N. Katz, vol. 1, *Of the Rights of Persons* (Chicago: University of Chicago Press, 1979), 435–41.

45. Ibid., 438–39.

46. Ibid., 440–41.

47. Nelson, *Americanization of the Common Law*, 46–53.

48. Ibid., 117–33, 159–64.

49. Ibid., 125.

50. *Benson v. Remington*, 2 Mass. Rep. 113 (1806).

51. Nelson, *Americanization of the Common Law*, 238 (n. 102); *Freto v. Brown*, 4 Mass. Rep. 675 (1808); *Jenney v. Alden*, 12 Mass. Rep. 375 (1815); *Whiting v. Howard*, 3 Pick. Rep. 201 (1825).

52. *Chase v. Elkins*, 2 Vermont Rep. 290 (1829).

53. Ibid., 291.

54. Ibid., 293.

55. Nelson, *Americanization of the Common Law*, 48; John Demos, *A Little Commonwealth: Family Life in Plymouth Colony* (London: Oxford University Press, 1970), 107–17.

56. *Jenney v. Alden*, 12 Mass. Rep. 38; *Galbraith v. Green*, 4 Serg. & Rawle 207 (1818); *Burlingame v. Burlingame*, 7 Cowen's Rep. 92 (1827); *Morse v. Welden*, 6 Conn. Rep. 547 (1827); *Varney v. Young*, 11 Vermont Rep. 258 (1839).

57. Tapping Reeve, *The Law of Baron and Femme, of Parent and Child, Guardian and Ward, Master and Servant, and of the Powers of Courts of Chancery, with an Essay on the Terms Heir, Heirs, and Heirs of the Body*, 2d ed., edited by Lucius E. Chittenden (Burlington, Vt.: Channery Goodrich, 1846), 290–91.

58. Compare Michigan *Revised Statutes*, sec. 26, 355 (1837/38), and Michigan *Compiled Laws*, vol. 2, sec. 27, 1495 (1872).

## Chapter Five

1. William Page to AHMS, March 2, 1836, Papers of the American Home Missionary Society, 1825–46, American Home Missionary Society Archives, The Amistad Research Center, Tulane University, New Orleans, La.

2. William Jones to AHMS, September 17, 1830, ibid.

3. William Jones to AHMS, March 20, 1831; Erie Prince to AHMS, March 21, 1831; William Jones to AHMS, July 27, 1831; and E. P. Hastings to AHMS, August 27, 1831, all in ibid.

4. Arvilla Powers Smith Diary, 1834–45, and Reminiscences, 1808–34, 1833, Michigan Historical Collections, Bentley Historical Library, University of Michigan, Ann Arbor, Mich.

5. Noah M. Wells and E. P. Hastings to AHMS, March 7, 1831, and E. P. Hastings to AHMS, January 20, February 15, 1834, all in Papers of the American Home Missionary Society, 1825–46, American Home Missionary Society Archives, The Amistad Research Center, Tulane University, New Orleans, La.

6. William Jones to AHMS, September 12, 1831, ibid.

7. "A Record of the Richland Presbyterian Church, 1831–1843," unpublished manuscript, in the possession of the church; E. P. Hastings to AHMS, February 4, 1832, and Isaac Barnes

to AHMS, April 27, 1832 (emphasis in original), both in Papers of the American Home Missionary Society, 1825–46, American Home Missionary Society Archives, The Amistad Research Center, Tulane University, New Orleans, La.

8. Edward M. Cook Jr., *The Fathers of the Towns: Leadership and Community Structure in Eighteenth-Century New England* (Baltimore: Johns Hopkins University Press, 1976), 119–41; Patricia Bonomi, *Under the Cope of Heaven: Religion, Society, and Politics in Colonial America* (New York: Oxford University Press, 1986).

9. On the nationalization of American denominations, see William Warren Sweet, *Religion and the Development of American Culture, 1765–1840* (New York: Charles Scribner's Sons, 1952), 54–128. On the organizational strategies of denominations, see T. Scott Miyakawa, *Protestants and Pioneers: Individualism and Conformity on the American Frontier* (Chicago: University of Chicago Press, 1964), and Donald G. Mathews, "The Second Great Awakening as an Organizing Process, 1780–1830: An Hypothesis," *American Quarterly* 21, no. 1 (Spring 1969): 23–43. On the stunning success of Baptists and Methodists after the Revolution, see Nathan O. Hatch, *The Democratization of American Christianity* (New Haven: Yale University Press, 1989). On the American Home Missionary Society, see Colin Brumitt Goodykoontz, *Home Missions on the American Frontier, with Particular Reference to the American Home Missionary Society* (Caldwell, Idaho: Caxton Printers, 1939), 165–269, and Frederick I. Kuhns, "The Operation of the American Home Missionary Society in the Old Northwest, 1826–1861" (Ph.D. dissertation, University of Chicago, 1947).

10. William Warren Sweet, *Religion on the American Frontier, 1783–1850*, vol. 2, *The Presbyterians* (New York: Harper & Brothers, 1936), 99–128, vol. 3, *The Congregationalists* (Chicago: University of Chicago Press, 1939), 13–43.

11. Charles L. Zorbaugh, "The Plan of Union in Ohio," *Church History* 6 (1937): 145–64; Ronald H. Noricks, "'Jealousies and Contentions': The Plan of Union and the Western Reserve, 1807–1837," *Journal of Presbyterian History* 60 (Summer 1982): 130–43.

12. Necia Ann Musser, "Home Missionaries on the Michigan Frontier: A Calendar of the Michigan Letters of the American Home Missionary Society" (Ph.D. dissertation, University of Michigan, 1967), 1:109–15; Rev. Philo R. Hurd, D.D., "An Historical Sketch of Congregationalism in Michigan, Brought Down to the Year 1884," *Michigan Pioneer and Historical Collections* 7 (1886): 103–11; John Comin and Harold Fredsell, *History of the Presbyterian Church in Michigan* (Ann Arbor, Mich.: Ann Arbor Press, 1950), 80–105; Frederick I. Kuhns, "The Breakup of the Plan of Union in Michigan," *Michigan History Magazine* 33, no. 2 (June 1948): 157–80.

13. Arvilla Powers Smith Diary, July 30, 1837, Michigan Historical Collections, Bentley Historical Library, University of Michigan, Ann Arbor, Mich. See also Musser, "Home Missionaries," 1:100–102.

14. *Record of the Richland Presbyterian Church*, January 12, 1833.

15. Ibid., January 1, 1833; William Jones to AHMS, December 16, 1832; E. P. Hastings and Noah M. Wells to AHMS, April 3, 1833; and Levi White to AHMS, August 15, 1833, all in Papers of the American Home Missionary Society, 1825–46, American Home Missionary Society Archives, The Amistad Research Center, Tulane University, New Orleans, La.

16. Luther Humphrey to AHMS, April 1, 1834, Papers of the American Home Missionary Society, 1825–46, American Home Missionary Society Archives, The Amistad Research Center, Tulane University, New Orleans, La.

17. Arvilla Powers Smith Diary, February 5, 1834, Michigan Historical Collections, Bentley Historical Library, University of Michigan, Ann Arbor, Mich.

18. "Record of the Richland Presbyterian Church," June 27, 1836, June 27, 1838.

19. Samuel W. Durant, *The Kalamazoo County History* (Philadelphia: Everts & Abbott, 1880), 471; "Record of the Richland Presbyterian Church," records of admission before 1836: October 14, 1831, January 12, 1833, March 7, 13, April 4, 1834; dismission: March 27, 1835.

20. Durant, *Kalamazoo County History*, 460, 470; "Record of the Richland Presbyterian Church," January 5, 1839.

21. "Record of the Richland Presbyterian Church," March 19, 1836; Durant, *Kalamazoo County History*, 471.

22. John D. Pierce to AHMS, May 1, 1837, Papers of the American Home Missionary Society, 1825–46, American Home Missionary Society Archives, The Amistad Research Center, Tulane University, New Orleans, La.

23. Kuhns, "American Home Missionary Society," 23.

24. Constitution, 1837, and Minutes, 1837–41, March 1, 1837, Records of the Michigan Association of Congregational Churches, Michigan Historical Collections, Bentley Historical Library, University of Michigan, Ann Arbor, Mich.

25. Durant, *Kalamazoo County History*, 471.

26. "Record of the Richland Presbyterian Church," April 14, 1836.

27. Ibid., February 10, 1838. Only Brown, Mills, and Woodruff signed the apology, which is out of order in the "Record of the Richland Presbyterian Church," so it was clearly their act alone, not that of the entire session.

28. Kuhns, "American Home Missionary Society," 30.

29. "Record of the Richland Presbyterian Church," January 23, 1839.

30. Minutes, 1837–41, June 2, 1841, Records of the Michigan Association of Congregational Churches, Michigan Historical Collections, Bentley Historical Library, University of Michigan, Ann Arbor, Mich.

31. O. P. Hoyt to AHMS, January 8, 28, 1844, Papers of the American Home Missionary Society, 1825–46, American Home Missionary Society Archives, The Amistad Research Center, Tulane University, New Orleans, La.

32. O. P. Hoyt to AHMS, June 3, 18, 1842, ibid.

33. Vernon D. Taylor to AHMS, March 2, 1841, ibid.

34. Durant, *Kalamazoo County History*, 460, 472, 482; Rev. S. N. Griffith, "Sketch of the Early History of Methodism in the Southwest Part of the State of Michigan," *Michigan Pioneer and Historical Collections* 2 (1901): 158–71. See also Elijah H. Pilcher, *Protestantism in Michigan: Being a Special History of the Methodist Episcopal Church and Incidentally of Other Denominations* (Detroit: R. D. S. Taylor & Company, 1878), 254–63.

35. Durant, *Kalamazoo County History*, 472.

36. Ibid., 342.

37. Francis Hodgman, *Early Days in Climax: Reminiscences* (Climax, Mich.: By the author, 1905), 3–4.

38. Ibid., 50.

39. The Barnes family's post-Richland activities are described in *The History of Allegan and Barry Counties, Michigan, with Illustrations and Biographical Sketches of Their Prominent Men and Pioneers* (Philadelphia: D. W. Ensign & Company, 1880), 260, 353–62.

# Chapter Six

1. Isaac Barnes to Lucius Lyon, January 1, 1845, Lucius Lyon Papers, William L. Clements Library, University of Michigan, Ann Arbor, Mich. The letter is not in Barnes's handwriting, which suggests that he was unwell.

2. Mumford Eldred Jr. to Isaac E. Crary, June 18, 1840, ibid. (emphasis in original).

3. Isaac Barnes to Lucius Lyon, February 28, 1836, ibid.

4. *Kalamazoo Gazette*, July 22, 1837, 2.

5. Ronald P. Formisano, *The Birth of Mass Political Parties: Michigan, 1827–1861* (Princeton: Princeton University Press, 1971), 23; *Kalamazoo Gazette*, March 24, 1838, 2.

6. Isaac Barnes to Lucius Lyon, May 26, 1835, Lucius Lyon Papers, William L. Clements Library, University of Michigan, Ann Arbor, Mich.

7. For Eldred's political activities outside Richland, see *Kalamazoo Gazette*, November 11, 1838, 2; September 11, 1840, 3; December 24, 1841, 2; October 7, 1842, 2; September 4, 1843, 2.

8. Mumford Eldred Jr. to Lucius Lyon, May 1, 1844, Lucius Lyon Papers, William L. Clements Library, University of Michigan, Ann Arbor, Mich.

9. Caleb Eldred to Lucius Lyon, December 2, 1844, and Mumford Eldred Jr. to Lucius Lyon, December 2, 1844, both in ibid.

10. All references to officeholding in Richland are drawn from Richland Township Records, 1833–61, Regional Historical Archives, Waldo Library, Western Michigan University, Kalamazoo, Mich.

11. Eldred's date of birth is unknown, but he was listed as between twenty and thirty years of age on the census of 1840.

12. Richard S. Alcorn, "Leadership and Stability in Mid-Nineteenth Century America: A Case Study of an Illinois Town," *Journal of American History* 61 (1974): 685–702; R. A. Burchell, "The Character and Function of a Pioneer Elite: Rural California, 1848–1880," *Journal of American Studies* 15 (1981): 377–90; Don H. Doyle, *The Social Order of a Frontier Community: Jacksonville, Illinois, 1825–70* (Urbana: University of Illinois Press, 1978), 92–118.

13. The annual rate of population turnover was calculated from the Richland Township Tax Rolls, 1844–60, Regional Historical Archives, Waldo Library, Western Michigan University, Kalamazoo, Mich.

14. For a detailed account of Eldred's extraordinary career as a land speculator, see Susan E. Gray, "Local Speculator as Confidence Man: Mumford Eldred Jr. and the Michigan Land Rush," *Journal of the Early Republic* 10, no. 3 (Fall 1990): 383–406.

15. Richland was so strongly Whig that the Democratic *Kalamazoo Gazette* liked to single out the township for ridicule. See *Kalamazoo Gazette*, July 4, 1840, 2. At other times, the editor of the *Gazette* despaired at the strength of anti-Democratic sentiment in the county. See *Kalamazoo Gazette*, November 10, 1848, 1.

16. See, for example, election returns for 1840–42 in *Kalamazoo Gazette*, November 3, 1840, 2; November 12, 1841, 2; November 25, 1842, 2; and Samuel W. Durant, *The Kalamazoo County History* (Philadelphia: Everts & Abbott, 1880), 467.

17. Mumford Eldred Jr. to Lucius Lyon, August 13, 1844, Lucius Lyon Papers, William L. Clements Library, University of Michigan, Ann Arbor, Mich. (emphasis in original).

18. Mumford Eldred Jr. to Lucius Lyon, December 2, 1844, ibid.

19. Mumford Eldred Jr. to Lucius Lyon, January 31, 1845, ibid. Eldred may have misrepresented himself to Lyon here, too. According to Durant, *Kalamazoo County History*, not long after he wrote to Lyon, Eldred resigned as postmaster in Richland with the understanding that the office would go to Elijah N. Bissell, a Democratic partisan. Bissell was supposed to run the post office from his home on the Grand River Road, well north of the village but hardly on the western side of the township. See ibid., 467, 474.

20. Ibid., 474.

21. Edward W. Bemis, "Local Government in Michigan and the Northwest," *Johns Hopkins University Studies in Historical and Political Science* 5 (March 1883): 5–25.

22. An excellent overview of northern antebellum politics is William E. Gienapp, " 'Politics Seems to Enter into Everything': Political Culture in the North, 1840–1860," in *Essays on American Antebellum Politics, 1840–1860*, edited by Stephen E. Maizlish and John J. Kushma (College Station: Texas A & M University Press, 1982), 14–69.

23. Basic works on party ideology include Daniel Walker Howe, *The Political Culture of the American Whigs* (Chicago: University of Chicago Press, 1979), and Harry L. Watson, *Jacksonian Politics and Community Conflict: The Emergence of the Second Party System in Cumberland County, North Carolina* (Baton Rouge: Louisiana State University Press, 1981), and *Liberty and Power: The Politics of Jacksonian America* (New York: Hill and Wang, 1990).

24. Andrew R. L. Cayton and Peter Onuf, *The Midwest and the Nation: Rethinking the History of an American Region* (Bloomington: Indiana University Press, 1990), esp. 79.

25. The Whig newspaper, variously known as the *Kalamazoo Telegraph* and the *Michigan Telegraph*, was published only between 1845 and 1849. See the maps giving Michigan election returns by county in Floyd Benjamin Streeter, *Political Parties in Michigan, 1837–1860: A Historical Study of Political Issues and Parties in Michigan from the Admission of the State to the Civil War* (Lansing: Michigan Historical Commission, 1918), 11–12, 75, 101–2, 134.

26. No township records survive for Climax. The Alamo Township Records span only the years 1838 to 1843 and do not contain full election returns.

27. Formisano, *Birth of Mass Political Parties*, 27–29.

28. Kenneth Winkle, *The Politics of Community: Migration and Politics in Antebellum Ohio* (Cambridge: Cambridge University Press, 1988). Winkle's work focuses on the attempts of Whig and Democratic partisans to control the eligibility of voters through poll lists. With a single exception, these lists have not survived for Richland, Climax, or Alamo. Durant, *Kalamazoo County History*, reprinted the poll list for the first Climax election of 1838 to show that both parties temporarily imported day laborers into the township to obtain their votes. See ibid., 331–32.

29. *Kalamazoo Gazette*, April 5, 1850, 2.

30. Formisano, *Birth of Mass Political Parties*, 170.

31. *Kalamazoo Gazette*, May 10, 1850, 2.

32. Durant, *Kalamazoo County History*, 467–68.

33. Formisano, *Birth of Mass Political Parties*, 141–54.

34. These ratios refer to the total voter turnout divided by the total number of offices.

35. Eliminated from the cohort for simplicity of calculation were 16 (8.8 percent) men who won and lost the same number of offices. Most of these each won and lost a single office, so their absence from the pool does not affect the outcome of the analysis.

36. Party affiliation was determined from newspaper accounts of township and county elections and of the work of partisan county committees and from settler biographies in antiquarian sources.

37. *Kalamazoo Gazette*, October 20, 1848, 2.

38. May sources include *Portrait and Biographical Record of Kalamazoo, Allegan, and Van Buren Counties, Michigan* (Chicago: Chapman Brothers, 1892), 514, and *History of Berkshire County, Massachusetts, with Biographical Sketches of Its Prominent Men*, vol. 3 (New York: J. B. Beers & Company, 1885), 523.

39. *Kalamazoo Gazette*, July 22, 1836, 2.

40. *Portrait and Biographical Record*, 574.

41. *Kalamazoo Gazette*, November 22, 1850, 2.

42. Formisano, *Birth of Mass Political Parties*, 31–55, 166–68.

43. Antiquarian sources, therefore, were the most useful sources in determining church membership.

44. May participated in the organization of the Congregational Association in 1837. See Minutes, 1837–41, March 1, 1837, Records of the Michigan Association of Congregational Churches, Michigan Historical Collections, Bentley Historical Library, University of Michigan, Ann Arbor, Mich.

45. Durant, *Kalamazoo County History*, 473.

46. Formisano, *Birth of Mass Political Parties*, 188–91; *Portrait and Biographical Record*, 261–64; Durant, *Kalamazoo County History*, 479–81.

47. See, for example, Paul Johnson, *A Shopkeeper's Millennium: Society and Revivals in Rochester, New York, 1815–1837* (New York: Hill and Wang, 1978); Mary P. Ryan, *Cradle of the Middle Class: The Family in Oneida County, New York, 1790–1865* (Cambridge: Cambridge University Press, 1981); John S. Gilkeson Jr., *Middle-Class Providence* (Princeton: Princeton University Press, 1986); and Stuart Blumin, *The Emergence of the Middle Class: Social Experience in the American City, 1760–1900* (Cambridge: Cambridge University Press, 1989).

48. The opposite poles of the debate are represented by Christopher Clark, *The Roots of Rural Capitalism: Western Massachusetts, 1780–1860* (Ithaca: Cornell University Press, 1990), and Winifred Rothenberg, *From Market Places to a Market Economy: The Transformation of Rural Massachusetts, 1750–1850* (Chicago: University of Chicago Press, 1992).

49. See, for example, Joan M. Jensen, *Loosening the Bonds: Mid-Atlantic Farm Women, 1750–1850* (New Haven: Yale University Press, 1986); Jon Gjerde, *From Peasants to Farmers: The Migration from Balestrand, Norway, to the Upper Middle West* (Cambridge: Cambridge University Press, 1985); and Jack Larkin, *The Reshaping of Everyday Life, 1790–1840* (New York: Harper and Row, 1989).

50. Henry Bishop, "Report of the Memorial Committee—Kalamazoo County," *Michigan Pioneer and Historical Collections*, 2d ed., 14 (1908): 127.

51. Durant, *Kalamazoo County History*, 476.

52. Peck sources include *Portrait and Biographical Record*, 907–8; Durant, *Kalamazoo County History*, 481–82; *Michigan Pioneer and Historical Collections*, 2d ed., 1 (1900): 88–89; and Henry Bishop, "Memorial Report—Kalamazoo County," *Michigan Pioneer and Historical Collections* 26 (1896): 128.

53. *Kalamazoo Gazette*, September 25, 1846, 2; February 12, 1847, 3.

54. Like Peck, Read was a stockbreeder and was active in the county agricultural society. See *Kalamazoo Gazette*, October 20, 1854, 2, and *Portrait and Biographical Record*, 630–31.

55. Durant, *Kalamazoo County History*, 476.

56. Lovell sources include *Portrait and Biographical Record*, 718–19, 728–30; *American Biographical History of Eminent and Self-Made Men: Michigan* (Cincinnati: Western Biographical Publishing Company, 1978), 42–43; and Abby Maria Hemenway, *Vermont Historical Gazetteer*, vol. 5, *The Towns of Windham County* (Brandon, Vt.: Carrie E. H. Page, 1891), 556.

57. An account of the election is in Durant, *Kalamazoo County History*, 329–30.

58. *Kalamazoo Gazette*, November 3, 1840, 2; November 12, 1841, 2; November 25, 1842, 2; November 19, 1847, 2. Lists of men elected to most offices between 1838 and 1879 are in Durant, *Kalamazoo County History*, 333–34.

59. These men were delegates to county Democratic conventions and served on township vigilance committees. See *Kalamazoo Gazette*, September 11, 1840, 2; October 17, 1842, 2; September 6, 1843, 2.

60. *Kalamazoo Gazette*, November 17, 1854, 2; September 5, 1856, 2.

61. *Kalamazoo Gazette*, November 9, 1849, 2; November 7, 1856, 2; November 9, 1860, 2.

62. *Kalamazoo Gazette*, July 1, 1853, 2. On the regulation of sales of alcohol in nineteenth-century Michigan, see Floyd B. Streeter, "History of Prohibition Legislation in Michigan," *Michigan History Magazine* 2, no. 2 (April 1918): 289–308.

63. Durant, *Kalamazoo County History*, 331.

64. Ibid., 345–46.

65. *Kalamazoo Gazette*, November 3, 1840, 2; November 25, 1842, 2.

66. See, for example, Gilkeson, *Middle-Class Providence*, 12–54.

67. Durant, *Kalamazoo County History*, 347.

68. For Clark's political affiliation, see *Kalamazoo Gazette*, February 17, 1860, 2.

69. *Kalamazoo Gazette*, September 11, 1857, 2.

## Conclusion

1. "Kalamazoo County: The Ninth Annual Reunion of the Pioneers of Kalamazoo County, August 14, 1879, Held in Dyckman's Grove in Schoolcraft," *Michigan Pioneer and Historical Collections*, reprint ed., 3 (1903): 517–32, reprinted from *Kalamazoo Daily Telegraph*, August 15, 1879.

2. "Meeting of Pioneers: Tenth Annual Reunion and Picnic of Kalamazoo County Pioneers—The State Society Meet with Them," *Michigan Pioneer and Historical Collections*, reprint ed., 3 (1903): 536–42.

3. See table A.14, "Reasons for Leaving Home: Kalamazoo County Men Born 1810–1839 and 1840–1869."

4. For a full account of this transformation, see Burton Bledstein, *The Culture of Professionalization: The Middle Class and the Development of Higher Education in America* (New York: W. W. Norton, 1976), esp. 80–128.

5. Samuel W. Durant, *The Kalamazoo County History* (Philadelphia: Everts & Abbott, 1880), 297, 339, 341, 468–69.

6. Gilkey family sources include ibid., 482–83, and *Michigan Pioneer and Historical Collections*, reprint ed., 6 (1907): 313–14.

7. George L. Gilkey, "The Gilkeys" (1950), unpaginated manuscript extract courtesy of Mary Gilkey Steward, Sullivan, Ind.; anecdote courtesy of Professor John Houdek of Western Michigan University, who has collected oral history accounts of the Gilkeys.

8. *Portrait and Biographical Record of Kalamazoo, Allegan, and Van Buren Counties, Michigan* (Chicago: Chapman Brothers, 1892), 523.

9. Ibid., 561.

# Index

of, 21–24, 197 (nn. 14, 15); speculation, 28–29, 33, 38–41, 137, 145–46, 176, 200 (n. 51); boom, 43–48
Langdon, Samuel, 161
Lanman, James, 4–5, 53–54
Lawrence, Daniel, 104, 136, 164
Lewis, William, 68
Livestock: raising, 58–64, 176. *See also* Agricultural production
Local exchange, 77–79, 89–90. *See also* Debt litigation; Indians; Merchants
Location geography: settlers', 10, 17–18, 27–28. *See also* Topography; Infrastructure, township
Lodge, Henry Cabot, 8
Lonsbury, Josephine Barrett, 93–95
Lovell, Catherine Eldred, 78–79, 165
Lovell, Cyrus, 26–27
Lovell, Enos, 163
Lovell, Enos T., 163–65
Lovell, George, 62, 163–64
Lovell, Lafayette W., 62, 163–65, 167
Lovell, Willard, 36, 163–64, 166, 218 (n. 56)
Lovell, Zerviah, 163
Lyon, Lucius, 139–42, 147–49

Mann, Bruce, 89
Maple sugar, 65, 71, 74–75, 78. *See also* Agricultural production; Indians: economy of
Markets: difficulty of securing, 52–58; seasonality of, 80–81. *See also* Local exchange; Trade; Transportation
Marsh, Justin, 56
Martin, John Frederick, 22
Mason, Edwin, 130, 132
Mason, Stephens, 46
Mathews, Lois K., 2, 6
May, Dwight, 171
May, Rockwell, 157, 159, 161
Medina, Ohio, 20–21, 127, 129, 131
Merchants, 31–32, 50–51, 68, 70, 75–79, 83–87, 134, 145–49, 165, 178–79. *See also* Eldred, Mumford, Jr.; Local exchange; Infrastructure, township; Trade: fur; Trade: long-distance

Metcalf, James, 18
Methodists, 123, 135–36, 213 (n. 9), 214 (n. 34)
Migration: routes, 1–2, 4, 10–11, 72, 193 (nn. 1, 5); Yankee system of, 9–13, 18
Milling, 52, 137, 145, 176; settlers' judgment of potential for, 18; as essential local infrastructure, 28, 31–32, 35, 38, 147. *See also* Location geography: settlers'; Topography
Mills, Augustus, 27, 154, 161–62
Mills, Elihu, 27
Mills, Henry, 27
Mills, Henry L., 82–84
Mills, Simeon, 27–28, 125, 127–32, 144–45, 162
Mills, Sylvester, 27, 31–32, 129
Mills, Timothy, 27, 32, 143, 145, 162
Mills, Willard, 27, 31–32, 129
Missions, Protestant Indian, 205–6 (nn. 19, 20); Slater, 68–71, 74, 90, 143, 148; Griswold, 73, 143; Old Wing, 73–75, 90, 143
Mitchell, William C., 82, 86–87
Mount Holyoke Seminary, 162

Nelson, William E., 113–14
Nevins, Alfred, 161
New England: as culture region, 1–2, 193 (nn. 1, 2)
Northrup, Cornelius, 26
Norton, Birdseye and Nathaniel, 21–22
Norton, Selden, 26

Osterud, Nancy Grey, 64
Ottawa, 16, 69, 71–75, 90

Page, William, 119–20
Panic of 1837–39, 45–48, 73. *See also* Cash: scarcity of; Internal improvements; Land: boom
Patrimony, as access to capital, 108–10; effect of education on, 173–74. *See also* Inheritance: law and practice in colonial New England; Labor: child's right to

own; Labor: parent's right to child's; Women: dower and guardianship rights; Women: as owners of property in land; Women: as wage earners

Peck, Horace M., 160–61

Percival, Samuel, 35

Pierce, Isaac, 36, 165–67

Pierce, James D., Lawrence S., Levi, and John M., 166

Pierce, John D., 122, 129–30

Pierce, Longworthy, 165–66

Pioneer Society of Kalamazoo County, 16, 169–73, 177. *See also* Rural elites: formation of

Plan of Union, 16, 123–24, 127, 130, 133–34, 213 (nn. 9, 12). *See also* Denominations, Calvinist

Plummer, Daniel, 26

Politics: patronage, 139–43, 147–50; partisan, 142–43, 150–59, 162–65. *See also* Antislavery; Rural elites: formation of; Infrastructure, township; Township government

Population turnover: effect of indebtedness on, 87–88; effect of family ties on, 102–3; effect on family-farming arrangements, 110; relationship to elite formation, 144, 172; effect on voter turnout, 154–56

Porter, James, Jr., 130

Porter, James, Sr., 26, 30, 125, 127, 130

Porter, John S., 157–58, 161

Potawatomi, 16, 34, 71–72, 75

Potts, Henry, 164

Powell, E. P., 5–6

Power, Richard Lyle, 4

Prairies: Kalamazoo County, 17–18, 27–28, 33–34, 196 (n. 5). *See also* Location geography: settlers'; Topography

Presbyterian General Assembly, 123–24, 129

Prince, Erie, 120

Produce: market garden, 65; orchard, 65. *See also* Agricultural production

Promissory notes, 81–83, 208 (nn. 44, 45). *See also* Debt litigation

Proprietorship, 18, 21–26. *See also* Barnes, Isaac; Hudson, David; Land: distribution, New England system of

Pulteney Purchase, 24–25

Ransom, Fletcher, 37, 62–63

Reed, Gilbert E., 161

Reeve, Tapping, 116

Religion. *See* American Home Missionary Society; Church; Denominations, Calvinist; Methodists; Plan of Union; Missions, Protestant Indian

Republican Party: dominance in local politics, 154, 157–58, 165, 167–68; as aspect of regional identity, 172

Reynolds, George W. and Sheldon, 97

Richland Prairie Seminary, 160–62, 177

Robe, James T., 135

Robinson, Rix, 75

Rohrbough, Malcolm, 41

Rourke, Constance, 4

Rowell, Andrew, 127

Rural elites: formation of, 159–62, 167–68, 171–72, 175–78, 215 (n. 12), 217 (nn. 47, 48, 49). *See also* Pioneer Society of Kalamazoo County; Politics: partisan

Saint Joseph Presbytery, 120, 126–27, 130

Sawyer, William, 163–64

Schob, David, 53–54

Schoolcraft, 50, 169, 171

Scott, A. H., 76–79

Second Great Awakening, 18, 136–37

Seeley, Elisha B., 84

Settlement systems, 10, 195 (nn. 23, 24). *See also* Location geography: settlers'

Seward, John, 120

Sheep raising, 61–63, 160. *See also* Agricultural production

Sheldon, George, 104

Sheldon, Thomas, 43

Shipping: Great Lakes, 48, 147. *See also* Trade: fur; Trade: grain

Shortridge, James R., 2–3

Silk worms, 56–57. *See also* Agricultural production

Slater, Leonard, 69–70